기초 기본 영문법

기초 기본 영문법

초판 1쇄 인쇄 2014년 6월 25일
초판 1쇄 발행 2014년 6월 30일

지은이 허헌구
펴낸이 金泰奉
펴낸곳 한솜미디어
등록   제5-213호

편집   박창서 김수정
마케팅 김명준
홍보   김태일

주소   143-200 서울시 광진구 구의동 243-22
전화   (02)454-0492(代)
팩스   (02)454-0493
이메일 hansom@hansom.co.kr
홈페이지 www.hansom.co.kr

값 13,000원
ISBN 978-89-5959-397-2 (03740)

※ 본서의 독창적인 내용의 무단전재를 금합니다.

Basic English Grammar

초급에서 고급까지
회화 + 독해 + 영작 + 시험을 위한

기초 기본 영문법

허헌구 지음

한솜미디어

| 머 리 말 |

영문법은 영어 문장을 만드는 방법이며 규칙이다. 영문법을 모르면 문장을 옳게 만들 수 없으므로 회화, 독해, 영작을 올바르게 할 수 없다.
영문법 지식 없이 아무리 현지에 가 열심히 공부를 해도 큰 효과를 올릴 수 없다. 영문법을 모르고 회화 정도 한대도 정상적인 회화가 아니며, 더욱이 책이나 신문 등은 제대로 해석할 수도 없다. 그러니 현지에 가더라도 영문법을 배운 후에 가는 것이 훨씬 효과적이다. 영문법을 모르고 영어를 잘할 수 있다는 것은 어불성설이다.
본 도서는 영어를 배우는 초보자나 영문법 지식이 다소 있는 자들을 대상으로 영어실력을 빠른 시일 안에 눈부시게 향상되도록 엮어진 책이다. 본문이나 연습문제의 문장들은 가능한 한 일상생활에서 많이 사용하는 실용 문장들로 했다. 문법 설명은 회화, 독해, 영작, 시험출제 위주로 간결 명료 시원하게 했다. 자세하고 충분한 문법 설명으로 문법에 자신감이 생기게 했고, 필수적이고 기본적인 충분한 연습문제로 실력을 다지게 했다.
그러므로 누구나 이 책을 숙달하면 회화 + 독해 + 영작 + 시험에 자신감이 생기면서 더 나은 실력 향상을 가져오게 하는 튼튼한 발판을 쌓게 되어 어휘의 확장과 함께 훨씬 더 좋은 성과를 올리게 될 것이다.
가끔 지루하고 어려운 구문들이나 어휘는 특히 독해를 위해서 넘어야만 하는 산들이다.
"No pains, no gains. 노력 없이는 얻는 것도 없다."

I want you to be a good improvement.

허헌구

| 차례 |

머리말 5

제1장 문장의 5형식
1. 문장의 구성요소 8
2. 문장의 5형식 9

제2장 어순(문장 성분의 순서)
* 어순의 규칙 16

제3장 영작과 독해하기
Ⅰ. **영작하기**
1. 주체의 말이 먼저 오고 수식의 말이 가까운 순서대로 온다 21
2. 주어 + 동사가 먼저 온다 21
3. 주어 + 동사 + 목적어 24
4. 문장 구성의 원리 25

Ⅱ. **독해(해석)하기**
1. 직독직해와 직청직해 28
2. 해석(독해)하기 29

제4장 부사
1. 부사의 용법 36
2. 부사(구)의 어순 38
3. 부사의 종류 42
4. 부사의 비교 42
5. 주의할 부사들 43
6. 접속부사 45

제5장 형용사
1. 형용사의 종류 51
2. 수량형용사 51
3. 형용사의 용법 52
4. 형용사의 어순 54
5. 형용사의 비교 55
6. 수사 59

제6장 to부정사
1. to부정사의 용법 67
2. to부정사의 의미상의 주어 71
3. 원형부정사의 용법 73
4. 동사 + to부정사 75
5. to부정사의 관용적 표현 76
6. 독립부정사의 관용어구 78
7. to부정사의 어순 78

제7장 동명사
1. 동명사의 명사적 용법 85
2. 동명사의 의미상의 주어 86
3. 동명사와 to부정사의 선택 87
4. 동명사의 관용적 표현 92
5. 동명사의 위치 96

제8장 분사
1. 분사의 종류 101
2. 분사의 용법 102
3. 분사구문 104

제9장 관계대명사
1. 관계대명사 who 114
2. 관계대명사 which 118
3. 관계대명사 that 119
4. 관계대명사 what 120
5. 선행사 + 전치사구 + 관대. 121
6. 한정적 용법과 계속적 용법 122
7. 관계대명사절의 삽입 122
8. 관계부사 123
9. 유사관계대명사 124
10. 복합관계대명사 125

제10장 수동태
1. 수동태를 만드는 법 131
2. 수동태의 시제 132
3. 주의해야 할 수동태 133

제11장 가정법
1. 가정법 현재 142
2. 가정법 과거 142
3. 가정법 과거완료 143
4. that절 속의 가정법 현재 144
5. 특별한 가정법 구문 144
6. If절의 대용어구 145
7. 혼합 가정법 147
8. 가정법 미래 147

제12장 일치와 화법
1. 주어와 동사의 수 일치 152
2. 시제의 일치 154
3. 화법 156

제13장 접속사
1. 등위접속사 165
2. 종속접속사 169

제14장 명사
1. 명사의 종류 179
2. 불가산명사 → 가산명사 181
3. 명사의 수 182
4. 명사의 격 185

제15장 관사
1. 부정관사의 용법 193
2. 정관사의 용법 195
3. 관사의 생략 199
4. 관사의 어순 202

제16장 대명사
1. 대명사의 종류 208
2. 인칭대명사 208
3. it의 특별용법 209
4. 재귀대명사 212
5. 지시대명사 213
6. 부정대명사 214
7. 의문대명사 219

제17장 전치사
1. 전치사의 용법 228
2. 전치사의 어순 229
3. 전치사의 후치 231
4. 전치사의 생략 232
5. 유사한 전치사와 접속사 234
6. 전치사의 종류 234

제18장 조동사
1. 특수 조동사 248
2. 일반 조동사 250

제19장 동사의 시제
1. 동사의 변형 267
2. 동사의 시제 269
3. 기본시제 270
4. 완료시제 275
5. 진행시제 278

제20장 특수구문
1. 강조 286
2. 도치 287
3. 생략 290
4. 삽입 291
5. 의문문과 부정문 292

※ 각 단원마다 필수 기본 연습문제

부록
Ⅰ. 악센트 규칙 297
Ⅱ. 필수 기본 관용어(숙어) 302
Ⅲ. 불규칙 동사표 323

제1장 문장의 5형식

1. 문장의 구성요소

(1) 주어(主語, Subject, ~은, ~는, ~이, ~가)
    주어는 문장에서 주체(핵심)가 되는 말이다.
    주어로는 명사(대명사) 역할을 하는 명사상당어구[명사, 대명사, 명사구, 명사절, to부정사(구), 동명사(구)]가 쓰인다.

(2) 동사(動詞, Verb, ~하다, ~상태다)
    동사는 사물의 동작이나 상태를 나타내는 말(품사)이다. 동사는 크게 목적어를 갖지 않는 자동사와 목적어를 갖는 타동사로 나눈다.

(3) 목적어(目的語, Object, ~을, ~를, ~에게)
    목적어는 동사의 대상(목적)이 되는 말이다. 목적어로는 주어와 마찬가지로 명사(대명사) 역할을 하는 명사상당어구가 쓰인다.

(4) 보어(補語, Complement)
    보어는 주어나 목적어를 '보충 설명'하는 말(수식어)이다.
    보어에는 주격보어와 목적격보어가 있다. 보어로는 명사상당어구(명사, 명사구, 명사절)와 형용사상당어구(형용사, 분사, 형용사구)가 쓰인다.

2. 문장의 5형식

(1) **1형식 문장 : S + V = 주어 + 완전자동사**
완전자동사는 보어나 목적어를 필요로 하지 않는 동사이지만, 자주 부사(구)와 함께 쓰여 문장의 의미를 더 보충한다.

Birds sing. 새들은 노래한다(지저귄다).
Many birds sing merrily in(on) the trees all day in summer.
많은 새들이 여름에 하루 종일 나무 (위)에서 즐겁게 노래한다.
merrily(부사), in the trees(부사구), all day(부사구),
in summer(부사구)

(2) **2형식 문장 : S + V + C = 주어 + 불완전자동사 + 주격보어**
불완전자동사는 주격보어를 필요로 하는 동사이다. 주격보어는 동사 바로 뒤에서 주어를 보충 설명해 주므로 「**주어 = 주격보어**」의 동격관계가 성립한다.
동사만으로 뜻이 불충분하기 때문에 부족한 뜻을 보충하여 주어나 목적어를 보충 설명해 주는 말이 보어이다. 주격보어로는 명사상당어구[명사, 명사구, 명사절, to부정사(구), 동명사(구)]와 형용사상당어구(형용사, 분사, 형용사구)가 쓰인다.

He is a teacher. (he = a teacher, 명사-주격보어)
The book is interesting. (분사-주격보어)
You are very kind to help me. (형용사구, you = very kind)
Seeing is believing. (동명사) She is beautiful. (형용사)
The fact is *that she doesn't come*. (명사절-주격보어)
My plan is *to master English*. (to부정사구-명사구-주격보어)
(my plan = to master English)

★ 주격보어가 필요한 불완전자동사에는 be동사류(stay, keep, lay, remain, stand, sit), become동사류(get, grow, go, fall, turn, come, run), 지각동사류(look, smell, taste, feel, sound, seem)가 있다.

불완전자동사 + 형용사(명사). (○)

불완전자동사 + 부사. (×)

He looks angry. (he = angry-주격보어) 그는 화나 보인다.

She seems hard. (형용사), He became a doctor. (명사)

The baby fell asleep. (형용사)

His books lay scattered all over the room. (과거분사)

그의 책들은 방안 전체에 흩어져 있다.

주의 : It was terribly cold last night.

(부사 terribly는 형용사 cold를 수식)

* be동사

① 있다 : The book is on the desk. 그 책은 책상 위에 있다.

② ~이다(하다) : She is kind. 그녀는 친절하다.

③ ~되다 : I want to be a musician. 나는 음악가가 되고 싶다.

(3) **3형식 문장 : S + V + O = 주어 + 타동사 + 목적어**

타동사는 목적어를 필요로 하는 동사이다. 명사는 주어, 목적어, 보어로 쓰이기 때문에 주어나 목적어로는 명사 역할을 하는 명사상당어구[명사, 명사구, 명사절, to부정사(구), 동명사(구)]가 쓰인다.

He made. 그는 만들었다.

완전한 문장이 되지 못한다. 여기서 made라는 과거동사는 '무엇을'이라는 목적어가 필요한 동사이므로 타동사로 쓰인다.

He made *coffee*. (명사-목적어)

그는 커피를 만들었다. (완전한 문장)
He made *a pot of strong coffee*. (명사구-목적어)
그는 한 주전자의 진한 커피를 만들었다.
I hoped *to master English*. (to부정사구-명사구-목적어)
He likes *playing tennis*. (동명사구-명사구-목적어)
I didn't know *that she was your sister*. (명사절-목적어)
He made *the kind of coffee I like*.
(관계대명사절의 명사절-목적어)

* He *made for* the park. 그는 공원 쪽으로 갔다. (자동사 + 전치사)
for the park는 부사구이므로 made는 완전자동사. (1형식 문장)

☆ 전치사구가 필요한 3형식 문장 : 주어 + 타동사 + 목적어 + 전치사구
타동사 중에는 문장의 의미를 분명하게 나타내기 위해서 전치사구(부사구)를 필요로 하는 경우가 있다.
I *explained* my plan *to* her. 나는 내 계획을 그녀에게 설명했다.
His voice *reminds* me *of* my old friend.
그의 음성은 내게 나의 오랜 친구를 생각나게 한다.
I *bought* a book *for* her.
나는 그녀에게 책을 사 주었다(나는 그녀를 위해 책을 샀다).

(4) 4형식 문장 : S + V + IO + DO = 주어 + 타동사 + 간접목적어 + 직접목적어
수여동사(~에게 ~을 주다)는 IO와 DO를 필요로 하는 동사이다.

I gave him a book. 나는 그에게 책을 주었다.
 = I gave a book to him.
Father bought me a book. 아버지는 나에게 책을 사 주었다.
 = Father bought a book for me. 아버지는 나를 위해 책을 샀다.

I asked her a question. 나는 그녀에게 질문을 했다.
= I asked a question of her.

★ 4형식 문장 → 3형식 문장

4형식 문장에서 간접목적어 앞에 전치사 to, for, of를 쓰고 직접목적어 뒤에 놓으면 간접목적어가 전치사구로 변해서 4형식 문장이 3형식 문장으로 바뀐다.

- 간접목적어 앞에 전치사 of가 필요한 동사 : ask, inquire, demand, beg
- to가 필요한 동사(~에게 ~하다) : give, pay, read, sell, show, tell, write, bring, teach, offer, lend, send, promise, telephone
- for가 필요한 동사(~위해 ~하다) : buy, get, find, save, call, make, order, choose, cook, bring

(5) 5형식 문장 : S + V + O + C = 주어 + 타동사 + 목적어 + 목적격보어

목적격보어(목적보어)는 목적어 바로 뒤에서 목적어을 보충 설명해 주므로 「목적어 = 목적격보어」의 동격관계가 성립한다. 목적격보어에는 주격보어와 마찬가지로 명사상당어구와 형용사상당어구가 쓰인다.

① 5형식 문장 : 주어 + 타동사 + 목적어 + 목적보어

She told him to close the door. (to부정사구-명사구-목적보어)
그녀는 그가 문을 닫도록 말했다. (him = to close the door)
I found the exam easy. (the exam = easy 형용사)
나는 그 시험이 쉽다는 것을 알았다(알아냈다).
We called the dog Ali. (the dog = Ali 명사)
우리는 그 개를 알리라고 불렀다.
I saw a dog running after her. (분사구 = 형용사구)
= I saw that a dog runs after her.

나는 개가 그녀를 따라가는 것을 보았다.
She made him *what he is today*. (명사절)
그녀가 오늘(날)의 그를 만들었다.
* He makes me angry. (○, 형용사)
　He makes me angrily. (×, 부사)

② **지각동사와 사역동사가 있는 5형식 문장**

〈지각동사/사역동사 참조 → 73p〉

지각동사(see, hear, feel 등) + 목적어 + 동사원형/현재분사
사역동사(have, let, make 등) + 목적어 + 동사원형/과거분사
want(believe, tell, ask 등) + 목적어 + to부정사

I heard her playing the piano.
(현재분사, her = playing the piano)
= I heard her play the piano. (동사원형, her = play the piano)
　나는 그녀가 피아노를 연주하는 것을 들었다.
He makes me clean the room. (동사원형, me = clean the room)
그는 내게 방을 청소하도록 시켰다.
I had the bicycle repaired.
(과거분사-수동관계, the bicycle = repaired)
나는 자전거가 수리되도록 시켰다.
I *asked* him *to* come tomorrow.
나는 그에게 내일 오라고 부탁했다.
(ask + 목적어 + to부정사, ~에게 ~하라고 요청(부탁)하다)

* 5형식 문장에서 목적어와 목적보어(to부정사) 사이에는 주어와 동사의 관계가 성립하기도 한다. 이 경우 목적어는 의미상의 주어로 은, 는, 이,

가로 해석한다.

I *believe* him (*to* be) honest. (to부정사구-목적보어)
= I believe (that) he is honest. 나는 그가 정직하다고 믿는다.
* I believe him (to be) a kind man. [목적보어 : to be + 형(명)]

★ 4형식 문장과 5형식 문장의 구별

5형식 문장의 목적보어가 명사일 때, 4형식 문장과 혼동하기 쉽다. 이 경우에는 목적어와 목적어 뒤에 오는 명사가 동격인지 살펴본다.

He made his son a toy. (his son ≠ a toy) → 4형식
그는 그의 아들에게 장난감을 만들어 주었다.
He made his son an astronaut. (his son = an astronaut) → 5형식
그는 그의 아들을 우주비행사로 만들었다.

★ 자동사로 오인하기 쉬운 타동사들

call, discuss, interview, mention, marry, greet, resemble, reach, approach, live, visit 등은 타동사이므로 전치사 없이 목적어가 온다.
I married with Sandra last week. (×)
I married Sandra last week. (○)
나는 산드라와 지난주에 결혼했다.

타동사로 오인하기 쉬운 자동사들(자동사 + 전치사 = 타동사 역할)

talk, complain, listen, graduate, look, laugh, wait, experiment, deal, depend 등은 자동사이므로 전치사가 있어야 목적어가 올 수 있다.
I wait Tina all day. (×)
I wait for Tina all day. (○)
나는 티나를 하루 종일 기다린다.

자동사로도 타동사로도 쓰이는 동사들

burn, close, open, drop, hang, grow, move, ring, stop, hurt, turn 등

The window broke last night. (그) 창문은 지난밤에 깨졌다.
He broke the window last night. 그는 (그) 창문을 지난밤에 깼다.

☆ 문법을 이해하거나 독해를 하거나 회화를 하거나 영작을 하려면 문장의 5형식을 알아야 한다. 모든 영어 문장은 5가지 문장 형식에 속한다. 긴 문장은 단지 수식어구(단어, 구, 절)가 붙어 있기 때문이다. 수식어구 속에는 보충 정보(설명)가 들어 있다.

☆ 두 개 이상의 단어가 모여서 하나의 품사 역할을 하는 것을 구(句, Phrase)라고 한다. 구에는 전치사구(형용사구, 부사구), to부정사구, 동명사구, 분사구가 있다. 전치사구는 대개 「**전치사 + 명사(대명사)**」로 되어 있다.

「**주어 + 동사**」가 있는 어군을 절(節, Clause)이라 하고, 모든 절은 완전한 문장을 이룬다.

절에는 형용사절, 부사절, 명사절이 있고, 절은 마치 형용사, 부사, 명사처럼 쓰인다.

종속절은 접속사나 관계사에 의해 주절과 연결된다. 문장의 중심이 되는 절을 주절(主節)이라 하고, 주절에 딸린 절을 종속절(從屬節)이라고 한다.

If it's fine tomorrow (종속절), we want to play tennis in the afternoon (주절).

in the afternoon (부사구)

제2장 어순(문장 성분의 순서)

★ **어순의 규칙**

(1) **주어 + 동사 + 목적어 순이다**
술어동사와 목적어 사이에는 다른 단어가 거의 오지 않는다.
She plays the piano. 그녀는 피아노를 연주한다.
She has found a wallet. 그녀는 지갑을 찾았다.

(2) **부사어구는 방법 + 장소 + 시간, 또는 장소 + 방법 + 시간 순이다**
〈부사(구)의 어순 참조 → 38p〉
S + V + O + (C) + 부사어구(how, where, when) + 부사어구 + …

① 부사어구는 대개 방법 + 장소 + 시간 순서로 온다. 왕래발착동사(come, go, arrive 등)일 때는 장소 + 방법 + 시간 순서로 오기도 한다. 방법과 장소 중 동사에 직접 영향을 주는 것이 먼저 오고, 긴 부사어구일수록 나중에 오는 것이 원칙이다. 목적어 뒤에서는 아무거나 먼저 오기도 하나, 대개 방 + 장 + 시 순서로 오는 것이 원칙이다. 시간부사구는 문두, 문미에 자유로이 올 수 있다. 장소부사구는 특별히 강조될 때에만 문두에 오고 보통은 문미 쪽에 온다
* 단순 문장에서 부사어구는 대개 문미 쪽에 온다.

He went home safely yesterday. (장-방-시)
= He went safely home yesterday. (방-장-시)

I went home by car yesterday. (장-방-시)
He arrived safely at the airport yesterday. (방-장-시)
Martin works hard at the office every day. (방-장-시)

나는 매일 내 동생과 함께 집에서 영어를 공부한다.
나는 공부한다/영어를/내 동생과 함께/집에서/매일.
I study English/with my brother at home every day. (○)
I study English/with my brother every day at home. (△)
I study English/at home with my brother every day. (△)
Every day I study English/with my brother at home. (○)
At home, I study English/with my brother every day. (○)

② 두 개 이상의 장소나 시간부사어구가 있을 때는 작은 단위가 큰 단위보다 먼저 온다. 문두에는 큰 단위가 온다.
I'll see her at nine on Saturday.
= On Saturday I'll see her at nine.
Many people take a walk in the park in Seoul.
= In Seoul, many people take a walk in the park.

(3) **빈도부사는 조동사(be)와 본동사 사이에 온다**
조동사가 여러 개이면 첫 번째 조동사 뒤에 오고, 조동사가 없을 때는 본동사 앞에 온다. be동사가 있으면 be동사 뒤에 온다. 즉 부사 not(never)의 위치와 같다.
Sarah often plays the piano in her room.
Sarah has often played the piano in her room.
Sarah is never tired of playing the piano.

(4) **목적어가 문두(문장 앞)에 올 때**

부정어가 문두에 오면 무조건 도치(조동사가 주어 앞에 옴)가 된다. 목적어가 문두에 올 때 혼돈이 생기면 목적어는 문두에 올 수 없다.

They discussed *most of these problems*.

= *Most of these problems* they discussed.

They discussed *none of these problems*.

= *None of these problems* did they discuss.

The dog bites the cat. 개가 고양이를 문다.

≠ The cat bites the dog. 고양이가 개를 문다.

Exercises

A. 다음 빈도부사들을 맞는 위치에 넣으시오.

1. I get tired when I walk with a dog. (never)
2. Mum goes shopping in the morning. (usually)
3. You can ask me for help. (always)
4. In summer we have barbecue parties in our garden. (sometimes)
5. There was milk in the bottle when I wanted to drink some. (hardly any)
6. You will hear of Ronny in the future. (often)

※ 1. I never get ⋯ 2. Mum usually goes ⋯ 3. You can always ask ⋯ 4. ⋯ we sometimes have ⋯ 5. There was hardly any milk ⋯ 6. You will often hear ⋯

B. 다음 단어들을 어순 규칙에 따라 완전한 문장으로 배열하시오.

1. sometimes, drives, Laura, to, sea, the, in, summer
2. You, wish, were, for the future, all the best, I
3. are, living room, the, in, news, the, my, watching, parents
4. I, written, have, him, a letter, today
5. his, lunch, brings, Lukas, always, to school
6. has, shown, just, the guide, to the visitors, the rooms
7. knows, from, someone, my, dad, town, this
8. repaired, for me, my bike, my father, last week
9. meet, often, friends, we, the, at, weekend
10. have, his name, him, asked, I
11. stands, our, always, in, the, tree, living room, Christmas
12. explained, the teacher, the sentences, the students
13. two, books, reads, three, my, or, mum, usually, every, week
14. He, not, understand, could, me
15. hear, our, hardly, neighbors, can, come, we, home, ever
16. envy, I, her, her nice dress
17. coffee, the secretary, will, for the boss, make
18. is, a pullover, for me, knitting, just, my mother
19. always, a country of immigrants, been, has, the United States
20. about 30,000 years ago, by way of the Bering Strait, came, from Asia, the first humans, to the Americas

※ 1. Laura sometimes drives to the sea in summer./In summer Laura sometimes drives to the sea.
2. I wish you were all the best for the future.

3. My parents are watching the news in the living room.
4. I have written him a letter today./Today I have written him a letter.
5. Lukas always brings his lunch to school.
6. The guide has just shown the rooms to the visitors.
7. My dad knows someone from this town.
8. My father repaired my bike for me last week./Last week my father repaired my bike for me.
9. We often meet friends at the weekend./At the weekend we often meet friends.
10. I have asked him his name.
11. Our Christmas tree always stands in the living room.
12. The teacher explained the students the sentences.
13. My mum usually reads two or three books every week.
14. He could not understand me.
15. We can hardly ever hear our neighbors come home.
16. I envy her her nice dress.
17. The secretary will make coffee for the boss.
18. My mother is just knitting a pullover for me.
19. The United States has always been a country of immigrants.
20. About 30,000 years ago the first humans came from Asia to the Americas (to the Americas from Asia) by way of the Bering Strait./The first humans came from Asia to the Americas (to the Americas from Asia) by way of the Bering Strait about 30,000 years ago.

제3장 영작과 독해하기

Ⅰ. 영작하기

1. **구, 절, 문장에서는 주체(핵심)가 되는 말이 먼저 오고, 수식하는 말이 가까운 순서대로 온다**

    방안에 있는 꽃들 flowers *in the room* (꽃들이 핵심)
    책상 위에 있는 책 the book *on the desk.* (책이 핵심)
    거리의 모퉁이에 at(on) the corner *of the street* (모퉁이 핵심)
    부엌에서 요리하고 있는 여자 the woman *cooking in the kitchen*
    서울에서 그녀와 함께 살 남자 the man *to live with her in Seoul*
    학교 앞에 있는 가게 the store *in front of the school*
    내가 공원에서 본 여자 the woman *that I saw in the(a) park*
    내가 공부했던 학교 the school *where I studied*

2. **영어는 대개 주어＋동사가 먼저 온다**

    영어는 주어와 동사로 먼저 결론을 내리고 나서, 이어서 결론을 보충 설명하는 수식어구들이 가까운 순서대로 온다. (그러나 한국어는 동사가 문장 끝에 오므로 결론을 맨 나중에 내리므로 어순이 크게 달라진다.)

(1) **문장을 만들 때 5형식을 구태여 일일이 따져가며 문장을 만들 필요는 없다**

    다만 습관적으로 주어 + 동사 + 목적어 + 수식어 … 순서로 문장을 만들어가면 된다.

(2) 주어가 없을 때는 가주어 it을 쓴다

집에 갈 시간이다. It's time to go home.
너를 다시 보니 좋다. It's nice to see you again.

(3) ~이 있다 : There is(are) …

공항으로 가는 버스가 있나요? Is there a bus to the airport?
마당에는 차 몇 대가 있다. There are some cars in the yard.

(4) 영작문은 유사하게 만들어질 수도 있다

She is beautiful. 그녀는 아름답다.
She seems beautiful. 그녀는 아름다워 보인다.
It seems that she is beautiful.
= She seems to be beautiful.
= It appears that she is beautiful. 그녀는 아름다워 보인다.
≒ The chances are that she is beautiful.
　 그녀는 아름다울 것 같다.
= She is likely to be beautiful. 그녀는 아름다울 것 같다.
= She may(might, should) be beautiful. 그녀는 아름다울 거다.
= She'll probably be beautiful. 그녀는 아마 아름다울 거다.

(5) S + V + 목적어/보어/부사어구

주어 + 동사 뒤에는 목적어, 보어, 부사어구 중 한 가지가 온다.
Tony can speak *French*. (목적어) ← 명사상당어구
Fred has been *ill*. (보어) ← 명사상당어구와 형용사상당어구
My uncle lives *in the USA*. (부사어구) ← 부사상당어구

She had him repair the bike within two days.
(목적어, 보어, 부사구)

한 문장 속에는 3종류가 연달아 오기도 한다.
그녀는 그에게 자전거를 이틀 이내에 수리하게 했다.

(6)   어구의 유형   쓰임
주어 + 동사 + ① to부정사   형용사, 부사, 명사
             ② 동명사   명사
             ③ 분사   형용사, 부사
             ④ 관계사, 관계대명사   형용사
                관계부사   형용사
             ⑤ 전치사구   형용사, 부사
             ⑥ 형용사   보어로 쓰임, 명사를 수식
             ⑦ 부사   동사, 형용사, 부사를 수식
             ⑧ 명사   주어, 목적어, 보어로 쓰임
             ⑨ 구와 절   형용사, 부사, 명사로 쓰임

나는 매일 학교에 간다. (한국어식)
나는 간다/학교에/매일. (영어식)
I go/to school/every day.

우리는 월요일 오후에 부산에 도착했다. (한)
우리는 도착했다/부산에/월요일 오후에. (영)
We arrived/in Pusan/(on) Monday afternoon.

그녀가 내일 온다고 그는 말한다. (한)
그는 말한다/그녀가 온다고/내일. (영)
He says/(that) she comes/tomorrow.

어제 우리는 버스를 타고 박물관에 갔다. (한)

어제 우리는 갔다/버스를 타고/박물관에. (영)
Yesterday we went/by bus/to the museum.

바로 지금 나는 부산에 있는 인터넷 카페에 앉아 있다.
바로 지금/나는 앉아 있다/인터넷 카페에/부산에 있는.
Right now(At the moment)/I am sitting/in an internet café/in Pusan.

옆집에 사는 *여자는* 선생이다.
The woman/who(that) lives next door/is a teacher.

3. **주어＋동사＋목적어**

목적어가 있을 경우 가능한 한 주어＋동사＋목적어를 먼저 쓰고 이어서 수식어구를 쓴다.
그녀는 영어를 매우 잘 말한다. (한국어식)
그녀는 말한다/영어를/매우 잘. (영어식)
She speaks/English/very well.
* 영어를 잘하려면 영어식 어순배열이 습관화되어야 한다.

우리는 많은 친구들을 파티에 초대했다. (한)
우리는 초대했다/많은 친구들을/파티에. (영)
We invited/a lot of friends/to the party.

나는 그녀를 아침에 가끔 지하철에서 본다. (한)
나는 가끔 본다/그녀를/지하철에서/아침에. (영)
I sometimes see/her/on a(the) subway/in the morning.

내가 아침에 그를 볼 때면 그는 늘 급하다.

내가 그를 볼 때면/아침에/그는 늘 급하다.
When I see him/in the morning,/he always is in a hurry.

나는 나의 사랑을 그녀에게 고백했다.
나는 고백했다/그녀에게/나의 사랑을.
I confessed/her/my love. = I confessed/my love/to her.

그녀는 나를 그녀의 부모님에게 소개했다.
그녀는 소개했다/나를/그녀의 부모님에게.
She introduced/me/to her parents.

만일 네가 그에게 돈을 빌려주면,/너는 그것을 결코 돌려받지 못할 거다.
If you lend him money, you'll never get it back.

나는 늘 너를 나의 가장 좋은 친구로 여겼다.
나는 늘 여겼다/너를/나의 가장 좋은 친구로.
I have always considered/you/my best friend.

나는 그녀에게 내 새 차를 운전하게 했다.
나는 하게 했다/그녀에게 운전을/나의 새 차를.
I let/her drive/my new car.

4. **문장 구성의 원리**

영어는 주어와 동사가 먼저 오고, 이어서 주어와 동사를 보충 설명하는 목적어나 보어가 동사 다음에 오고, 목적어나 보어를 보충하는 말이 그 다음에 오고, 보충하는 말을 다시 보충하기 위한 말들이 계속해서 그 다음에 오면서 문장은 길어진다. 즉 뒤 단어가 앞 단어를 보충 설명하는 과정이 연속되면서 문장은 길어지고, 이렇게 만들어진 긴 문장들이 다시 접속사나 관계사로 연결되면서 문장은 더 길어진다.

S + V + O + (C) + 수식어구 + 수식어구…
S(+ 수식어구) + V + O(+ 수식어구) + C(+ 수식어구) + 수식어구 + 수식어구…

★ 예를 들어 부사상당어구(부사, 부사구, 부사절)에는 전치사구, 전치사구 + 관계대명사절, to 부정사(구), 분사구, 종속절 등이 있는데, 이들도 앞 단어를 보충 설명한다.
He works *quickly*. (부사) 그는 빨리 일한다.
He makes the coffee *reasonably quickly*. (부사구)
She can't talk, *while making coffee*. (분사구문-부사구)
= She can't talk *while she makes coffee*. (부사절-종속절)
He went *to the kitchen to make coffee*. (전치사구-부사구)
He made the coffee <u>in the kitchen he always works in</u>.
(전치사구 + 관계대명사절)-부사구
I am glad *to see you* again. (to부정사구-부사구)
She stood *waiting for a friend*. (분사구(문)-부사구)

부모님을 뵙기 위해, 나는 여자친구와 함께 버스로 시골로 갔다. (한)
나는 갔다/시골로/버스로/여자친구와 함께/부모님을 뵙기 위해. (영)
I went/to the countryside/by bus/with my girlfriend,/to see my parents.
* 전치사구(부사구)는 연거푸 올 수 있다.

경찰은 그 사건을 본 누군가에게 말하기를 원한다. (한)
경찰은 원한다/누군가에게 말하기를/그 사건을 본. (영)
The police want/to talk to anybody/who saw the accident.

제인은 우리가 그녀를 우리들의 집에서 우리와 함께 머물도록 초대했기 때문에 매우 행복해 했다. (한)
제인은 매우 행복해 했다/우리가 그녀를 초대했기 때문에/우리와 함께 머물도록/우리들의 집에서. (영)
Jane was very happy/because we invited her/to stay with us/at our house.

나는 그에게 무슨 일이 일어났는지 누구에게도 말하지 말 것을 약속하게 했다.
나는 그에게 약속하게 했다/그는 누구에게도 말하지 말 것을/무슨 일이 일어났는지.
I made him promise/that he wouldn't tell anybody/what happened.

우리는 집으로 돌아오는 차 안에서 토론 끝에 주말에 이 마을에서 친구들과 함께 축구 차기로 결정했다.
우리는 결정했다/축구 차기로/친구들과 함께/이 마을에서/주말에/토론 끝에/차 안에서/집에 돌아오는 길에.
We decided/to play soccer/with friends/ in this town/on the weekend[(on) weekends]/at the end of a discussion/in the car/on the way back home.

구나 절로 이루어진 복잡한 문장에 접속사나 관계사가 연결되면서 문장은 더 길어진다.

There are many differences between me and this man. He has all that he wants, and nothing to do but to spend money and enjoy a pleasant life, while I have to work hard to get dry bread enough to keep myself and my children alive. What has he done that he should be so lucky, and what have I done that I should be so miserable?

나와 이 남자 사이에는 많은 차이점들이 있다. 그는 모두 가지고 있다, 그가 원하는 것을, 그리고 아무것도 할 것이 없다, 돈을 소비하는 것과 즐거운 삶을 즐기는 것 이외에는, 반면에 나는 힘들게 일을 해야만 한다, 마른 빵을 충분히 얻기 위해서, 내 자신과 내 아이들을 계속 살아있게 하기 위하여. 그는 무엇을 했기에, 그는 그토록 행운이 있어야만 하고, 그리고 나는 무엇을 했기에 이렇게 비참해야만 하는가?

Ⅱ. 독해(해석)하기

1. 직독직해와 직청직해

우리는 지난주에 조부모님을 방문했다. (한국어식)
우리는 방문했다/조부모님을/지난주에. (영어식)
We visited/grandparents/last week.

우리는 방문했다. (누구를?)/조부모님을 (언제?)/지난주에.
이런 식으로 직독하면서 즉시 해석하는 것을 직독직해라고 부른다. 영어를 읽으면서 빨리 이해하려면 영어민식의 직독직해하는 습관이 필수적이다. 영어민은 해석을 하기 위해 앞뒤로 왔다 갔다 하면서 해석하는 것이 아니라 들으면서(읽으면서) 자연히 차례로 이해가 되어 버린다. 그러므로 직독직해를 잘하는 학생일수록 영어민의 사고방식과 영어의 어순구조를 빨리 터득하게 되므로 자연히 영어를 빨리 배우게 된다.

★ 직독직해의 기본 원리와 끊어읽기
① 동사 앞에서 끊는다. [주어가 형용사구(절)의 수식을 받아 길 때]

② 구 앞에서 끊는다. (전치사구, 부정사구, 동명사구 앞에서)
③ 절 앞에서 끊는다. (접속사절, 관계사절)
④ 구두점 앞에서 끊는다.

Obama also struggled/with the absence of his father,/who he saw only once more/after his parents divorced,/when Obama Sr. visited Hawaii/for a short time/in 1971.
오바마는 또한 고투했다/그의 아버지의 부재로,/그를(아버지를) 그는 단지 한 번 더 보았다/ 그의 부모가 이혼한 후에,/오바마 아버지가 하와이를 방문했을 때/잠깐 동안/1971년에.

2. **해석(독해)하기**

아무리 긴 문장이라도 뒷말은 앞말을 가까운 순서대로 보충 설명하면서 수식해 나갔으므로, 해석도 구 단위, 절 단위로 끊어서 순서대로 해석해 나간다.

Clinton's grandparents were strict disciplinarians,/who instilled in him/the importance of a good education./"My grandparents had a lot to do/with my early commitment to learning,"/Clinton later recalled./"They taught me to count and read./I was reading little books/when I was 3."
클린턴의 조부모님은 엄격히 교육하는 분들이었다,/그들은 그에게 가르쳤다/좋은 교육의 중요성을./"나의 조부모님은 많은 것을 해야만 하셨다/나의 배우려는 조기 약속으로."/라고 클린턴은 후에 기억했다./"그 분들은 나에게 계산하는 것과 읽는 것을 가르치셨다./나는 작은 책들을 읽고 있었다/내가 3살 때."

Clinton's mother returned to Arkansas/with a degree in nursing/

in 1950,/and later that year/she married an automobile salesman/named Roger Clinton./Two years later,/the family moved from Hope to Hot Springs, Arkansas./Although neither his parents nor his grandparents were religious,/Clinton became a devoted Baptist/from a very young age./On Sunday mornings,/he woke himself up,/put on his best dress clothes/and walked half a mile/to Park Place Baptist Church/to attend services alone.
클린턴 엄마는 아칸소 주로 돌아왔다/간호학 학위를 받고/1950년에,/그리고 그해 늦게/그녀는 한 자동차판매원과 결혼했다/로저 클린턴이라고 불리는./2년 후에,/그 가족은 호프에서 핫 스프링스(아칸소 주)로 이사했다./비록 그의 부모님도 그의 조부모님도 종교적이지 않았을지라도,/클린턴은 헌신적인(열성적인) 침례교도가 되었다,/매우 어린 나이에./어느 일요일 아침에,/그는 혼자 일어나서,/그의 가장 좋은 옷을 입고,/반 마일을 걸었다/침례교회 공원으로,/홀로 예배에 참석하기 위해서.

Then he returned home,/and when he knocked at the door of Cassim's house/it was opened by a slave called Morgiana,/who was the cleverest and best/of all his brother's servants.
그가 집으로 돌아온 그때,/그리고 그가 캐심의 집문을 노크했을 때,/문은 모르기아나라고 불리는 종에 의해 열렸다,/그는 가장 영리하고 가장 좋았다/모든 그의 형의 하인들 중에서.

So it was agreed/that one of the robbers should disguise,/go into the town,/and try to find out/who the man was/whom they had found in their cave,/and whose body had been stolen away.
그래서 동의되었다/도둑들 중 하나가 가장을 하고,/마을 안으로 들어가야 하는 것이,/그리고 찾아낼 것을 노력해야 하는데/그 남자는 누구였으며/그들이 그들의 동굴 속에서 누구를 발견한 것이었으며,/그리고 누구의 시체가 도난당한 것인지를.

In the city of Bagdad,/far away in Persia,/there lived a poor man called Hindbad./He was a porter,/and one hot afternoon/ as he was carrying a very heavy load,/he stopped to rest/in a quiet street/near a beautiful house/which he had never seen before.
바그다드의 도시에서,/페르시아에서 멀리 떨어진,/힌드바드라로 불리는 한 가난한 사람이 살았다./그는 짐꾼이었다,/그리고 뜨거운 어느 날 오후에/그는 매우 무거운 짐을 운반하고 있었을 때,/그는 휴식을 하려고 멈췄다/조용한 거리에서,/아름다운 집 가까이/그가 결코 전에 본 적이 없는.

A legion of buyers like Mr. Calvin,/buoyed/by a growing economy and a soaring stock market,/are shedding/whatever reluctance,/or self-imposed restraint,/they had during the recession/ by entering showrooms/and leaving with trophy cars.
캘빈 씨와 같은 구매자들의 지역은,/들떠 있었다/성장하는 경제와 급상승하는 주식시장에 의해,/떨쳐버리고 있다/마음에 내키지 않는 무엇이든지,/또는 스스로의 자제력도,/그들은 불경기 동안에/전시장에 입장해서/전시품 차와 함께 떠남으로써.

Some economists,/like Simon Tilford,/deputy director of the Center for European Reform/in London,/argue/that the euro zone is already stuck/in the same kind of economic quicksand/ that trapped Japan for decades,/and that the European Central Bank must aggressively stimulate/growth now,/not only by cutting rates/but also by taking steps to pump money/into the economy.

몇몇 경제학자들은,/사이먼 틸포드와 같은,/유럽개혁센터의 부국장인/런던에 있는/주장한다/유로존이 이미 빠져있다고,/똑같은 종류의 경제 늪 속에/일본이 수십 년 동안 갇혀 있었던,/그래서 유럽중앙은행이 적극적으로 촉진시켜야만 한다고/성장을 지금,/금리인하뿐만 아니라/돈을 펌프하기 위한 조치를 취하는 것도/경제에.

이러한 긴 문장들을 듣고 이해하거나, 읽고 해석하기 위해서는 영어식 직청직해와 직독직해가 필수적이다. 한국어식으로는 도저히 따라 듣거나 따라 해석할 수 없기 때문이다. 직독직해의 능력이 길러지면 문장의 구와 절이 덩어리 단위로 끊어서 들리고 끊어서 이해되므로 아무리 긴 문장이라도 어휘만 알면 이해하게 된다. 직독직해가 처음에는 이상하게 느껴지지만, 습관화되면 자연스러워진다. 직독직해가 되어야만 구나 절이 쉽게 숙달된다.

★ 복잡한 긴 복문을 한국어식으로 독해할 경우, 주절의 동사를 찾기 힘든 경우가 있다. 종속절들이 주절 앞뒤로 여러 개 올 경우 접속사나 관계대명사가 생략된 종속절인지 살펴보아야 한다. 그러나 영어식 직독직해 방법으로는 종속절과 주절의 동사를 구태여 찾아 구별할 필요가 없다.

That Sarah likes her new car (which) her father bought her when she had no money is clear.
= That Sarah likes her new car is clear (which) her father bought her when she had no money.
사라가 돈이 없을 때 그녀의 아버지가 그녀에게 사준 그녀의 새 차를 사라가 좋아하는 것은 분명하다. (한국어식 해석)
사라가 그녀의 새 차를 좋아하는 것은 분명하다/그녀의 아버지가 그녀에게 사준/그녀가 돈이 없을 때. (영어식 해석)

* 간단한 문장은 한국어식으로 해석하더라도 긴 문장은 영어식으로 해석하는 것이 좋다. 최선의 방법은 간단한 문장에서부터 스스로 영어식으로 순서대로 해석하는 습관을 기르는 것이다.

Exercises

A. 다음을 영작하시오.
1. 그녀는 그녀의 남편을 위해 식사를 요리했다.
2. 물론 우리가 도착했을 때 비가 오고 있었다.
3. 너는 교실에서 누구의 책을 발견했니?
4. 누가 너에게 이 선물을 주었니?
5. 나의 아버지는 몇 년 전에 새 차를 샀다.
6. 우리는 새 꽃들을 봄마다 정원에 심는다.
7. 그는 오늘 아침 기차로 갔을 리가 없다.
8. 만일 내가 기차로 일하러 간다면 나는 신문을 읽을 수 있다.
9. 내가 돈이 있다면 그 집을 살 수 있을 텐데.
10. 나는 규칙들을 아이들에게 설명했다.
11. 개를 가진 사람들은 늘 친절하다.
12. 건강식품은 어른뿐만 아니라 아이들에게도 좋다.
13. 해마다 수천의 사람들이 교통사고로 죽는다.
14. 프랭클린 루즈벨트는 미국의 대통령으로 네 번 선출되었다.
15. 나는 어제 클럽에서 오직 그만 보았다.
16. 나는 이 책을 나의 휴가 중에 읽으려고 한다.
17. 잭이 정말로 무엇을 원하는지 아는 것은 불가능하다.
18. 지난 반세기에는 많은 경제적 어려움들이 있었다.

※ 1. She cooked a meal for her husband.
2. Of course it was raining when we arrived.
3. Whose book did you find in the classroom?
4. Who gave you this present?
5. My father bought a new car some years ago.
6. We plant new flowers in the garden every spring.
7. He can't have gone by train this morning.
8. If I go to work by train, I can read the paper(newspaper).
9. If I had money, I could buy the house. (가정법 과거)
10. I explained the rules to the children(kids).
    = I explained the children the rules.
11. People who have dogs are always friendly(kind).
12. Health food is good for children as well as adults.
13. Every year thousands of people are killed (die) in a car accident.
14. Franklin Roosevelt was elected President of the United States four times.
15. I saw only him at(in) the club yesterday./Yesterday I saw only him at(in) the club.
16. I'm going to read this book on my holiday.
17. It is impossible to know what Jack really wants.
18. In the last(past) half century there were many economic(financial) difficulties.

제4장 부사

부사(副詞)는 동사, 형용사, 부사 앞에 놓여 그 말을 수식하여 그 뜻을 더 풍부하게 만드는 품사이다.

(1) **부사를 만드는 법 : 「형용사 + ly」**
    quick(빠른) → quickly(빠르게)   usual(보통의) → usually(보통)
    easy(쉬운) → easily(쉽게)   true(진실의) → truly(진실로)
    sure(확실한) → surely(확실하게)
    careful(주의 깊은) → carefully(주의 깊게)
    basic(기본적인) → basically(기본적으로)
    certain(확실한) → certainly(확실하게)

(2) **형용사와 부사가 같은 형태**
    early(이른-일찍), fast(빠른-빨리), wide(넓은-널리), long(오랜-오래), right(옳은-올바로), hard(어려운-심하게), high(높은-높게), far(먼-멀리), much(많은-많이), late(늦은-늦게), wrong(틀린-틀리게), close(가까운-가까이), just(공정한-바로), near(가까운-가까이)

(3) **형용사와 부사가 같은 형태에 -ly를 붙이면 다른 뜻으로 되는 부사**
    near(가까운-가까이)-nearly(거의), high(높은-높게)-highly(매우), hard(어려운-열심히)-hardly(거의~않다), late(늦은-늦게)-lately(최근에), right(올바른-올바르게)-rightly(당연히), high(높은-높게)-highly(상당히), most(가장 많은-가장 많이)-mostly(대개), deep

(깊은-깊게)-deeply(매우), close(가까운-가까이)-closely(접근하여), just(공정한-바로)-justly(정당하게)

1. **부사의 용법**

(1) 부사는 동사, 형용사, 부사, 문장 전체를 수식한다
She speaks English well. (부사 well이 동사를 수식-방법)
I met her before(last year). (부사 before가 동사를 수식-시간)
She is very beautiful. (부사 very가 형용사를 수식)
She speaks English very well. (부사 very가 부사를 수식)
Fortunately, she got a new job. (부사가 문장 전체를 수식)
We met *in the tennis court* yesterday.
(부사구가 동사를 수식-장소)
* 방법, 장소, 시간을 나타내는 부사(구)는 대개 동사를 수식한다.

(2) 다음 동사들 바로 뒤에는 형용사는 올 수 있고, 부사는 올 수 없다

① be동사 뒤에
You *are lucky* that I was there to help you.
We *were happy* when we heard your voice.
The holidays will *be wonderful*.
The weather has *been terrible* this week.

주의 : She is seriously ill. (O) 그녀는 심하게 아프다.
be동사 뒤에 부사 seriously는 형용사 ill을 수식하고 있다.

② feel, look, smell, seem, sound, taste 등의 지각동사(불완전자동사) 뒤에는 주격보어로 형용사가 온다.

I *feel awful* about this mistake.

Jack *looked angry(tired)* yesterday, didn't he?

This *smells good*. What is it?

This song *sounds great*. Who is singing?

Your spaghetti always *tastes* so *good*.

★ 부사가 목적어(전치사 + 목적어)와 연관될 때는 지각동사 + 목적어 뒤에 부사가 온다.

The doctor felt *my pulse* carefully.

의사는 내 맥박을 조심스럽게 쟀다.

I tasted *the spaghetti* slowly. 나는 스파게티를 천천히 맛보았다.

Jack looked at *me* angrily. 잭은 화나서 나를 쳐다보았다.

The teacher looked angrily at *his pupils*.

선생은 화나서 그의 학생들을 쳐다보았다.

③ get, go, grow, become '되다'의 의미가 있는 동사 뒤에

Stop this noise or I'll *go crazy*. Let's go inside. It's *getting cold*.

Bill *grows impatient* easily. Sarah *became angry* when she saw me.

④ be동사 뒤에는 형용사나 명사가 올 수 있다.

She is beautiful. (O) She is a student. (O)

She is beautifully. (×) She sings beautifully. (O)

Her English is very good. 그녀의 영어는 매우 좋다. (형용사)

She speaks English well. 그녀는 영어를 잘 말한다. (부사)

예외 : My homework was *over*. (부사) 내 숙제는 끝났다.

⑤ be동사 뒤의 주격보어들

be + 명사(형용사, 전치사구(부사구), to부정사, 동명사, 종속절)

He is a teacher. (be + 명사)

My plan is to learn English. (be + to부정사구)

She is beautiful. (be + 형용사), Seeing is believing. (be + 동명사)

He is at the library. (be + 부사구(전치사구))

The problem is that we don't have any money.
(be + 종속절-명사절)

2. 부사(구)의 어순

(1) **부사가 형용사, 부사, 구, 절을 수식할 때는 그 말 바로 앞에 온다**

She is very *beautiful*. (형용사)

She sings very *beautifully*. (부사)

He went to school <u>soon after</u> breakfast. (구, ~후 곧)

She had dinner <u>long before</u> he came home. (절, 훨씬 이전에)

(2) **자동사를 수식하는 부사는 대개 자동사 뒤에, 타동사를 수식하는 부사는 대개 목적어 뒤에 온다**

She runs fast. He studies English hard.

She can speak English fluently.

= She can fluently speak English.

I love her really. = I really love her.

(3) **부사(구)는 술어동사와 목적어 사이에는 거의 오지 않는다**

그러나 목적어가 부사(구)보다 훨씬 길 때는 「긴 것은 뒤로」의 원칙에 따라 드물게 예외적으로 부사(구)가 술어동사와 목적어 사이에 오기도 한다.

I recovered *yesterday* the stolen bike.

= I recovered the stolen bike *yesterday*.

Never put off *until tomorrow* what you can do today. (명사절)
오늘 할 수 있는 일을 내일로 미루지 마라.
= 내일까지 미루지 마라/네가 오늘 할 수 있는 것을.
* 목적어가 긴 경우 부사는 대개 동사 앞에 온다.
He loudly denied *that he had stolen the book*. (목적절-명사절)

(4) 전치사 수반동사와 함께 쓰이는 부사는 전치사 앞에, 또는 전치사의 목적어 뒤에 온다
She *looked* kindly *at* me. 그녀는 나를 상냥하게 쳐다보았다.
= She *looked at* me kindly.
* 전치사의 목적어가 절일 때 부사는 전치사 앞에 온다.
She *looked* kindly *at* people who got off the bus.
그녀는 상냥하게 사람들을 쳐다보았다/버스에서 내리는.

(5) 빈도부사는 조동사(be동사) 뒤에 본동사 앞에 온다. 조동사가 여러 개이면 첫 번째 조동사 뒤에 온다. 즉, 부사 not(never)의 위치와 같다
never, hardly, seldom, sometimes, often, usually, always, frequently, ever, scarcely 등

He always works hard. He has always been kind to others.
I have never heard such a rumor.
나는 결코 들은 적이 없다/그런 소문을.

(6) 방법(상태)부사는 자동사 뒤에, 목적어가 있으면 목적어 뒤에 온다
Susan laughed loudly. Jack carried the baggage carefully.
Linda watched the monkeys curiously.

(7) 문장부사(문장 전체를 수식)는 문두(문미), 조동사 앞뒤에 자유자재로 오지만

장소, 시간부사어구가 있으면 이들 앞에 온다

certainly, probably, surely, generally, mostly, fortunately, happily, suddenly, eventually, originally, normally, actually, frankly 등

Happily, he has passed the exam.
= He happily has passed the exam.
= He has happily passed the exam.
= He has passed the exam happily.
He has passed the exam happily at school today.

(8) 시간부사(구)는 문두나 문미에 온다. 장소부사(구)는 강조할 때만 문두에 온다

Tomorrow I go to meet my girlfriend.
= I go to meet my girlfriend tomorrow.
In America, many people eat in restaurants.
= Many people eat in restaurants in America.

(9) 두 개 이상의 부사(구)가 겹칠 때는 대개 「방법 + 장소 + 시간」 순이지만, 왕래 발착 동사일 때는 「장소 + 방법 + 시간」 순으로 되기도 한다

She arrived home safely last night. (장 + 방 + 시)
= She arrived safely home last night. (방 + 장 + 시)
She played the piano elegantly in the hall last night.
(방 + 장 + 시) 그녀는 피아노를 연주했다/우아하게/홀에서/지난밤에.

(10) 짧은 부사구는 앞쪽에, 긴 부사구는 뒤쪽에 오기도 한다

Our grandfather died *at half past three* last night.
= Our grandfather died last night *at half past three*.

우리 할아버지는 돌아가셨다/지난밤 3시 반에.

(11) 부사와 부사구가 겹칠 때는 대개 부사가 부사구보다 먼저 온다
We walked west *through the city*.
우리는 서쪽으로 걸었다/도시를 지나.

(12) 「시간이나 장소」는 작은 단위 → 큰 단위 순서로 온다
I met him at a hotel in Seoul in Korea. (장소)
I met her at eleven, Monday, April, 15th, 2014. (시간)

(13) 방향을 나타내는 부사구가 겹칠 때는 이동되는 순서로 온다
He ran from the school down the hill over the bridge through the field to the village.
그는 학교로부터 언덕 아래로 다리 위로 벌판을 지나 마을로 달렸다.

(14) 전치사와 결합이 안 되는 부사
명사와 부사로 쓰이는 단어들은 움직이는 동사 뒤에서는 부사로만 쓰이므로 「전치사 + 부사」형으로는 쓰이지 않는다. 그러므로 다음 단어들은 부사로 쓰였을 경우 방향 전치사 to와 결합하지 못한다.
home 집으로, here 여기에, upstairs 위층에, ahead 앞에, 앞으로, right 우측으로, forwards 앞으로, downtown 시내로, abroad 해외로, back wards 뒤쪽으로, there 저기에, inside 안으로, outside 바깥으로, downhill 비탈 아래로
I go to home. (×, 부사) I go home. (○, 부사)
I stay at home. (○, 명사)

(15) else(그 밖의, 다른) 부사는 수식하는 말 뒤에 온다
What else did he say? 그 밖에 무엇을 그는 말했니?

I don't want anything else, thanks.
나는 원하지 않는다/그 밖에 (다른) 어떤 것을, 고맙다.

(16) 구동사를 만드는 부사

pick up, put up, bring back, give up, take up, turn on(off), throw away, take off(on), try on(off), set down 등

「타동사 + 부사」(turn on)로 구동사(동사구)를 이룰 때, 목적어가 명사이면 동사와 부사 사이에 오거나 부사 뒤에 온다. 목적어가 대명사이면 동사와 부사 사이에만 온다. 짧은 것은 앞에 긴 것은 뒤로 가는 습성 때문이다.

Turn on the light. = Turn the light on. 불을 켜라.
Turn it on. (○) Turn on it. (×)

그러나 자동사 + 전치사는 다르다.
Listen to the girl. (○) Listen the girl to. (×)

3. 부사의 종류

① 부사 : He stands in front of the theater *impatiently*.

② 부사구 : He stands in front of the theater *very impatiently*.

③ 전치사구(부사구) : He stands in front of the theater *with his girlfriend*.

④ to부정사구(부사구) : He stands in front of the theater *to meet his girlfriend*.

⑤ 분사구문(부사구) : He stands there *waiting for his girlfriend*.

⑥ 종속절(부사절) : He stands there *in order that he waits for his girlfriend*.

4. 부사의 비교

형용사와 같이 원급, 비교급, 최상급을 만든다.
little → less → least, early → earlier → earliest
well → better → best, much → more → most
badly → worse → worst, late → later → latest
far → further/farther → furthest/farthest
quickly → more quickly → most quickly

5. 주의할 부사들

(1) very와 much

very는 형용사와 부사의 원급을 수식하고, much는 비교급과 동사를 수식한다. 최상급 수식은 the very와 much가 쓰인다.
It's very good to meet you. 매우 좋다/너를 만나는 것은.
I like vegetable dishes *very much*. (very much가 동사를 수식)
나는 야채 요리들을 좋아한다/매우 많이.

The bike runs very fast.
The bus runs much faster than the bike.
The plane is much the fastest vehicle in the world.
= The plane is the very fastest vehicle in the world.
　비행기는 단연코 가장 빠른 운송수단이다/세상에서.

(2) already, yet, still

already(이미, 벌써)는 긍정문에, yet는 부정문(아직)과 의문문(이미, 벌써)에 쓰인다.
already가 의문문에 쓰이면 놀라움을 나타낸다.
still(아직도, 여전히)은 모든 종류의 문장에 쓰인다.
I have finished the work already.

나는 그 일을 끝마쳤다/벌써(이미).
Have you finished the work already?
너는 그 일을 끝마쳤니/벌써? (놀랍다)
I have not finished the work yet.
나는 그 일을 끝내지 않았다/아직.
Have you finished the work yet?
너는 그 일을 끝마쳤니/벌써(이미)?
The book which I ordered hasn't still arrived.
내가 주문한 책은 아직(도) 도착하지 않았다.

(3) too, either, also
'역시, ~도, 또한'이라는 뜻으로 too는 긍정문에, either는 부정문에 쓰인다.
also는 모든 종류의 문장에 쓰이며, 문장 중간에 온다.
I am a student, too. = I am also a student. 나 역시 학생이다.
He doesn't smoke cigarettes. I don't, either.
그는 담배를 피우지 않는다. 나도(나 역시) 피우지 않는다.

(4) so와 neither
대답문의 도치 : so 역시(도)~하다, neither 역시(도)~아니다.
She likes tea. So do I. = I like tea, too.
She doesn't like coffee. Neither do I. = I don't like it, either.
그녀는 커피를 좋아하지 않는다. 나도 그것을 좋아하지 않는다.
* Neither answer is correct. (둘 중) 어느 대답도 옳지 않다.
Either you or he has to go there.
너나 그나 둘 중 하나는 거기에 가야만 한다.

(5) enough

enough는 형용사와 부사를 뒤에서 수식하고, 명사를 앞뒤에서 수식한다.

She is rich enough to buy a new house. (형용사 수식)
She has enough money to buy a new house. (명사 수식)
= She has money enough to buy a new house. (명사 수식)
그녀는 충분한 돈을 가지고 있다/새 집을 사기 위해.

(6) no

① no + 명사 = not ~ any + 명사, no + 명사 → none(대명사)
There were no books. = There weren't any books.
Is there any pen on the desk? No, there is none(no pen).

② no matter + 의문사(what, how, where, which, when)는 양보의 의미로 '아무리 ~할지라도'의 뜻이다.
No matter how impatient Jack is = However impatient Jack is
No matter how impatient Jack is, he never takes offense.
잭은 아무리 참을성이 없을지라도 결코 화를 내지 않는다.

6. **접속부사**

접속부사는 앞뒤 문장을 연결하면서 뒤 문장을 꾸며주는 부사이다. 접속부사는 대개 격식체(학술적 문장)에서 사용되며, 일상체(회화체)에서는 거의 사용되지 않는다. 접속부사는 두 번째 문장의 ① 문두에, ② 주어와 동사 사이에, ③ 문미에 온다.

Peter passed the exam because he studied hard.
= Peter studied hard. Therefore, he passed the exam. (격식체)
= Peter studied hard, so he passed the exam. (일상체)

= Peter studied hard. He, therefore, passed the exam.
= Peter studied hard. He passed the exam, therefore.

Peter is rich, but James is poor. (일상체)
= Peter is rich. However, James is poor. (격식체)
= Peter is rich. James, however, is poor.
= Peter is rich. James is poor, however.

Exercises

A. 형용사와 부사 중 어느 것이 적합한지 고르시오.

1. The driver was (serious, seriously) hurt in the accident.
2. The damage to the building was very (serious, seriously).
3. My grandfather always talks (serious, seriously).
4. Look, I've got (free, freely) tickets for the concert. Would you like to come along? No, thanks. I (hard, hardly) know them. I think they are (most, mostly) for older people.
5. She is always (high, highly) (elegant, elegantly).
6. (Surprising, Surprisingly), he (real, really) came to the party.
7. Be careful, you idiot! You (near, nearly) crashed into me! Oh, I'm (deep, deeply) sorry! But if I don't hurry, I'll be (late, lately) again and this will land me in (deep, deeply) trouble.
8. Mt Palomar Observatory is on a (high, highly) hill (near, nearly) Los Angeles. Many (high, highly) respected astronomers work there.
9. Angela speaks French very (good, well).

10. Both teams seemed to be very (nervous, nervously).
11. Your idea sounds (great, greatly).
12. When James heard the news, he became very (sad, sadly).
13. The patient felt very (weak, weakly).
14. What a (hard, hardly) test! I'll call you (direct, directly) when I get the results.
15. How are Bill and Jenny? I don't know. I haven't seen them (late, lately). Have you? No, I haven't. I (near, nearly) visited them last week, but then I didn't have the time.
16. Can I make a (direct, directly) phone call from here to America? Yes, you can. The first minute is (free, freely), then it's 50 p per minute.
17. He didn't look very (good, well) today.
18. He looks (angry, angrily).
19. He looked (angry, angrily) at the children who had broken the vase.
20. They said I could speak (free, freely), but then they were (deep, deeply) disappointed when I said what I did not like.
21. That's what I hate (most, mostly); (hard, hardly) work and (hard, hardly) any free time.

※ 1. seriously 2. serious 3. seriously 4. free, hardly, mostly 5. highly, elegant 6. Surprisingly, really 7. nearly, deeply, late, deep 8. high, near, highly 9. well 10. nervous 11. great 12. sad 13. weak 14. hard, directly 15. lately, nearly 16. direct, free 17. good(well) 18. angry 19. angrily 20. freely, deeply 21. most, hard, hardly

B. 괄호 안에 적합한 형용사나 부사를 보기에서 골라 넣으시오.

friendly, early, late, good, well, high, hard, fast

1. I know Richard (   ). He is a (   ) friend of my elder brother. They like mountains, and so they often leave (   ) in the morning to go climbing. They love to spend the day (   ) up in the rocks. Usually they return (   ) in the evening.
2. Richard is an (   ) riser. Even after a (   ) day of mountain climbing he does not sleep (   ). But he is always (   ) and has a (   ) word and smile for everybody.
3. He often thinks of the (   ) mountains that he loves so much. He is a (   ) and (   ) climber, but he is very careful, too. He practices (   ), usually two hours every afternoon.
4. Richard is also a (   ) skier, but I think sometimes he skis too (   ). I hope I will be like Martin when I get older.

※ 1. well, good, early, high, late 2. early, hard, late, friendly, friendly 3. high, good, fast, hard 4. good, fast

C. 괄호 안의 부사를 맞는 위치에 넣으시오. 한 개 이상일 수도 있음.
1. Steve practiced football. (yesterday)
2. Thomas Muster plays a match. (today, here)
3. Columbus set his foot on the American continent. (never)
4. I am interested in good films and books. (always)
5. Grandma has told me about her schooldays. (often)
6. You will remember her when you see her. (hardly)
7. Dad drives to work. (frequently)

8. We make a barbeque in the garden. (sometimes)

9. Lisa smiled at me. (happily, today)
10. The visitors were waiting. (outside, patiently)
11. I'll have to work. (tomorrow, hard)
12. It rained. (yesterday, heavily, here)
13. Let's go! (now, quickly, inside)
14. The book sold 300,000 copies. (quickly)
15. They thought that I was dead. (probably)
16. You think that I don't know what I'm talking about. (obviously)
17. Our dog barks when he sees a stranger. (always, loudly)

18. They wanted to sack me. *(actually)*
19. I didn't know what to think. *(really)*
20. The commission accepted my proposal. *(eventually)*
21. I didn't realize how difficult it would be. *(honestly)*
22. The union demanded a 6 per cent wage increase. *(originally)*
23. The committee meets once every month. *(normally)*
24. The man could have killed the cat. *(easily)*

※ 1. Yesterday Steve practiced football./Steve practiced football yesterday. 2. Thomas Muster plays a match here today/Today Thomas Muster plays a match here. 3. Columbus never set his foot on the American continent. 4. I am always interested in good films and books. 5. Grandma has often told me about her schooldays. 6. You will hardly remember her when you see her. 7. Dad frequently drives to work. 8. We sometimes make a barbeque in the garden. 9. Lisa smiled at me happily today./Today Lisa smiled at me happily. 10. The visitors were waiting patiently outside./Outside the visitors were waiting patiently. 11. I'll have to work hard tomorrow./Tomorrow I'll have to work hard. 12. It rained heavily here yesterday./Yesterday it rained heavily here. 13. Let's go inside quickly now! 14. The book quickly sold ··· 15. They probably thought ··· 16. You obviously think ··· 17. Our dog always barks loudly when ··· 18. They actually wanted to sack me./They wanted to sack me actually. 19. I really didn't know what to think./Really, I didn't know ···/I didn't know what to think really. 20. The commission eventually accepted my proposal./Eventually, the commission accepted my proposal./The commission accepted my proposal eventually. 21. I honestly didn't realize how difficult it would be./Honestly, I didn't realize ···/I didn't realize ··· be honestly. 22. The union originally demanded a 6 per cent wage increase./Originally, the union demanded ···/The union demanded ··· increase originally. 23. The committee normally meets once every month./Normally, the committee meets ···/The committee meets once every month normally. 24. The man could easily have killed the cat./The man could have killed the cat easily.

제5장 형용사

형용사(形容詞)는 사물의 성질, 상태(모양, 크기, 색깔, 수량) 등을 나타내는 품사이다.

1. **형용사의 종류**
   ① 성상형용사 : 사물의 성질, 상태를 나타내는 형용사
    a kind girl, a pretty girl, a small car
   ② 대명형용사 : 대명사가 명사를 수식하여 형용사 역할을 함
    this(some, which, any, my) + book
   ③ 수량형용사 : 수량형용사에는 수사와 부정 수량형용사가 있다.
   • 수사에는 기수, 서수, 배수가 있다.
   • 부정 수량형용사 : many, much, little, some, any, few 등
   ④ 관사형용사 : 명사를 한정 수식함 : a (an, the) book

2. **수량형용사**

(1) **수 형용사 many와 양 형용사 much**
    I have many(a lot of, lots of, plenty of) friends here.
    We need much(a lot of, lots of) water to live every day.
    We have a great deal of wine. a great(good) deal of = a lot of
    She doesn't eat a lot(much). 그녀는 많이 먹지 않는다.
    A *number of* women play tennis. (많은 여자들, 복수 취급)
    The number of women playing tennis is small.

(여자들의 수, 단수 취급)

(2) few와 little

few는 수에 쓰이는 형용사이고, little은 양에 쓰이는 형용사이다. a가 붙으면 '조금, 약간'의 뜻이고, a가 없으면 '거의 없다, 매우 적다'의 뜻이다.

I have a few friends here. 나는 몇 명의 친구가 있다/여기에.
I have few friends here. 나는 친구가 거의 없다(매우 적다)/여기에.
I have a little money now. 나는 돈이 조금 있다/지금.
I have little money now.
나는 돈이 거의 없다(매우 조금 있다)/지금.
Many a little makes a mickle. 티끌 모아 태산.

3. 형용사의 용법

형용사의 용법에는 한정적 용법(명사를 수식)과 서술적 용법(보어로 쓰임)이 있다.

(1) 한정적 용법

형용사가 명사 앞에서 명사를 수식한다.
-thing이 붙은 대명사를 뒤에서 수식한다.
He is a diligent man. 그는 부지런한 남자다.
I want to buy something nice for her.
나는 사고 싶다/멋진 어떤 것을/그녀를 위해.
Still waters run deep. 잔잔한(조용한) 물이 깊다(깊게 흐른다).
(말 없는 사람이 생각이 깊다.)

(2) 서술적 용법

① 형용사가 주어나 목적어를 보충 설명하는 보어 역할을 하는데, 이를 형용사의 서술적 용법이라고 한다.
She is beautiful. (주격보어) 그녀는 아름답다.
He seems ill. (주격보어) 그는 아파 보인다.
He makes her happy. (목적격보어) 그는 그녀를 행복하게 한다.

② a로 시작하는 형용사는 대개 동사 뒤에서 서술적 용법(보어)으로만 쓰인다.
afraid 두려워하는, alike 닮은, alive 살아 있는, alone 고독한, asleep 잠든, ashamed 부끄러워하는, awake 깨어 있는, aware 알고 있는

The baby is asleep. 그 아기는 잠들었다.
She is afraid of dogs. 그녀는 개를 두려워한다.
His grandmother is still alive. 그의 할머니는 아직 살아계시다.
Both the sisters are alike in many ways.
그 두 자매는 닮았다/여러 면에서.

(3)　the + 형용사 = 복수 보통명사

　　The rich are not always happy.
　　부자들이라고 늘 행복한 것은 아니다.
　　The young should be kind to the old.
　　젊은이들은 친절해야 한다/노인들에게.
　　Blessed are the poor in spirit. (도치)
　　심령이 가난한 자는 복이 있나니.
　　← The poor in spirit are blessed.
　　　(주부가 술부보다 더 무거운 부자연스러운 문장)

4. 형용사의 어순

⟨형용사(분사)의 어순 참조 → 102p⟩

(1) 형용사의 전치수식

명사를 수식하는 형용사는 명사 앞에 오는 것이 원칙이다.

① 형용사의 위치는 대개 「관사 + 부사 + 형용사 + 명사」(관부형명)의 순이다
This is a very interesting movie. 이것은 매우 재미있는 영화이다.

② 관사(지시형용사) + 수량형용사 + 성상형용사 + 명사[한(한정사)수형명]
Those three tall boys are my friends.
저 세 키 큰 소년들은 내 친구들이다.

③ 두 개 이상의 성상형용사가 올 때
관사(지시, 소유) + 서수(기수) + 크기 + 나이 + 성질 + 색깔 + 출처 + 재료 + 명사 순이다. 그러나 이들 규칙들은 잘 지켜지지 않는다. 짧은 형용사는 앞쪽에, 긴 형용사는 뒤쪽에 오기도 한다. 또는 주관적인 형용사는 앞쪽에, 객관적인 형용사는 뒤쪽에 오기도 한다.
a big old Chinese vase. 크고 오래된 중국 꽃병.
a new yellow plastic tablecloth. 새 노란 플라스틱 책상보.
a small blue Korean car. 작은 청색 한국 차.

(2) 형용사의 후치수식

① -thing, -body, -one, -where로 끝나는 대명사는 형용사가 뒤에서 수식함
Is there anything interesting on TV.
재미있는 어떤 것이 있니/TV에?

② 영어의 「긴 것은 뒤로」의 습성에 따라 to부정사(구), 형용사구, 형용사절이 명사(대명사)를 수식할 경우 명사 뒤에서 수식한다.

I want a book *to read*.
나는 읽을 책을 원한다. (형용사구-to부정사)

I love her *(who, whom) I met at school*.
(형용사절-관계대명사절)

The flowers *in the room* are beautiful. (형용사구-전치사구)

I'm reading the book *which was written in English*. (형용사절)

The woman *talking with Tom* is my aunt.
(형용사구-현재분사구)

I'm reading the book *written in English*. (형용사구-과거분사구)

* 동사 + 목적어(사물) + 과거분사(목적보어) ← 수동관계

5. **형용사의 비교**

   형용사는 다른 것과 비교할 때에는 원급, 비교급, 최상급을 쓴다.

   as (tall, good) **as**, (taller, better) **than**, **the** (tallest, best)

(1) **형용사의 규칙변화**

   ① 원급에 -(e)r, -(e)st를 붙여 비교급, 최상급을 만든다.

old	older	oldest
wise	wiser	wisest

   ② 「단모음 + 단자음」으로 끝나는 어미는 자음을 겹치고 -er, -est를 붙인다.

big	bigger	biggest
tat	tatter	tattest

③ 「자음 + y」로 끝나는 어미는 y를 i로 고쳐 -er, -est를 붙인다.

happy	happier	happiest
easy	easier	easiest

④ 대다수 2음절어와 3음절 이상의 형용사나 부사는 more, most를 붙인다.

useful	more useful	most useful
important	more important	most important

(2) 형용사의 불규칙변화

good	better	best(좋은)
well	better	best(잘, 건강한)
ill	worse	worst(아픈)
bad	worse	worst(나쁜)
many(much)	more	most(많은)
little	less	least(적은-양)
little	smaller	smallest(작은-크기)
old	elder	eldest(형-동생-UK)
old	older	oldest(늙은-나이)
late	later	latest(늦은-시간)
late	latter	last(뒤의-순서)
far	farther	farthest(먼-거리)
far	further	furthest(더한-정도)

(3) 형용사의 원급(동등 비교)

　　as 원급 as : ~만큼 ~한

　　not as 원급 as = not so 원급 as : ~만큼 ~하지 않다

I am as tall as he. 나는 그만큼 크다.
I am not as(so) tall as he. 나는 그만큼 크지 않다.

(4) 형용사의 비교급

① 비교급 + than : ~보다 더 ~하다

I am taller than he(him). 나는 그보다 더 크다.
= He is not as tall as I(am). 그는 나만큼 크지 않다.
= He is not as tall as me.
= He is less tall than I(am).
= He is less tall than me.
* than 뒤에 주격이나 목적격이 오는데, 주격은 격식체로 사용빈도가 매우 낮고, 목적격은 일상체로 자주 쓰인다.
* Better late than never. 늦더라도 안 하는 것보다 더 낫다.
  ← (It is) better … (안 하는 것보다 늦은 것이 더 낫다)

② The + 비교급, the + 비교급 : ~할수록 점점 더 ~하다

The sooner, the better. 빠르면 빠를수록 좋다.
The higher up we go, the colder it becomes.
높이 올라갈수록 점점 더 추워진다.
The situation is getting more and more dangerous.
상황은 *점점 더* 위험지고 있다.

③ **비교급 앞에** : much, even, far, by far, still, a lot 는 '훨씬, 더욱'
   최상급 앞에 : much, even, far, by far, the very 는 '단연코, 바로'의 뜻을 나타낸다.

The love of the heart is much more truthful than physical love.
마음의 사랑이 훨씬 더 진실하다/물질적인 사랑보다.

This is the very (much) cheapest bike in this shop.
이것은 단연코(바로) 제일 싼 자전거이다/이 가게에서.

④ **라틴어 비교에는** than 대신 to를 쓴다.
prefer~ to ~을 더 좋아하다, junior to ~보다 손아래의, prior to ~보다 앞선, superior to ~보다 우수한, inferior to ~보다 열등한, senior to ~보다 손위의
I prefer coffee to tea. = I like coffee more than tea.

(5) 형용사의 최상급

① 형용사의 최상급 앞에는 the를 붙인다. 최상급 뒤에서 장소나 그룹을 나타내는 단수명사 앞에는 in을 쓴다. 구성원을 나타내는 복수명사 앞에는 '누구들 중에서'를 의미하는 of나 among을 쓴다.
Seoul is the largest of all the cities in Korea.
Seoul is the largest city in Korea.
He is the strongest boy in the class.
= No (other) boy in the class is as strong as he.
= No boy in the class is stronger than he(him).
= He is stronger than any other boys in the class.
= He is the strongest of all (the) boys in the class.
* Hunger is the best sauce. 시장이 반찬이다.

② 부사의 최상급에는 the를 붙이지 않는다.
He studies hardest in our class.
그는 가장 열심히 공부한다/우리 반에서.

③ 소유격 + 최상급일 때는 the를 붙이지 않는다.

It is my greatest pleasure to meet you finally.
나의 가장 큰 기쁨이다/너를 드디어 만나는 것은.
You are my best friend.

④ 최상급이 보어로 쓰일 때는 the를 붙이지 않는다.
The building is highest here.　Winter is coldest.

─────────────────────────────────────── (참고)

6. 수사

수량형용사 중의 하나인 수사에는 개수를 나타내는 기수와 순서를 나타내는 서수와 비율을 나타내는 배수가 있다. 서수 앞에는 the가 붙는다.

기수 : one(하나), two(둘), three, four, five, six, ten, eleven, twelve, thirteen, twenty, hundred, thousand….

서수 : the first(1st)첫 번째, the second(2nd)두 번째, the third(3rd), the fourth(4th), fifth, sixth, twelfth, …

배수 : two times(두 배, 두 번), three times(세 배, 세 번), four times (네 배, 네 번), …

The first step is always the hardest (step).
첫 걸음이 늘 가장 어렵다.

(1) 정수

100 = a(one) hundred	1001 = a(one) thousand and one
200 = two hundred	2000 = two thousand
20,000 = twenty thousand	200,000 = two hundred thousand
2,000,000 = two million	30,000,000 = thirty million

23,456 = twenty three thousand, four hundred (and) fifty six.

(2) 수

분자는 기수로, 분모는 서수로 읽는다. 분자가 2 이상이면, 분모에 -s를 붙인다.

1/2 = one half(a half)   1/3 = one third(a third)
2/6 = two sixths   2 3/4 = two and three fourths

(3) 소수

2.34 = two point three four   0.58 = zero point five eight

(4) 연도, 월, 일

연도는 두 자리씩 끊어 읽는다.
1989 = nineteen eighty nine   1900 = nineteen hundred
2007 = two thousand seven   1905 = nineteen five
1970년대 = 1970s = nineteen seventies, in (the) 1970s
       = 1970년대에
July 4(th) = July (the) fourth = the fourth of July.

(5) 전화번호와 시각

전화번호는 한 자씩 읽는다. 0는 [ou]나 zero로 읽는다.
675-4563   six seven five, four five six three
9 : 20 a.m. = nine twenty a.m. (eiem) 오전 9시 20분, twenty past nine
3 : 40 p.m. = three forty p.m. (pi:em) 오후 3시 40분, twenty to four

(6) 셈

2 + 3 = 5   2 plus 3 is(are, equals, make, makes) 5
3 - 3 = 0   3 minus 3 is(equals) 0(zero)
3 × 2 = 6   3 times 2 is(equals) 6
             = 3 multiplied by 2 is(equals) 6
6 ÷ 2 = 3   6 divided by 2 is(equals) 3

(7) 불특정한 수의 지칭
   hundreds of miles 수백 마일
   two hundred miles 2백 마일
   millions of people 수백만 사람들
   three million people 3백만 사람들
   dozens of cases 수십의 사건들
   two dozen cases 2십 여건의 사건들
   a glass of water 한 잔의 물
   two glasses of water 두 잔의 물
   a cup of coffee 한 잔의 커피
   two cups of coffee 두 컵의 커피
   a ten-year-old girl 10살의 소녀
   The girl is ten years old 그 소녀는 10살이다.

* 하이픈(-)으로 연결된 단위명사는 형용사 역할을 하므로 복수형을 쓰지 않는다. 기수 다음의 단위명사도 형용사 역할을 하므로 복수형을 쓰지 않지만, 단위명사 뒤에 전치사 of가 있으면 복수인 경우 복수형으로도 쓰인다. (dozens of cases)

* A journey of a thousand miles begins with one step.
  (총칭 → 관사) 천리 길(여행)도 한 걸음부터 (시작한다)

Exercises

A. 괄호 안의 형용사나 부사를 적합한 급으로 고치시오.

1. Did you see Billy yesterday? Yes, he looked really (ill). What's wrong with him? I think he's got the flu. I hope he'll get (well) soon. So do I. There's nothing (bad) than lying in bed when the sun is shining.
2. Our school is a large building, but the new church is (large). The train station is the (large) building in town, but it's much (little) than Victoria Station in London.
3. Today was the (happy) day in my life: Laura said she loved me! She is really the (lovely) and (wonderful) girl in the world.
4. Which pizzeria is (near), "da Antonio" or "Sorrento?" the (late), I think. It's just around the corner.
5. I love science, but Jenny, my (old) sister, hates it. How (old) is she? Sixteen. She's three years (old) than I.
6. You look tired! Well, I had to walk all the day from the station, and it was (far) than I thought.
7. Have you read Stephen King's (late) book? Yes, I think it's the (good) he has ever written. Well, I think "The Stand" was even (good).
8. In Amsterdam, they showed us the (narrow) house in town. It is only three meters (wide).

※ 1. ill, better, worse 2. larger, largest, smaller 3. happiest, loveliest, most wonderful 4. nearer, latter 5. elder, old, older 6.

farther 7. latest, best, better 8. narrowest, wide

B. 다음 문장을 비교급 문장으로 만드시오.
1. England is (large) Wales.
2. Nothing is (interesting) juicy stories about celebrities.
3. Forgetting is (easy) remembering.
4. Writing a poem is (difficult) composing a business letter.
5. It's actually much (simple) it looks.
6. Two heads are (good) one.
7. Some statistics are (bad) meaningless.
8. The average woman still earns much (little) the average man.
9. There's nothing (boring) watching the commercials on TV.
10. He wanted (much) I was prepared to give.

※ 1. England is larger than Wales.
2. Nothing is more interesting than juicy stories about celebrities.
3. Forgetting is easier than remembering.
4. Writing a poem is more difficult than composing a business letter.
5. It's actually much simpler than it looks.
6. Two heads are better than one.
7. Some statistics are worse than meaningless.
8. The average woman still earns much less than the average man.
9. There's nothing more boring than watching the commercials on TV.

10. He wanted more than I was prepared to give.

C. 다음 문장을 최상급 문장으로 만드시오.
1. Buying this car was one of the (big) mistakes I ever made.
2. Actually, it's one of the (safe) and (economical) cars on the road today.
3. Silvia is one of the (nice) girls I ever met.
4. She's one of the (sensitive) people I know.
5. The car is not always the (sensible) mode of transport.
6. Franklin D. Roosevelt was one of the (great) US presidents and had the (long) term of office.
7. Drunk driving is one of the (dangerous) crimes we have in this country.
8. She's one of the (friendly) and (solid) people I know.
9. Parenting is the (important) job in our society and the one that has been neglected (much).
10. Brian was the (tall) and (handsome) of the group.

※ 1. biggest 2. safest, most economical 3. nicest 4. most sensitive 5. most sensible 6. greatest, longest 7. most dangerous 8. friendliest(most friendly), most solid(solidest) 9. most important, most 10. tallest, handsomest(most handsome)

D. 형용사와 부사 중 적합한 것을 괄호 안에 넣으시오. 그리고 동시에 비교급, 최상급이 필요한지 생각하시오.
1. Do you know Nicole Brown? I think I do. Is she the (beautiful) girl who sings and dances so (good)? Yes, that's her. She seems (nice), doesn't she? Yes, she does. But I don't know

her very (good) I think you know her much (good) than I.

2. Why are you running around so (nervous), Bob? Well, I am (real) (nervous). You see, Sophie has an (important) job interview today, and she said she would call me (direct) as soon as it was over. Was Sophie (excited), too, this morning? Not (real); she seemed very (calm) when she left the house. Of course, she had studied (hard) for this interview. She should (easy) get the job. I think she is the (good) for it!

3. Ah, this smells (wonderful)! What is it, Mom? Apple pie. It is (typical) American. Would you like a piece? Yes, please! It tastes (wonderful), too.

4. Do you like Mr. Brown? No, I don't. I think he is a (boring) teacher. He often shouts at us (angry), and we (hard) know why. Also, he speaks very (dry) and he never tells any jokes.

5. What's wrong with Martin? Why does he look so (sad)? Haven't you heard? He had a (bad) accident last Thursday, and now his (new) racing bike is broken. What happened? Well, he was riding too (fast) and I think a little (careless), too, when he crashed into a tree. (lucky), he didn't break anything. That's (good)! He was (real) (lucky).

6. What's this (terrible) smell? Has a stink bomb exploded somewhere? No, that's the cheese Dad brought back from France. Don't you like it? You can say it (free)! Like it? I think it's (awful). He should eat the thing (quick) and throw away the wrapping. I'm (deep) sorry that you don't like it. You see, it tastes (excellent), too.

※ 1. beautiful, well, nice, well, better 2. nervously, really, nervous, important, directly, excited, really, calm, hard, easily, best 3. wonderful, typically, wonderful 4. boring, angrily, hardly, drily 5. sad, bad, new, fast, carelessly, Luckily, good, really, lucky 6. terrible, freely, awful, quickly, deeply, excellent

제6장 to부정사

to부정사, 동명사, 분사는 자체로서 쓰이거나, 또는 구를 만들어 문장을 수식하면서 긴 문장을 만든다. 구에는 to부정사구, 동명사구, 분사구, 전치사구(형용사구, 부사구)가 있다. 4구 3절(관계사절, 접속사절, 간접의문문)을 어느 정도 숙달하면 영어는 쉬워진다.

to부정사(~하는 것, ~할)는 동사의 성질을 지니고, **형용사**, **부사**, **명사**로 쓰이므로 문장에서 to부정사의 쓰임은 매우 광범위하고 매우 빈번하다. 부정사(不定詞)는 인칭, 수, 시제에 의하여 제약을 받지 아니하고 항상 동사원형으로 쓰인다.
부정사에는 to부정사(to 있는 부정사 = to동사원형)와 원형부정사(to 없는 부정사 = 동사원형)가 있다.

1. **to부정사의 용법**

    to부정사는 **형용사**(명사를 수식, 보어로 쓰임), **부사**(동사, 형용사, 부사, 문장 전체를 수식), **명사**(주어, 목적어, 보어로 쓰임)처럼 쓰인다.

(1) **to부정사의 명사적 용법**

    to부정사는 명사(~하는 것은, ~하는 것을, ~하는 것)처럼 주어, 목적어, 보어로 쓰인다.

    To learn English is not difficult. (to부정사구-명사구-주어)
    영어 습성상 문두에는 to부정사를 잘 사용하지 않으므로(주부 부분이

무겁기 때문에), 가주어 it을 문두에 놓고, to부정사구를 문장 뒤로 보낸다.

→ *It* is not difficult *to learn English*.
　(it은 가주어, to부정사구는 진주어)
My dream is *to master English*. (to부정사구-명사구-보어)
I want *to learn English*. (to부정사구-명사구-목적어)

I found *it* difficult *to learn English*. (5형식 문장)
(it은 가목적어-to부정사구는 진목적어)
* 5형식 문장에서 목적어 자리에 긴 to부정사구를 두지 않기 때문에 가목적어 + 목적보어 + 진목적어 순으로 된다. (be동사만 생략됨)

(2) **to부정사의 형용사적 용법**
　to부정사는 형용사(~할, ~하는)처럼 명사(대명사)를 수식하는 한정적 용법과 보어로 쓰이는 서술적 용법이 있다. 동사가 명사를 수식하려면 to부정사가 명사를 뒤에서 수식한다.
　She has no house to live in. (명사 + to부정사)
　She gave me something to eat. (대명사 + to부정사)
　그녀는 내게 주었다/먹을 어떤 것을.

★ **(be + to부정사)의 용법 = to부정사의 서술적 용법**
　to부정사가 be동사 뒤에 오면 주격보어(주어를 보충 설명)로 쓰이며, 예정(5가지 중 가장 많이 쓰임), 의무(명령), 운명, 가능, 목적(의도)을 나타낸다.
① 예정
I *am to* leave in the afternoon. 나는 떠날 예정이다/오후에.
　= I am going to leave in the afternoon. (be going to = will)
　= I will leave in the afternoon.

② 의무(명령)

You *are to* learn English. 너는 영어를 배워야 한다.

= You should(have to, must) learn English.

③ 운명

He was never to see his girlfriend again.

그는 결코 보지 못했다/그의 여자친구를 다시.

④ 가능

Nobody *is to* be seen on the street.

= Nobody can be seen on the street. 아무도 볼 수 없다/거리에서.

⑤ 목적

If you are to succeed, you should study harder.

네가 성공하려면 더 열심히 공부해야 한다.

(3) **to부정사의 부사적 용법**

to부정사는 부사처럼 목적, 원인, 이유, 결과, 조건을 나타내며, 부사처럼 동사, 형용사, 부사를 수식한다. 독립부정사는 문장 전체를 수식한다.

부사적 어미는 ~하기 위해, 하려고, 하러, 하고, 하(다)니, 해도, 해서, 하면서, 하므로, 하기에(~할), ~으로, 하면, ~없이 등이 있다.

① 목적

I bought an English grammar book in order to study English.

= I bought an English grammar book to study English.

  나는 영문법 책을 샀다/영어를 공부하기 위해.

We eat to live, not live to eat. (동사 + to부정사-동사를 수식)

우리는 *살기 위해 먹는다/ 먹기 위해 사는 것이 아니라.*

② 원인

I am glad to see you again. 나는 기쁘다/너를 다시 *보니.*

③ 이유

　　I am very stupid to say such a thing.
　　나는 매우 어리석다 /그런 것을 말하다니.

④ 결과

　　She grew up to be a good doctor.
　　= She grew up and became a good doctor.
　　　그녀는 자라서 좋은 의사가 되었다.

⑤ 조건

　　I would be happy to live with her.
　　나는 행복할 텐데(할 거다)/그녀와 함께 산다면.

⑥ to부정사가 형용사(분사)를 뒤에서 수식(형용사 + to부정사)

　　This house is very comfortable to live in.
　　= It is very comfortable to live in this house.
　　　매우 편안하다/이 집에서 살기에(사는 것은).
　　They are ready(prepared) to help.
　　그들은 도울 준비가 되어 있다.

⑦ to부정사가 부사를 뒤에서 수식(부사 + to부정사)

　　He is old enough to be home alone. [enough(too) + to부정사]
　　그는 충분한 나이다/혼자 집에 있기에.
　　That baggage is too heavy for me to lift.
　　그 짐은 너무 무거워 내가 들 수 없다.
　　= 그 짐은 내가 들기에 너무 무겁다.

⑧ 독립부정사가 문장 전체를 수식

Needless to say, he is not true. (말할 필요도 없이)
To make matters worse, it begins to rain. (설상가상으로)

2. to부정사의 의미상의 주어

(1) to부정사의 의미상의 주어를 쓰지 않는 경우
① 문장의 주어와 to부정사의 의미상의 주어가 같을 때(주절과 종속절의 주어가 같을 때)
② 문장의 목적어와 의미상의 주어가 같을 때(주절의 목적어와 종속절의 주어가 같을 때)
③ to부정사의 의미상의 주어가 일반인일 때(종속절의 주어가 일반인일 때)
④ 누구나 인정하는 일반적 사실을 기술할 때

이들 네 가지 경우에는 to부정사의 의미상의 주어를 쓰지 않는다.

I hope that I pass the exam.
(문장의 주어 = to부정사의 의미상의 주어)
= I hope to pass the exam. 나는 희망한다/시험에 합격하기를.

I told her that she comes tomorrow.
(문장의 목적어 = to부정사의 의미상의 주어)
= I told her to come tomorrow.
나는 그녀에게 오라고 말했다/내일.
It is important that people learn English.
(to부정사의 의미상의 주어 = 일반인)
= It is important to learn English. 중요하다/영어를 배우는 것은.
Seeing is to believe. 보는 것은 믿는 것이다. (일반적 사실의 기술)

Teaching is to learn. 가르치는 것은 배우는 것이다.

(2) to부정사의 의미상의 주어를 쓰는 경우

① 문장의 주어와 to부정사의 의미상의 주어가 다를 때, to부정사의 의미상의 주어는 to부정사 바로 앞에 「for + 목적격」을 쓴다.
The problem was so difficult that I couldn't answer it.
= The problem was too difficult *for me* to answer.
그 문제는 너무 어려워서 내가 답할 수 없었다.

To play tennis is difficult. (to부정사구는 주어로 잘 쓰지 않으므로)
→ It is difficult to play tennis. 어렵다/테니스를 치는 것은.
It is difficult *for me* to play tennis. 어렵다/내가 테니스를 치는 것은.
(it은 가주어, for me는 의미상의 주어, to play tennis는 진주어)

★ It is difficult *for me* to play tennis. (○)
I am difficult to play tennis. (×, I ≠ difficult)
위 문장에서 사람을 주절의 주어로는 쓸 수 없다. 어려운 것은 테니스를 치는 활동(움직임)이지, 사람이 아니기 때문이다.
necessary, difficult, impossible, pleasant, convenient 등의 형용사가 보어로 쓰일 때, 사람은 주어가 될 수 없다.

② 사람의 성질(성격)을 나타내는 형용사(clever, good, kind, foolish, nice, intelligent, brave, careful) 뒤에 오는 to부정사의 의미상의 주어는 「of + 목적격」을 쓴다.
It is very good *of you* to come with us.
매우 좋다/네가 우리와 함께 가(오)는 것은.
It is very kind of you to help me.

= You are very kind to help me. (you = very kind)

3. 원형부정사(동사원형, 원형동사)의 용법

(1) 동사 + 목적어 + 동사원형(목적보어)

지각동사와 사역동사의 목적보어(목적격보어)로 동사원형이 쓰인다.
목적보어가 있는 이들 문장들은 5형식 문장을 이룬다.

① **지각동사 + 목적어 + 동사원형/현재분사**

동사원형이 지각동사(see, watch, hear, feel, hear, listen to, look at, notice, observe)의 목적보어로 쓰일 때.
I see her play tennis. (동사원형), (her = play tennis-목적보어)
= I see her playing tennis. (현재분사)
= I see that she plays tennis. 나는 그녀가 테니스 치는 것을 본다.

I heard her sing a song. 나는 그녀가 노래 부르는 것을 들었다.
She noticed him hesitate. 그녀는 그가 망설이는 것을 알아챘다.
He watched his son study English.
그는 그의 아들이 영어 공부하는 것을 지켜보았다.

② **사역동사 + 목적어 + 동사원형/과거분사**

동사원형이 사역동사(have, make, let)의 목적보어로 쓰일 때.

★ 사역동사 + 목적어 + 동사원형[목적어(사람)와 뒤의 동사가 능동관계일 때]
   사역동사 + 목적어 + 과거분사[목적어(사물)와 뒤의 동사가 수동관계일 때]
I had her sing a song. (능동-동사원형)
= I got her to sing a song.
나는 그녀에게 노래를 부르도록 시켰다(부르게 했다).

I made him clean the room. (능동-동사원형)
나는 그에게 방을 청소하도록 했다(시켰다).
I had our house painted. (by someone-수동-p.p)
나는 우리 집이 페인트칠 되도록 시켰다.
She had him repair the bike. (능동-동사원형)
그녀는 그에게 자전거를 수리하도록 시켰다.
He had the bike repaired. (수동-과거분사)
그는 자전거가 수리되도록 시켰다.
* He has repaired the bike. 그는 자전거를 수리했다.

③ get + 목적어 + to부정사/과거분사

사역동사 get은 목적어(사람)와 목적보어가 능동관계일 때는 목적보어로 to부정사가 쓰이고, 목적어(사물)와 목적보어가 수동관계일 때는 목적보어로 과거분사가 쓰인다.
I got him to do the work. (능동)
나는 그에게 그 일을 하도록 시켰다(했다).
I got my car's oil changed. (수동)
나는 내 차의 오일을 바꾸게 했다.

④ help + 목적어 + 동사원형/to부정사

사역동사 help는 목적보어로 동사원형이나 to부정사가 쓰인다.
I helped him clean the room.
나는 그가 방 청소하는 것을 도와주었다.
= I helped him to clean the room.

⑤ 동사 + 목적어 + to부정사

지각(사역)동사 이외의 타동사들은 목적보어로 대개 to부정사를 갖는다.

want, ask, expect, like, know, report, suppose, discover 등

I want him to study hard. 나는 그가 열심히 공부하기를 원한다.
I didn't expect him to succeed so well.
나는 그가 그렇게 잘 성공하리라고 기대하지 않았다.

(2) 동사원형(do)이 쓰이는 관용어구
　　had better + do : ~하는 것이 좋다, ~해야 한다
　　would rather + do : 차라리 ~하는 게 낫다
　　may well + do : ~하는 게 당연하다
　　may as well + do : ~하는 게 낫다, ~하는 편이 낫다
　　be going to + do : ~하려고 하다, ~할 예정이다
　　cannot but + do : ~하지 않을 수 없다
　　have to + do : ~해야 한다

★ Linda wants to help him. 린다는 그를 돕기를 원한다.
　Linda wants him to help. 린다는 그가 돕기를 원한다.
　want와 would like 뒤에는 that절이 안 오고 to부정사가 온다.

4. 동사+to부정사
동사+목적어+to부정사(목적보어)
I expect to pass the test. 나는 시험에 합격하기를 기대한다.
I expect Tom to pass the test.
나는 탐이 시험에 합격하기를 기대한다.
I like to go now. 나는 지금 가고 싶다.
I like her to go now. 나는 그녀가 지금 가는 것을 좋아한다.
He wants to know. 그는 알기를 원한다.
He wants me to come with her.

그는 내가 그녀와 함께 오(가)기를 원한다.
I taught her to drive. 나는 그녀에게 운전하는 것을 가르쳤다.
I helped him move(to move) the desk.
나는 그가 책상을 옮기는 것을 도왔다.
She encouraged me to become a singer.
그녀는 내가 가수가 되도록 격려했다.

★ to부정사의 to 생략

to부정사구가 and로 연결될 때 두 번째 to부정사구의 to는 생략된다.
I want to sit in the garden and (I want to) read a book.
I want her to sit beside me and (to) talk with me.
* I *believe* him (to be) kind. (to부정사구-목적보어)

5. to부정사의 관용적 표현(to부정사구를 절로 고침)

(1) too + 형용사(부사) + to = so ~ that ~ can't :
~하기에 너무 ~하다(너무 ~해서 ~할 수 없다)
He is too poor to buy a car. 그는 차를 사기에 너무 가난하다.
= 그는 너무 가난해서 차를 살 수 없다.
= He is so poor that he cannot buy a car.
그는 너무 가난해서 차를 살 수 없다.

(2) 형(부) + enough to = so ~ that ~ can : ~하기에 충분히 ~하다
(enough는 부사나 형용사를 뒤에서 수식)
그는 차를 사기에 충분히 부유하다.
He is rich enough to buy a car.
= He is so rich that he can buy a car.
그는 아주 부유해서 차를 살 수 있다.

★ so ~ that 용법

① so (형, 부) that S + V : 너무 ~해서 ~하다

② ···, so (so that) S + V : 그래서 ~하다(결과)

③ ··· so(so that) S + may(can, will) : ~하기 위하여(목적)

(3) so ~ as to = enough to : ~할 만큼 ~하다

so as to : ~하기 위하여

그는 새 집을 살만큼 아주 부유하다.

He is so rich as to buy a new house.

= He is rich enough to buy a new house.

= He is so rich that he can buy a new house.

= He is rich, so(so that) he can buy a new house.

그는 부유하다, 그래서 그는 새 집을 살 수 있다.

그는 늦지 않기 위해 일찍 일어났다.

He got up early so as not to be late.

= He got up early in order not to be late.

= He got up early in order that he may not be late.

= He got up early so(so that) he may not be late.

(4) 의문사 + to부정사

Do you know how you play tennis?

= Do you know how to play tennis?

너는 아니/어떻게 테니스를 치는지? (너는 아니/테니스 치는 법을?)

I really don't know what to do in the future.

나는 정말 모른다/장차(미래에) 무엇을 해야 할지.

I don't know when to begin the tennis game.

나는 모른다/테니스 시합이 언제 시작하는지.

6. **독립부정사의 관용어구(숙어)**

    to be frank(plain) with you 솔직히 말하면
    to begin(start) with 우선(첫째로)
    to be brief(short) 간단히 말하면
    to be exact 정확히 말하(자)면
    to conclude 결론적으로 말하면
    to do him justice 공평히 말하면
    to make matters worse 설상가상으로
    to be honest 정직하게 말하면
    to make a long story short(to sum up, to come to the point)
        요약하면(요약해서 말하면)
    to say nothing of(not to speak of, not to mention)
        ~은 말할 것도 없고,
    strange to say 이상한 말이지만
    to tell the truth 사실을 말하(자)면
    to be sure 틀림없다(확실하다)
    so to speak 말하자면
    needless to say 말할 필요도 없이

7. **to부정사의 어순**

(1) 주어, 목적어, 보어 자리에 온다(to부정사의 명사적 용법)

(2) 명사 뒤에 온다(명사나 대명사를 뒤에서 수식)
    There's a lady to see you. 당신을 보려는 숙녀가 있다.

(3) 형용사 뒤에 온다(형용사를 뒤에서 수식)
    English is easy(difficult, hard) to learn.

It is impossible to know what Sarah really wants.
아는 것은 불가능하다/사라가 정말 무엇을 원하는지.
We are ready to go there. 우리는 갈 준비가 되어 있다/거기에.

(4) 특정한 동사 뒤에 온다(동사를 뒤에서 수식)

agree, forget, learn, hope, seem, try, want, decide, expect, would like 등

Tony *forgot to* do his homework last night.
토니는 그의 숙제를 하는 것을 잊었다/어젯밤(지난밤)에.
We aren't *allowed to* talk during tests.
(우리는) 말해서는 안된다/시험 동안.
Linda *wants to* go shopping on Saturday.

(5) 동사 + 목적어 + to부정사(목적보어로 목적어를 보충 설명함)

He doesn't want us to make any noise.
그는 우리가 어떤 소음을 내는 것을 원하지 않는다.
= 그는 우리에게 원하지 않는다/어떤 소음을 내는 것을.
I asked her to come. 나는 그녀에게 오라고 부탁했다.
He told us to meet in the car park.
그는 우리에게 말했다/주차장에서 만난다고(만나는 것을).
He reminded everybody to bring his raincoats.
그는 모두에게 상기시켰다/자신의 우비를 가져오라고.

(6) 관계대명사절 자리에 온다

I haven't got a clean shirt (that) I can put on.
= I haven't got a clean shirt *to put on*.
　나는 깨끗한 셔츠가 없다/입을.

Chris doesn't know anybody (who) he could talk to.
= Chris doesn't know anybody to talk to.
크리스는 어느 누구도 알지 못한다/이야기할.

(7) 의문사 뒤에(의문사 + to do) 온다

Can anybody tell me how I can get to the bus station?
= Can anybody tell me how to get to the bus station?
누군가 내게 말해 줄 수 있니/어떻게 버스 정거장에 가는지?
They didn't know what they should do.
= They didn't know what to do. 그들은 몰랐다/무엇을 할지.
The problem is where to park the car.
문제는 차를 주차하는 곳이다.

(8) 분리부정사

I'm delighted to finally meet you.
나는 매우 기쁘다/너를 마침내 만나니.
You don't know her well enough to really understand her.
당신은 그녀를 충분히 잘 알지 못한다/그녀를 정말 이해하기에.
The company wants to more than double its turnover.
그 회사는 배 이상 원한다/그것의 매출액을.

(9) to부정사가 수동형으로 오기도 한다

'~되어지다(된다, 받다)'의 의미로 to부정사의 수동형이 온다.
The sports group seems to be sponsored by someone.
그 운동 단체는 후원을 받는 것 같다/누군가에 의해.
Drastic measures are not to be expected.
극단적인(과격한) 조치(정책)는 기대되지 않는다.

Exercises

A. 괄호 안의 동사가 to부정사인지 to 없는 부정사(동사원형)인지 결정하시오.
1. The window was too dirty (to see) through.
2. He came (to help) the old lady.
3. Have you done this (to annoy) your parents?
4. He made her (to answer) the letter at once.
5. I've forgotten how (to spell) that word.
6. Mr. Brown wouldn't (to let) his son (to drive).
7. You ought (to phone) her immediately.
8. The boss told me when (to repair) the engine.
9. Can you tell me how (to get) to the cinema?
10. Neil Armstrong was the first man (to land) on the moon.
11. The roof must (to be repaired) at once.
12. I don't consider it (to be) true.
13. The fans waited for the pop star (to arrive).
14. He opened the door (to let) the dog in.

※ 1. to see 2. to help 3. to annoy 4. answer 5. to spell 6. let, drive 7. to phone 8. to repair 9. to get 10. to land 11. be repaired 12. to be 13. to arrive 14. to let

B. 괄호 안에 동사를 적합한 to부정사나 동명사로 고치시오.
('~하는 것을' 과정을 중시하면 to부정사이고, '~것을' 명사를 중시하면 동명사임)
1. How old were you when you learned (drive)?
2. Several officials admitted (take) bribes.
3. The candidate carefully avoided (make) any promises.

81

4. Linda failed (make) a good impression at the job interview.
5. He denied (commit) the crime.
6. Can you show me how (change) the film in this camera?
7. When you have finished (write) your text, use the spellchecker any spelling errors.
8. Even on the worst day at work I can't imagine (do) anything else.
9. Do you want me (come) with you?
10. Can you remind me (call) Paul tomorrow?
11. A witness mentioned (see) a white pickup at the scene of the robbery.
12. It's hard to find a place (park) downtown.
13. I need a few days (think) about your proposal.
14. I don't recollect ever (see) her before.
15. I resent (be) called an egoist.
16. Do you think it is safe (drink) this water?
17. He said the road was impassable and suggested (go) by boat.
18. It's foolish of Sarah (quit) her job when she needs the money.
19. Everybody tells me (come) to Sarah's party, but I don't want (go).
20. I really don't mind (wait) for a few minutes, but I can't promise (wait) for half an hour!

※ 1. to drive 2. taking 3. making 4. to make 5. committing 6. to change 7. writing 8. doing 9. to come 10. to call 11. seeing 12. to park 13. to think 14. seeing 15. being 16. to drink 17.

going 18. to quit 19. to come, to go 20. waiting, to wait

C. 다음 문장을 to부정사구문으로 바꾸시오(종속절 → 구).

   1. We're looking for a place where we can stay.
   2. Jeju island is the place where we can go sightseeing.
   3. There are six menus from which you can choose.
   4. She only wants someone to whom she can chat.
   5. He's not a man who can be trusted.
   6. Peter was the only one who spoke against the plan.
   7. You're the man who can do it.
   8. When Tom had lost his purse he didn't know where he should go to.
   9. They didn't know whether they should accept the invitation.
   10. The doctor told me how I should take this medicine.

※ 1. ⋯ a place to stay 2. the place to go sightseeing 3. menus to choose from 4. someone to chat to 5. a man to be trusted 6. only one to speak against the plan 7. the man to do it 8. where to go to 9. whether to accept the invitation 10. how to take this medicine

D. 관계대명사절을 to부정사구로 바꾸시오(종속절 → 구).

   1. He was the first European that sailed around the world.
   2. As always, John and Peter were the last guests that arrived at the party.
   3. Route 66 was the best road that you could take to California.
   4. There were a lot of problems which had to be solved.
   5. Experts say that Peter is the only person that understands this

machine.

6. We had so much time left that we saw all the sights.
7. Linda is so happy that she doesn't worry about tomorrow.
8. It is so late that we can't do anything now.
9. We urgently need somebody who can look after our children.
10. Mr. Smith was the only person who was hurt in the accident.

※ 1. He was the first European to sail around the world.
2. As always, John and Peter were the last guests to arrive at the party.
3. Route 66 was the best road to take to California.
4. There were a lot of problems to be solved.
5. Experts say that Peter is the only person to understand this machine.
6. We had enough time left to see all the sights.
7. Linda is too happy to worry about tomorrow.
8. It is too late to do anything now.
9. We urgently need somebody to look after our children.
10. Mr. Smith was the only person to be hurt in the accident.

제7장 동명사

1. **동명사의 명사적 용법**

    동명사(動名詞, ~하는 것, ~한 것)는 동사의 성질을 지니고 명사 역할을 한다. 동명사는 「**동사원형 + -ing**」의 형태이다. 동사를 명사로 쓰려면 동명사를 써야 한다. 동명사는 동작(움직임) 동사에 -ing를 붙여 만든다.

    ★ **동명사는 명사처럼 주어, 목적어, 보어로 쓰인다**

    일반적으로 동명사(명사)가 동사 앞에 오면 주어로, 동사 뒤에 오면 목적어로, be동사 뒤에 오면 보어로, 전치사 뒤에 오면 전치사의 목적어로 쓰인다.

    Playing tennis is my hobby.
    테니스 치는 것은 내 취미이다. (주어-명사구)
    My hobby is *playing tennis*.
    내 취미는 테니스 치는 것이다. (보어-명사구)
    They began *playing tennis*.
    그들은 테니스 치기를 시작했다. (목적어-명사구)
    I look forward to *playing tennis*.
    나는 테니스 치는 것을 고대한다. (전치사의 목적어-명사구)
    Learning makes a good man better and a bad man worse.
    The most important thing is *listening*. (보어)

2. 동명사의 의미상의 주어

(동명사도 to부정사처럼 의미상의 주어가 있다.)

(1) 동명사의 의미상의 주어를 쓰지 않는 경우
① 문장의 주어와 동명사의 의미상의 주어가 같을 때(주절과 종속절의 주어가 같을 때)
② 문장의 목적어와 의미상의 주어가 같을 때(주절의 목적어와 종속절의 주어가 같을 때)
③ 동명사의 의미상의 주어가 일반인일 때(종속절의 주어가 일반인일 때)
④ 누구나 아는 일반적 사실을 기술할 때

이 네 가지 경우에는 동명사의 의미상의 주어를 쓰지 않는다.

He likes (that) he plays tennis.
(문장의 주어 = 동명사의 의미상의 주어)
= He likes playing tennis. 그는 테니스 치기를 좋아한다.

My boss scolded me (that) I neglected my work.
(문장의 목적어 = 의미상의 주어)
= My boss scolded me for having neglected my work.
내 상사는 나를 꾸짖었다/내 일을 소홀히 했다고.
[scold~for ~라고(때문에) 꾸짖다]

It is difficult that people speak English fluently.
(동명사의 의미상의 주어 = 일반인)
= Speaking English fluently is difficult.
유창하게 영어를 말하는 것은 어렵다.

Seeing is believing. (일반적 사실의 기술)
보는 것은 믿는 것이다. (백문이 불여일견, 百聞以不如一見)
Teaching is learning. 가르치는 것은 배우는 것이다.

(2) **동명사의 의미상의 주어를 쓰는 경우**
문장의 주어와 동명사의 의미상의 주어가 같지 않을 때, 동명사의 의미상의 주어가 일반인이 아닐 때는 동명사의 의미상의 주어를 써야 한다.
동명사의 의미상의 주어는 소유격과 목적격을 쓴다. 소유격은 격식체(학술적 문장체)이고, 목적격은 일상체(일상어, 회화체)이다.

I am sure (that) they will win the game.
(be sure of ~을 확신하다)
= I am sure of their(them) winning the game.
나는 확신한다/그들이 그 시합을 이길 것이라고(것을).

I am proud of my daughter's being a doctor. (소유격)
= I am proud of my daughter being a doctor. (목적격)
나는 자랑스러워한다/나의 딸이 의사라는 것을.

3. 목적어로 동명사와 to부정사의 선택

★ 목적어로 to부정사로 할지 동명사로 할지의 선택은?
 ① 숙어적으로 생각한다. (agree to인가 agree ~ing인가)
 ② 미래지향적(~할 것)인가 과거·현재지향적(~한 것)인가
 ③ 긍정적, 소망적이면 to부정사이고, 습관적(취미적), 상상적, 부정적이면 동명사이다.
 ④ 대체로 '~하는 것을' 과정을 중시하면 to부정사이고, '~것을' 명사를 중시하면 동명사이다.

It is nice to meet old friends.
좋다/오랜 친구들을 만나는 것은. (만나는 것-과정적, 미래적)
It was nice meeting old friends.
좋았다/오랜 친구들을 만난 것은. (만난 것-명사적, 과거적)

(1) to부정사만을 목적어로 취하는 동사

learn 배우다, agree 동의하다, appear(seem) ~처럼 보이다, threaten 위협하다, arrange(prepare) 준비하다, ask 묻다, 부탁하다, choose 선택하다, plan 계획하다, decide 결정하다, wish 희망하다, expect 기대하다, fail 실패하다, want 원하다, hesitate 망설이다, hope 희망하다, intend 의도하다, would like ~하고 싶다, manage 겨우 ~하다, need 필요로 하다, offer 제안하다, seek 찾다, pretend ~인 척하다, promise 약속하다, refuse 거절하다, afford ~할 여유가 있다 등

이들 동사들을 다 외울 수는 없다. appear to, want to, would like to, seem to, fail to, decide to, agree to, refuse to, expect to, happen to 등으로 평소에 문장을 통하여 숙어적으로 알아 두는 것이 좋다.

to부정사(~하는 것, ~할 것, ~하려는 것)만을 목적어로 취하는 동사들은 대개 미래지향적 동사로 소망적, 긍정적인 의미를 나타낸다.

I want to play tennis.
나는 테니스 치기를 원한다. (치기를-미래적, 소망적)
We decided to play tennis.
우리는 테니스 치기로 결정했다. (치기로-미래적)
What would you like to eat now?
무엇을 지금 먹고 싶니? (소망적)
We *agreed to* help them.

우리는 그들을 돕기로 동의했다. (돕기로-미래적)
I can't *afford to* buy a new car.
나는 새 차를 살 여유가 없다. (할-미래적)
He *seems to* have plenty of money.
그는 많은 돈을 가지고 있는 것처럼 보인다. (~인 것처럼, ~것같이)

(2) **동명사만을 목적어로 취하는 동사**

admit 시인하다, consider 고려하다, deny 부인하다, enjoy 즐기다, stop 중지하다, escape 피하다, finish 끝내다. forgive 용서하다, give up 포기하다, imagine 상상하다, mention 말하다, include 포함하다, miss 놓치다, postpone(delay, put off) 연기하다, practice 연습하다, quit 그만두다, recommend 추천하다(권하다), risk 위태롭게 하다, suggest 제안하다, dislike 싫어하다, mind 꺼리다, avoid 피하다, keep (on) 계속하다 등

enioy ~ing, mind ~ing, suggest ~ing, keep ~ing, think ~ing, give up ~ing, stop ~ing, avoid ~ing 등으로 평소에 숙어적으로 암기하는 것이 좋다.

동명사(~하는 것, ~한 것, ~하던 것)만을 목적어로 취하는 동사들은 대개 과거·현재지향적 동사로 습관적(취미적), 상상적(사고적), 부정적 의미를 나타낸다.

I enjoy reading books.
나는 책을 읽는 것을 즐긴다. (습관적, 취미적)
Would you mind opening the window?
창문을 열어 주시겠습니까(창문을 여는 것을 꺼려하십니까)?
(현재적, 부정적)
Suddenly we stopped talking.

갑자기 우리는 이야기하던 것을 멈췄다. (현재적, 부정적)
Jane has given up trying to lose weight.
제인은 체중을 줄이는 노력을 포기했다. (과거적, 부정적)
I can't imagine her riding on the horse.
나는 그녀가 말을 타는 것을 상상할 수 없다. (현재적, 상상적)
We are thinking of buying a car.
우리는 차를 사는 것에 관해 생각하고 있다. (현재적-사고적)

(3) to부정사와 동명사 둘 다 목적어로 취하는 동사

advise 충고하다, attempt 시도하다, begin(start) 시작하다, forget (알고 있던 것을) 잊다, hate 싫어하다, intend 의도하다, like(love) 좋아하다, prefer 선호하다, regret 후회하다, remember 기억하다(나다), try ~하려고 하다, continue 계속하다, propose 제안하다

★ 빈번한 반복적인 행동에는 to부정사나 동명사 둘 다 쓸 수 있다

I like getting up early. = I like to get up early.
I like being(to be) alone. 나는 좋아한다/혼자 있기를.
I hate running in the morning. = I hate to run in the morning.
나는 달리는 것을 싫어한다/아침에.
I love talking with people. = I love to talk with people.
나는 좋아한다/사람들과 이야기하는 것을.
I prefer living in the country.
 = I prefer to live in the country(countryside).
   나는 선호한다/시골에서 사는 것을.
It has started raining. = It has stated to rain. 시작했다/비오기.

좋아하고, 싫어하고, 시도하고, 시작하고, 잊고, 기억하는 것 등은 과거-현재와 미래에도 빈번히 반복적으로 일어나는 행동으로 to부정사와 동명

사가 모두 쓰인다.

(4) to부정사와 동명사를 목적어로 쓸 때, 의미가 달라지는 동사들

I remember locking the door.
나는 기억한다/그 문을 잠근 것을. (과거적)
I remember to lock the door.
나는 기억한다/그 문을 잠그는 것을. (미래적)
I forgot to meet her. 나는 잊었다/그녀를 만나는 것을. (미래적)
I forgot meeting her. 나는 잊었다/그녀를 만난 것을. (과거적)
I regret to tell you that you did not pass the exam.
나는 당신에게 말하려니 유감스럽다/당신이 시험에 합격하지 못한 것을. (미래적)
I regret telling you that you did not pass the exam.
나는 당신에게 말한 것을 후회한다/당신이 시험에 합격하지 못한 것을. (과거적)
I tried to play tennis. 나는 테니스 치기를 노력했다. (적극적)
I tried playing tennis.
나는 테니스를 (취미 삼아) 쳐보았다. (소극적)
I stopped to smoke. 나는 담배 피우려고 멈췄다.
I stopped smoking. 나는 담배 피던 것을 멈췄다(담배를 끊었다).

(5) to부정사, 동명사, 분사구문의 부정은 이들 앞에 not, never 등의 부정어를 놓는다

I remember not(never) locking the door. (동명사)
나는 기억한다/그 문을 잠그지 않은 것을.
I remember not(never) to lock the door. (to부정사)
나는 기억한다/그 문을 잠그지 않는 것을.

Not(never) knowing what to do, I am so bored now.
(분사구문) 무엇을 할지 몰라서 나는 지금 너무 지루하다.

4. 동명사의 관용적 표현

(어려운 구문들은 습득될 때까지 가끔 읽는 것이 좋다)

(1) There is no~ ing : ~하는 것은 불가능하다
There is no buying him a new car.
= It is impossible for him to buy a new car.
불가능하다/그가 새 차를 사는 것은.

(2) cannot help ~ing : ~하지 않을 수 없다, ~할 수밖에 없다
I cannot help studying English. 나는 영어를 공부할 수밖에 없다.
= I cannot but study English.

(3) It is no use ~ing : ~해도 소용없다
It is no use discussing the problem any longer.
= It is no use to discuss the problem any longer.
소용없다/그 문제를 더 이상 논의하는 것은.

(4) It goes without saying that : ~말할 필요가 없다, ~은 당연하다
It goes without saying that she is diligent.
= It is needless to say that she is diligent.
말할 필요가 없다/그녀가 부지런(성실, 근면)하다는 것은.

(5) be worth ~ing : ~할 가치가 있다
His suggestion is worth thinking.
그의 제의는 생각할 가치가 있다.

= It is worthwhile to think his suggestion.

(6) feel like ~ing : ~하고 싶다

I feel like traveling for a while. = I want to travel for a while.

= I feel inclined to travel for a while.

(7) make a point of ~ing : ~하는 것을 규칙으로 한다

I make a point of playing tennis every Sunday.

= I make it a rule to play tennis every Sunday.

나는 테니스 치는 것을 규칙으로 한다/일요일마다.

(8) be on the point of ~ing : 막 ~하려고 하다

He was on the point of having dinner.

그는 막 저녁을 먹으려고 했다.

= He was about to have dinner.

(9) on~ ing : ~하자마자, ~할 때

On returning home, she had dinner.

= As soon as she returned home, she had dinner.

그녀는 집에 돌아오자마자 저녁을 먹었다.

(10) be busy ~ing : ~하느라 바쁘다

I am busy preparing for the test recently.

나는 시험 준비를 하느라 바쁘다/요즘.

(11) above ~ ing : ~일 리가 없는

He is above doing such a thing.

= He is the last man to do such a thing.

그는 그런 일을 할 사람이 아니다.

(12) besides ~ing : ~뿐만 아니라
Besides teaching English, he studies English.
= In addition to teaching English, he studies English.
그는 영어를 가르칠 뿐만 아니라 배우기도 한다.

(13) be far from ~ing : ~ 하기는커녕, 결코 ~하지 않다
He is far from stealing. 그는 결코 훔치지 않는다.
= He never steals.
Far from being clever, he is stupid. 영리하기는커녕 그는 어리석다.

(14) come(go) near ~ing : 하마터면 ~할 뻔하다
She came(went) near being run over by a car.
그녀는 하마터면 차에 치일 뻔했다.
= She nearly(barely, narrowly) escaped from being run over by a car.
그녀는 거의 피할 수 없었다/차에 치이는 것으로부터.

(15) never(cannot) ~without ~ing : ~할 때마다 ~한다(2중 부정은 긍정)
They never have a meeting without arguing loud.
= Whenever they have a meeting, they argue loud.
그들은 회의를 가질 때마다 시끄럽게 논쟁한다.

(16) by ~ing : ~함으로써
By stopping smoking, I will be healthy.
금연함으로써 나는 건강할 거다.

(17) What do you say to ~ing : ~하자, ~하는 게 어때?

What do you say to play soccer? 축구 하는 게 어때?

= How about playing soccer?

= What do you think of playing soccer?

= Why don't we play soccer? 축구 할까?

= Let's play soccer. 축구 하자.

(18) have a difficult time ~ing : ~하느라 고생한다,

~하느라 어려운(힘든) 시간을 보낸다

= I have a difficult time studying English recently.

= I have difficulty studying English recently.

= I have trouble(problem) studying English recently.

나는 고생한다(애먹는다)/영어 공부하느라(고)/요즘(최근에).

(19) prevent(keep, stop) from ~ing : (~때문에) ~하지 못하다, ~하는 것을 방지하다(막다)

How do you prevent this from happening?

= How do you keep(stop) this from happening?

어떻게 이 일이 일어나는 것을 방지할 수 있니?

: = 추가설명(that is, 즉)   ; = 접속사 구실(and, but, because)

(20) go + 동명사

오락이나 놀이 활동을 하는 관용어구에 go 다음에 동명사가 온다.

go skiing, go running, go biking, go hiking, go boating, go shopping, go hunting, go sightseeing, go bowling, go camping, go swimming, go dancing 등

(참고)

5. 전치사의 목적어로 쓰이는 동명사의 위치(대부분 숙어적이다)

형용사(명사, 동사) + 전치사 + 동명사

동사를 전치사의 목적어로 쓰려면 동명사를 써야 한다.

(1) be + 형용사 + 전치사 + -ing

I'm *afraid of* go to the doctor's. (×)

I'm afraid of going to doctor's. (○)

Are you *interested in* riding a bicycle?

자전거를 타는 데 관심이 있니?

Jack *is crazy about* dancing. 잭은 춤추는 데 미쳤다.

(2) 명사 + 전치사 + -ing

The boat was *in danger of* sinking.

그 보트는 가라앉을 위험에 있었다.

What are the *advantages of* getting up early?

일찍 일어나는 장점은 무엇이니?

Is that a *reason for* staying away? 그것이 멀리 머무는 이유니?

(3) 동사 + 전치사 + -ing, 동사 + 전치사 + 목적어

동사 + 전치사 + -ing + 목적어, 동사 + 전치사 + 목적어 + -ing

동사 + 목적어 + 전치사 + -ing

We *talked about* the theme. 우리는 그 테마에 대해 이야기했다.

We *talked about* going to Europe.

우리는 유럽으로 가는 것에 관해 이야기했다.

I'm *thinking of* buying a car. 나는 차를 사는 것을 생각하고 있다.

I'm *looking forward to* meeting her.

나는 그녀를 만나기를 고대하고 있다.

She is *looking forward to* Tom coming home soon.

그녀는 탐이 곧 집에 오기를 고대하고 있다.
I *congratulated* Tom *on* getting a new job.
나는 탐에게 새 직업을 얻은 것을 축하했다.
She *accused* me *of* telling lies.
그녀는 내가 거짓말한 것을 비난했다.
I was accused of telling lies.
나는 거짓말을 한 것에 대해 책망을 받았다.
I forgot to *thank* him *for* helping me.
나는 그가 나를 도운 것에 대하여 감사하는 것을 잊었다.

(4) 부사구로서의 전치사 + -ing

I always check the tires before going by car on a long journey.
나는 늘 타이어를 점검한다/차로 긴 여행을 가기 전에.
We started to walk *instead of* waiting for the bus.
In spite of trying hard Barry always makes a lot of mistakes.
배리는 열심히 노력함에도 불구하고 늘 많은 실수를 한다.
You won't pass the exam without studying.

* 동명사는 형용사의 수식을 받기도 한다.
A good beginning is half the battle. (형용사가 동명사를 수식)
= The beginning is half of the whole. (총칭 → 관사)
= Well begun is half done. 시작은 반이다.
　← (What is) well begun is half done.

Exercises

A. 괄호 안의 동사를 적합한 to부정사나 동명사로 고치시오.

to부정사는 동사, 형용사, 부사, 명사를 수식하고, 동명사는 명사 역할(전치사의 목적어)

1. The company has agreed (pay) compensation.
2. The new drug appears (be) highly effective.
3. We chose (ignore) the warning.
4. Would you like (have) dinner with me one evening next week?
5. I would rather (go) by train than (walk).
6. The teacher had no pen (write) with.
7. He entered the room without (see) me.
8. This book is easy (understand).
9. I couldn't help (laugh).
10. After this debacle, the minister considered (resign).
11. I'm dying (read) her new novel.
12. I wish you'd quit (worry) about money.
13. Lock the door before (leave) the house.
14. It's possible (get) the missing parts.
15. The student was very proud of (win) the prize.
16. I forgot (tell) you that I don't like (play) cards.
17. She threatened (report) him to the police.
18. Are you thinking of (buy) a car?
19. Bill apologized for (shout) at me and he asked me (forgive) him.
20. Tim says he tried (call) me last night, but I don't remember (hear) the phone (ring).

21. Did you remember (write) to grandma and (say) thank you for the birthday present? Yes, I did, and I apologized for not (write) sooner.

22. I can't (open) this box. Can you show me how (do) it?-Let me (see)!

※ 1. to pay 2. to be 3. to ignore 4. to have 5. go, walk 6. to write 7. seeing 8. to understand 9. laughing 10. resigning 11. to read 12. worrying 13. leaving 14. to get 15. winning 16. to tell, playing 17. to report 18. buying 19. shouting, to forgive 20. to call, hearing, ringing 21. to write, to say, writing 22. open, to do, see

B. 괄호 안의 단어를 이용하여 동명사 문장으로 만드시오.

1. Tim promised he wouldn't smoke any more. (to give up)
2. The guide said we could also visit the gallery. (opportunity of)
3. He is very proud. He has passed his exam. (proud of)
4. He is not very happy. He doesn't earn enough money. (complain about)
5. Tony has a dream. He wants to be a pop star. (dream of)
6. Don't rely on Eric. (be no use)
7. My mother is very busy. She's preparing dinner. (be busy)
8. I will be pleased to meet your sister next week. (be looking forward to)
9. You shouldn't read that book. (not be worth)
10. It wasn't easy for us to find the way. (difficulties in)
11. I play tennis every weekend. (be fond of)

12. My brother is not at home. You needn't phone him. (be no use)
13. He finally got his driving license. (succeed in)
14. We had dinner. Then we went for a walk. (after)
15. He is a very good dancer. (good at)

※ 1. Tim promised to give up smoking. 2. The guide said we had the opportunity of visiting the gallery. 3. He is very proud of having passed his exam. 4. He complains about not earning enough money. 5. Tony dreams of being ⋯ 6. It's no use relying on Eric. 7. My mother's busy preparing dinner. 8. I'm looking forward to meeting ⋯ 9. It's not worth reading ⋯ 10. We had difficulties in finding ⋯ 11. I'm fond of playing tennis ⋯ 12. It's no use phoning him. 13. He succeeded in getting ⋯ 14. After having dinner, we ⋯ 15. He is very good at dancing.

제8장 분사

1. **분사의 종류**

    분사(分詞)는 동사와 형용사 역할을 하며, 현재분사(동사원형 + ing)와 과거분사의 두 가지 형이 있다.

    (1) 현재분사(~하는, ~하고 있는)는 능동, 진행의 의미가 있다
    falling prices 떨어지는 가격(자동사의 현재분사-진행의 의미)
    an exciting game 흥미롭게 하는 게임
    (타동사의 현재분사-능동의 의미)

    (2) 과거분사(~해버린, ~되어진(된))는 완료, 수동의 의미가 있다
    fallen prices 떨어진 가격(자동사의 과거분사-완료의 의미)
    an cxcited game 흥미로워진 게임(타동사의 과거분사-수동의 의미)

    (3) ① be동사 + 현재분사 = 진행형
    I am studying English now.
    I was studying English yesterday.
    ② be동사 + 과거분사 = 수동형
    I am invited to Tom's party.
    ③ have + 과거분사 = 완료형
    I have ever been to New York.

    (4) 현재분사와 동명사

현재분사와 동명사는 「**동사원형**＋ing」로 같은 형태이지만 용법은 다르다.

동명사는 명사의 역할을 하므로 '~하기 위한 것'으로 목적, 용도를 나타내고, 현재분사는 형용사의 역할을 하므로 '~하는, 하고 있는'으로 동작, 상태를 나타낸다.

a sleeping bag = a bag (which is used) for sleeping.
잠자기 위한 백 = 침낭, 침구 (용도-동명사)
a living room = a room for living
살기 위한 방 = 거실 (용도-동명사)
a sleeping baby = a baby who is sleeping.
잠자는 아기 = 자고 있는 아기 (상태-현재분사)

2. **분사의 용법**

분사는 '~하는, ~된'의 의미로 형용사의 일종으로 형용사처럼
① 명사를 수식하고(한정적 용법)
② 보어로 쓰이며(서술적 용법)
③ 그 외에 분사구문을 만든다

(1) **분사의 한정적 용법**

분사는 형용사처럼 명사 앞뒤에서 명사를 수식한다. 단독분사는 명사 앞에서, 수식어가 붙은 분사구는 명사 뒤에서 명사를 수식한다. 분사의 위치는 형용사의 위치와 같다.

★ 형용사(분사)의 어순-긴 것은 뒤로

① **단독형용사＋명사** : 전치수식(단독 단어일 때)
I saw a *big* dog. (형용사의 한정적 용법)

Barking dogs seldom bite. (분사의 한정적 용법)
짖는 개는 거의(좀처럼) 물지 않는다.

② **명사 + 형용사구** : 후치수식(2개 이상의 단어일 때)
The woman *under the tree* is Julia. (전치사구-형용사구)
The woman *talking with Tom* is Julia. (분사구-형용사구)
탐과 함께 이야기하고 있는 여자는 줄리아다.

③ **대명사 + 형용사** : 후치수식
(-thing, -body, -one, -where로 끝나는 대명사)
Choose something *you like*. (형용사절)
Let's play something *interesting*. 놀자/재미있는 어떤 것을.

④ **대명사 + 형용사구** : 후치수식
Give me something *good to see*.
내게 주시오/보기에 좋은 어떤 것을.
Do you know her *standing by the door*?
너는 아니/문 옆에 서 있는 그녀를?

(2) **분사의 서술적 용법(주어나 목적어를 보충 설명 = 보어)**
분사는 형용사처럼 주격보어, 목적격보어로 쓰인다.

① 주격보어
The soccer game is very exciting.
(the soccer game = very exciting)
그 축구경기는 매우 흥미진진하다.
He sat watching TV. 그는 TV를 보면서 앉아 있었다.
He sat surrounded by his family.

그는 그의 가족에 둘러싸여 앉아 있었다.
She came running. 그녀는 뛰어왔다.

② 목적보어(목적격보어)

I saw him *working hard*. (him = working hard)
나는 그가 열심히 일하는 것을 보았다. (△)
나는 열심히 일하는 그를 보았다. (○)
He made me wash a car. (○) 그는 내게 차를 씻게 했다.
He made me washing a car. (×) 그는 차를 씻는 나를 했다.
현재분사는 사역동사의 목적격보어가 될 수 없다.
그러나 지각동사의 목적격보어는 될 수 있다.
He saw me washing a car. (○) 그는 차를 씻는 나를 보았다.

(3) 과거분사의 부사구 역할

The flight will leave *as scheduled* at 7:00.
비행기는 출발할 거다/*예정대로* 7시에.
How's the price of Lotte Mart *compared to* E-mart?
롯데마트의 가격은 어떠니/이마트와 *비교해서*?

3. 분사구문

분사(현재분사, 과거분사)를 이용하여 부사절을 부사구로 바꾼 것을 분사구문이라고 한다. 분사구문은 일종의 분사구이다. 분사구문은 주로 격식체(학술적 문장체)에 쓰이며, 일상체에서는 잘 사용하지 않는다. 그러나 분사구문은 글에 자주 나오므로 독해를 위해서 알아두어야 한다.

(1) 부사절 → 분사구문 만드는 방법

① 부사절의 접속사를 없앤다.
② 부사절과 주절의 주어가 같을 경우 부사절의 주어를 생략한다. 주어

가 같지 않을 경우 부사절의 주어를 그대로 둔다.
③ 부사절의 동사를 「**동사 + ing**」형으로 바꾼다.
④ 분사구문에서 과거분사 앞에 being이나 having been은 생략할 수 있다.
  (being) + 과거분사(현재분사), (having been) + 과거분사

Though this building was built in 1950s, it still looks very good.
 = (Being) built in 1950s, this building still looks very good.
 = Built in 1950s, this building still looks very good.
  비록 이 건물은 1950년대에 지어졌지만 여전히 매우 좋아 보인다.

After he finished his homework, Jack went to bed.
 = After finishing his homework, Jack went to bed.

After he had finished his homework, Jack went to bed.
 = After having finished his homework, Jack went to bed.
 = After finishing his homework, Jack went to bed.
  잭은 그의 숙제를 끝마친 후에 잠자리에 들었다.

★ 현대 영어는 having + p.p 대신 p.p의 현재분사를 사용하기도 한다. After he had finished나 After he finished는 의미상의 차이가 거의 없기 때문에 having finished나 finishing 둘 다 쓸 수 있다.

(2) **분사구문의 용법 = 분사의 부사구적 용법**
  분사구문은 부사구이므로 부사처럼 시간, 이유(원인), 조건, 양보, 부대상황(동시동작), 계속 등을 나타낸다.

① 이유·원인(as, since, because)
　　나는 피곤했기 때문에 집에 머물렀다.
　　As I was tired, I stayed at home. (주절의 주어 = 종속절의 주어)
　　= (Being) tired, I stayed at home. (과거분사 앞 being은 생략 가능)
　　= As tired, I stayed at home.
　　* 의미의 혼동을 피하기 위해 접속사를 그대로 두기도 함.

② 시간(while, when, as, after)
　　나는 테니스를 치고 있는 동안에 줄리아를 만났다.
　　While I was playing tennis, I met Julia.
　　= (Being) playing tennis, I met Julia.
　　　(현재분사 앞 being은 생략 가능)
　　= Playing tennis, I met Julia.

③ 조건(if)
　　날씨가 좋으면 우리는 외출할 거다.
　　If it is fine, we will go out. (주절의 주어 ≠ 종속절의 주어)
　　= It being fine, we will go out.

④ 양보(though = although = even though(if))
　　비록 나는 열심히 공부했지만 시험에 떨어졌다.
　　Though I studied hard, I failed the exam(test).
　　= Studying hard, I failed the exam.
　　* 분사구문의 접속사나 해석은 주절에 의해 결정된다.

⑤ 계속(and)
　　우리는 7시에 떠나서 12시에 부산에 도착한다.
　　We leave at seven, *and we arrive* in Pusan at twelve.

= We leave at seven, *arriving* in Pusan at twelve.
우리는 7시에 떠난다, 그리고 12시에 부산에 도착한다.

* 분사구문이 주절 뒤에 올 때, 즉 S + V, -ing형이면 후치 분사구문이다. 후치 분사구문의 해석은 ㉠ ~하면서(동시동작)이거나 ㉡ and + 동사(연속동작, 그리고 ~하다)로 해석한다.

⑥ 부대상황(동시동작, while, when, as)
While Peter lived in the country, he worked hard.
피터는 시골에 살면서(사는 동안) 열심히 일했다.
= Living in the country, Peter worked hard.

* with 부대상황 : with + 목적어 + 목적보어(분사) : ~하면서(한 채로)
With night coming on, it's getting dark. (밤이 오면서)
The boy comes in, with his clothes wetted in the rain.
그 소년은 들어온다/그의 옷이 젖은 채로/빗속에.

★ 전치사 + -ing
① by + -ing = ~함으로써, ~하는 것으로, ~하면서
② in + -ing = ~하는데, ~하느라
③ on + -ing = ~하자마자, when ~할 때, ~하면
④ with + -ing = ~하면서(~한 채로), ~하는 동안(while)

(3) **독립분사구문**
부사절의 주어가 주절의 주어와 다르더라도 일반인(we, you, they, people)일 경우 생략한다. 생략된 분사구문을 독립분사구문이라고 한다.

독립분사구문의 관용어구(숙어)

broadly(roughly) speaking 대충 말하(자)면
strictly speaking 엄격히 말하(자)면
considering ~을 고려하면
frankly speaking 솔직히 말하면
generally speaking 일반적으로 말하면
judging from(by) ~으로 판단하건대(미루어 보아)
granting(granted, admitting) (that) : (= though)
    비록 ~일지라도(인정하더라도)
provided(supposing, assuming) (that) : (= if) 만약 ~한다면
seeing (that) ~ 으로 보아
talking of ~말인데(~대해서 말인데)

Exercises

A. 보기의 동사를 현재분사로 만들어 적합한 괄호 안에 넣으시오.

Laugh, get, run, walk, dance, rise, try, guess, plant, go, wait, climb, drive

1. I saw you (   ) flowers in your garden yesterday. Don't you think it's too early for that?
2. We heard you (   ) out last night. Where did you go? To a disco. Tony and I always go (   ) at the weekend.
3. Robert fell and broke his leg when he came (   ) down the stairs after someone had knocked at the door.

4. A few days ago Joe noticed some men (　) into the neighbor's house through the kitchen window. He knew the neighbors were not at home because he had seen them (　) in their car and (　) away. So he called the police, and they caught the men (　) to run away with the neighbors' TV.

5. I watched you (　) up and down outside the movie in the rain. Why didn't you go in? We couldn't! They kept us (　) until ten minutes before the film started.

6. What a sad story! I can still feel the tears (　) to my eyes!

7. What a stupid mistake! I can still hear the people (　) at me.

8. (patient to doctor) Please tell me what's the matter with me. Don't keep me (　)!

※ 1. planting 2. going, dancing 3. running 4. climbing, getting, driving, trying 5. walking, waiting 6. rising 7. laughing 8. guessing

B. 현재분사를 이용하여 두 문장을 연결하시오. 가능하면 두 가지 방법으로도 연결하시오.

1. Lisa was sitting by her desk. She was studying for an exam.
2. We stood outside the supermarket. We waited for Richard.
3. Mum was lying on the sofa. She was talking to Aunt Liz on the phone.
4. Dad opened his umbrella and walked out into the rain.
5. David left the house and waved back at his wife.

※ 1. Lisa was sitting by her desk, studying for an exam./Sitting by

109

her desk, Lisa was studying for an exam. 2. We stood outside the supermarket, waiting for Richard./Standing outside the supermarket, waiting for Richard. 3. Mum was lying on the sofa, talking to Aunt Liz on the phone./Lying on the sofa, Mum was talking to Aunt Liz on the phone. 4. Opening his umbrella, Dad walked out into the rain./Walking out into the rain, Dad opened his umbrella. 5. Leaving the house, David waved back at his wife./David left the house, waving back at his wife.

C. 다음 문장을 분사구문으로 만드시오.

1. When I walk home from school, I always pass by Mr. John's toy shop.
2. While Fred was visiting New York City, he made a day trip to Washington.
3. As Mum was tired after the dinner party, she went to bed early.
4. As Mary did not know what to do, she called the information desk.
5. After the guests had left, we cleaned up the living room.
6. Before I leave for school in the morning, I always feed my dog.
7. Susan got many letters and telegrams after she had won the quiz.
8. When Sarah heard about the accident, she broke down and cried.
9. After we had reached the top of the mountain, we took a photo.

※ 1. Walking home from school, I always pass by Mr. John's toy shop.
2. (While) visiting New York City, Fred made a day trip to Washington.
3. (Being) tired after the dinner party, Mum went to bed early.
4. Not knowing what to do, Mary called the information desk.
5. The guests having left (The guests leaving), we cleaned up the living room.
6. Before leaving for school in the morning, I always feed my dog.
7. Susan got many letters and telegrams, after winning(having won) the quiz.
8. On hearing about the accident, Sarah broke down and cried.
9. After reaching(having reached) the top of the mountain, we took a photo.

D. 관계대명사절을 현재분사(동사+ing)구로 바꾸시오.
1. The road that connects the two towns is very narrow.
2. We should all keep an eye on old people who live alone.
3. An increasing number of youngsters who apply for work are hardly literate.
4. People who stayed at the hotel were always very taken with the view.
5. We're a company full of smart, creative people who strive to do our jobs better every day.
6. The number of patients who suffer from this disease has increased rapidly in recent years.
7. The students who attend her workshops come from all over

the world including Britain and Australia.

※ 1. The road connecting the two towns is very narrow.
2. We should all keep an eye on old people living alone.
3. An increasing number of youngsters applying for work are …
4. People staying at the hotel were always very taken with the view.
5. We're company full of smart, creative people striving to do …
6. The number of patients suffering from this disease has …
7. The students attending her workshops come from all over …

E. 현재분사구문을 관계대명사절로 바꾸시오.
1. The burglars looked everywhere, even behind the pictures hanging on the walls.
2. Unemployment is one of the major problems facing our society.
3. The name 'Mississippi' is derived from an Indian word meaning 'great waters' or 'father of waters'.
4. Anyone seeing me there would have thought I was a lunatic.
5. The majority of the people living in this part of the city cannot afford to have computers in their homes.
6. Most of the big companies advertising on TV include their web address in their ads(advertisements).

※ 1. The burglars looked everywhere, even behind the pictures

that(which) hung on the walls.
2. Unemployment is one of the major problems that(which) face our society.
3. The name 'Mississippi' is derived from an Indian word that(which) means 'great waters' or 'father of waters'.
4. Anyone who(that) saw me there would have thought I was a lunatic.
5. The majority of the people who(that) live in this part of the city cannot afford to have computers in their homes.
6. Most of the big companies that(which) advertise on TV include their web address in their ads.

제9장 관계대명사

절은 주어와 동사를 가진 어군으로 보충 정보(설명)를 제공하면서 긴 문장을 만든다. 절은 기능에 따라 형용사절, 부사절, 명사절로 분류한다. 절의 종류에는 관계사절(관계대명사절, 관계부사절), 접속사절, 간접의문문이 있다. 구(句)나 절(節)은 하나의 품사처럼 형용사, 부사, 명사로 쓰인다.

두 문장을 연결하는 관계대명사는 접속사와 대명사의 구실을 겸한다.

선행사	주격	소유격	목적격
사람	who(that)	whose	whom(who, that)
동물·사물	which(that)	whose(of which)	which(that)
사람·동물·사물	that	–	that
사물(선행사 포함)	what	–	what

1. 관계대명사 who : 선행사가 사람일 때

(1) 주격 who(that)

　　The boy is my friend. He is a tennis player.
　　The boy is my friend. + He is a tennis player.
　　→ The boy **who**(**that**) is a tennis player is my friend.
　　　테니스 선수인 그 소년은 내 친구이다.
　　* 첫 번째 동사는 종속절의 동사이고, 두 번째 동사는 주절의 동사이다.

My daughter is a doctor. She lives in Seoul.
My daughter is a doctor and she lives in Seoul.
→ My daughter who(that) lives in Seoul is a doctor.
　서울에 사는 내 딸은 의사이다.
* 주격 관계대명사 who는 주어 역할을 하므로 주격 관계대명사 뒤에는 주어가 없는 불완전한 문장이 온다. 그러나 관계대명사절 전체는 완전한 문장이다.

☆ 관계대명사절은 **선행사(명사, 대명사)**를 수식하는 형용사절로 형용사처럼 쓰인다.
Someone who wants to come is welcome.
오기를 원하는 어떤 사람이라도 환영한다.
Everything (that) he said is untrue.
그가 말한 모든 것은 진실이 아니다.

★ 주격 관계대명사의 생략

① **주격 관계대명사 + be동사는 생략할 수 있다.**
문장에서 명사 뒤에 갑자기 형용사어구(형용사, 현재분사, 과거분사, 형용사구)가 있으면, 대개 주격 관계대명사 + be동사가 생략된 것으로 본다. 생략되어 줄여진 문장의 형용사어구는 앞에 있는 선행사(명사, 대명사)를 형용사처럼 수식한다.

The boy (who is) ***studying*** in the room is my son. (현재분사 앞)
The people (who were) ***interviewed*** are students. (과거분사 앞)
The book (which is) ***on the desk*** is hers. (형용사구 앞)
We have a lot of toys (which are) ***useful*** for children.
(형용사 앞)

= We have lots of toys useful for children.
우리는 많은 장난감들이 있습니다/아이들을 위한 유용한.
* 관계대명사절의 동사의 수는 선행사의 수에 일치시킨다.

② 주격관계대명사절에 be동사가 없다면, 주격 관계대명사를 생략하고 동사에 ing를 붙여 현재분사로 만드는 것이 빈번하다.
The woman who lives next door is a teacher.
= The woman living next door is a teacher.
옆집에 사는 여자는 선생이다.

She has a dog which runs very fast.
= She has a dog running very fast.
그녀는 매우 빨리 달리는 개를 가지고 있다.

③ there(it) is 명사 + (that) + 동사
There(it) is a man (that, who) wants to meet you.

(2) **목적격** whom(who, that)
The boy is my friend. You will meet him tonight.
→ The boy **who(whom, that)** you will meet tonight is my friend.
네가 오늘 밤에 만날 소년은 내 친구이다.
* whom은 격식체(문장체)로 문장에 가끔 나오고, who는 일상에서 많이 쓰이는 일상체(회화체)이다.

★ 목적격 관계대명사의 생략

① 목적격 관계대명사 + 주어 + 동사 …, 목적격 관계대명사 뒤에 주어 + 동

사가 있으면 목적격 관계대명사를 생략할 수 있다.

The boy (who, whom, that) you will meet tonight is my friend.
= The boy you will meet tonight is my friend.

② said (that) S + V … , think (that) S + V …
타동사 + that 뒤에 주어 + 동사가 있으면 접속사 that도 생략할 수 있다. 동사의 목적어 역할을 하는 명사절을 이끄는 접속사 that도 생략할 수 있다. 문장에서 동사 뒤에 갑자기 주어 + 동사가 있으면 접속사 that이 생략된 것으로 본다.

I believe (that) she is honest. (that절이 목적절)
It's important (that) he comes. (that절 앞에 형용사)
That he likes his new bike is clear. (that절이 주어)
The problem is (that) I have no money. (that절이 보어)
The fact (that) he likes his new bike is clear.
(선행사가 있는 that 주어절)

★ 일상체(회화체)에서 that을 생략하는 경우
명사(형용사) + that + S + V : 선행사(先行詞)가 있는 that은 생략 가능
동사 + that + S + V : 선행사가 없는 that은 목적절(타동사), 보어절에서는 생략 가능하고 주어절에서는 생략하지 않는다.

③ 관계대명사 앞에 전치사가 있는 목적격 관계대명사는 생략할 수 없다. 단 전치사가 관계대명사절 뒤로 가면 목적격 관계대명사는 생략할 수 있다.
문장에서 명사(대명사) 뒤에 갑자기 주어 + 동사가 있으면 목적격 관계대명사가 생략된 것으로 본다. 전치사 뒤에는 목적격이 오므로 전치사 뒤에서는 who가 아닌 whom이 와야 한다.

I met a man with who I played tennis. (×)

I met a man with whom I played tennis. (○)
= I met a man (whom, who, that) I played tennis with.
= I met a(the) man I played tennis with.
나는 함께 테니스를 친 남자를 만났다.

(3) 소유격 whose

The woman is a doctor. Her name is Julia.
→ The woman is a doctor and her name is Julia.
→ The woman whose name is Julia is a doctor.
이름이 줄리아인 그 여자는 의사이다.
I met the man. His car was stolen.
→ I met the man whose car was stolen.
나는 차를 도난당한 그 남자를 만났다.

2. 관계대명사 which : 선행사가 동물이나 사물일 때

(1) 주격 which(that)

The books are boring. They don't have any pictures.
→ The books which(that) don't have any pictures are boring.
어떤 그림들이 없는 책들은 지루하다.
* The cat (which, that) I have is very lovely.

(2) 목적격 which(that)

The books have dirty pages. I bought them yesterday.
The books (which, that) I bought yesterday have dirty pages.
내가 어제 산 책들은 더러운 페이지들이 있다.
The book *(which)* you are looking for is here.
= The book *for which* you are looking is here.

네가 찾는 책은 여기에 있다.

(3) 소유격 whose(of which)

The books cannot be sold. Their pages are dirty.
→ The books whose(of which) pages are dirty cannot be sold.
페이지들이 더러운 책들은 팔릴 수 없다.

3. 관계대명사 that : 선행사가 사람이나 동물이나 사물일 때

(1) 선행사가 사람 + 동물(사물)이면 관계대명사 that을 쓴다
사람과 사물이 함께 선행사가 되는 경우에는 관계대명사 that을 쓴다.
This is a photo of the farmer and his horse that are working on a(the) farm.
이것은 농부와 그의 말의 사진이다/농장에서 일하고 있는.
The boy that(who) sits in the garden is my brother.
Choose a(the) job that(which) fits your aptitude.
직업을 선택하라/네 적성에 맞는.

(2) 선행사 앞에 최상급, the only(very, same, first, last) 등의 수식어가 붙거나 선행사가 all(every, each, no, some) + 명사, little, such, -body, -thing 등으로 불특정한 것을 나타낼 때 관계대명사는 주로 that을 쓰지만, 선행사가 사람을 가리키면 who, 사물을 가리키면 which를 쓰기도 한다.
You are the only person that(who) can help us now.
Julia is the only one who(that) passed the test.
줄리아는 유일한 사람이다/그 시험에 합격한.
This is all the money that(which) I have.
이것은 모든 돈이다/내가 가지고 있는.

(3) 관계대명사 that 앞에는 전치사가 올 수 없으나, that절 뒤에는 올 수 있다

This is the house in which our family live. (○)

This is the house in that our family live. (×)

This is the house that our family live in. (○)

이것은 집이다/우리 가족이 사는.

(4) 관계대명사 that과 접속사 that의 비교

접속사 that 뒤에는 완전한 문장이 오지만, 관계대명사 that 뒤에는 주어나 목적어나 소유격이 없는 불완전한 문장이 온다. 왜냐하면 관계대명사 스스로 주어나 목적어나 소유격으로 되었기 때문이다.

I know that she is coming(will come) here tomorrow.

(that 뒤에 완전한 문장이 옴 → 접속사 that)

I know the woman that is comming here tomorrow.

(that 뒤에 주어가 없는 불완전한 문장이 옴 → 주격관계대명사 that)

4. 관계대명사 what = the thing that(which)

관계대명사 what절 '~ 하는 것은, ~하는 것을'은 명사절로 선행사를 포함하고 있다.

I'm giving you what you want.

나는 네게 줄 거다/네가 원하는 것을.

= I'm giving you the thing that(which) you want.

관계대명사 what절은 명사절이므로 명사처럼 문장에서 주어, 목적어, 보어로 쓰인다.

She gave me a book. She bought it yesterday.

→ She gave me a book *which* she bought yesterday.

　(형용사절) 그녀는 책을 내게 주었다/그녀가 어제 산.

→ She gave me *what she bought yesterday*. (명사절-목적어)

그녀는 내게 주었다/그녀가 어제 산 것을.

What is beautiful is not always good. (명사절-주어)
아름다운 것이 늘 좋은 것은 아니다.
He is not what he was. (명사절-보어)
그는 그였던 것이 아니다. (그는 예전의 그가 아니다.)
You reap what you sow. 뿌린 대로(것을) 거둔다. (명사절-목적어)

5. 선행사＋전치사구＋관계대명사

① 선행사를 수식하는 전치사구가 있을 경우 선행사와 관계대명사 사이는 멀어진다.

The <u>members</u> of the tennis club <u>who</u> are interested in tennis have meeting tomorrow.
테니스 클럽의 회원들은/테니스에 관심 있는/내일 회의가 있다.
I received <u>the money</u> from my parents <u>which</u> I will buy a bike.
나는 돈을 받았다/내 부모님으로부터/내가 자전거를 살.

② 주어를 수식하는 형용사절이 길면, 주어＋동사로 먼저 결론을 쓰고 동사 뒤에 형용사절(관계대명사절)을 쓴다.
주부 부분이 너무 길고 술부(서술부) 부분이 너무 짧으면 균형이 안 잡힌 부자연스러운 문장이 되지만, 술부 뒤에 추의 역할을 하는 부사어구가 오면 술부에 무게가 생겨 자연스러운 문장이 된다.

The car that my father bought last year broke down.
(주부가 술부보다 더 무거운 부자연스러운 문장)
＝*The car broke down that my father bought last year.*
  (술부 이하가 주부보다 더 무거운 자연스러운 문장)
＝The car that my father bought last year broke down yester-

day.
나의 아버지가 작년에 산 차는 어제 고장 났다. (자연스러운 문장)

6. **관계대명사의 한정적 용법과 계속적 용법**
   관계대명사절은 형용사절이므로 선행사(명사, 대명사)를 수식하는 한정적 용법과 앞 문장을 이어서 계속 보충 설명하는 계속적 용법이 있다. 계속적 용법일 때는 관계대명사 앞에 콤마(,)가 찍히고, 해석은 문장 앞에서부터 차례로 한다. 관계대명사 that과 what은 계속적 용법에는 쓰이지 않는다.

Where is the book (that) you borrowed from me last week?
(한정적 용법) 그 책은 어디에 있니/네가 나한테서 지난주에 빌린?
This is Tom, who has shown us the way. (계속적 용법)
이 사람은 탐이다, 그는 우리에게 그 길을 보여 주었다.
He said he had met her, which I can't believe.
그는 말했다/그가 그녀를 만났다고, 그것을 나는 믿을 수 없다.
He went to Pusan, where he stays for two weeks. (관계부사)
그는 부산에 갔다. 그곳에서 그는 2주 동안 머문다.

7. **관계대명사절의 삽입**
   삽입된 관계대명사절은 생략해도 문장구조에는 영향을 미치지 않는다.
The child, who is quite young, can already read and write.
그 아이는/꽤 어린/벌써 읽고 쓸 수 있다.
Mr. Brown, whose father is a millionaire, lives in New York.
브라운 씨는/아버지가 백만장자인/뉴욕에서 살고 있다.
The shops, which sell bikes, are closed today.
상점들은/자전거를 파는/오늘 문을 닫았다.

8. 관계부사

관계부사는 두 문장을 연결하는 접속사 구실을 한다.

관계부사 = 전치사 + 관계대명사(which)
       = 관계대명사(that, which) ⋯ 전치사

선행사	관계부사 = 전치사	+ 관계대명사
장소(the place)	where = in(at, on)	+ which
시간(the time)	when = in(at, on)	+ which
이유(the reason)	why = for	+ which
방법(the way)	how = in	+ which

I love the town. I was born there.
= I love the town and I was born there.
= I love the town *in which* I was born.
= I love the town which(that) I was born in.
= I love the town that I was born in.
　(목적격 관계대명사 생략 가능)
= I love the town I was born in.
= I love the town *where* I was born. (선행사 + 관계부사)
= I love where I was born. (관계부사 앞 선행사는 생략 가능)
= I love the town I was born in. (선행사 뒤 관계부사는 생략 가능)
　나는 마을을 좋아한다/내가 태어난.
Where there is a will, there is a way. 뜻이 있는 곳에 길이 있다.

Tell me the way. You solved the problem in this way.
= Tell me the way *in which* you solved the problem.
= Tell me the way that(which) you solved the problem in.

= Tell me the way you solved the problem.
= Tell me how you solved the problem.
　　내게 말해 다오/네가 그 문제를 푼 방법을.

* 선행사가 방법인 the way인 경우 the way + how형은 쓰지 않는다. 방법이란 말을 두 번 연거푸 쓰는 것이 되므로 둘 중에 하나만 쓴다.

――――――――――――――――――――――――――――― (참고)

9. 유사관계대명사

접속사 as, but, than이 관계대명사와 유사하게 쓰인다.

(1) 유사관계대명사 as

as, but, than 등은 접속사이지만, 선행사(명사)에 특별한 수식어가 붙을 경우 관계대명사처럼 쓰이는데, 이 경우 유사관계대명사라고 한다.

He is not such a fool as you thought.
그는 네가 생각한 그런 바보가 아니다.
This is the same bike as I lost.
이것은 내가 잃어버린 같은 종류의 자전거이다.
This is the same bike that I lost. (똑같은, 동일한, 바로 그)
Read such books as will enrich your life.
그런 책들을 읽어라/네 삶을 풍요롭게 할.

as는 계속적 용법으로, 앞 문장을 보충 설명하는 which 대신 쓰이기도 한다.
He is from American, as is clear from his accent.
그는 미국 출신이다, 그것은 분명하다/그의 악센트로부터.

(2) 유사관계대명사 but

선행사 앞에 부정어 no, not, never, hardly 등이 있을 경우, 유사관계대명사 but은 'that~ not, ~하지 않는'의 의미를 띤다. but 다음에 부정어가 없어도 부정의 의미를 띤다.

There is *no* rule of language *but* has some exceptions.
= There is no rule of language that does *not* have any exceptions.
언어의 규칙은 없다/어떤 예외가 없는.

(3) 유사관계대명사 than

than은 주로 선행사 앞 비교급과 함께 쓰여 관계대명사 역할을 한다.
I have more money than is needed.
I have more money than I need.
나는 더 많은 돈을 가지고 있다/내가 필요로 하는 것보다.

10. 복합관계대명사

(관계대명사 + ever) = 복합관계대명사, (관계부사 + ever) = 복합관계부사의 형태로 선행사가 없다. 관계대명사 that과 관계부사 why는 복합형이 없다.

복관대명사	명사절	양보의 부사절
whoever	누구든지(= anyone who)	누가 ~하더라도(= no matter who)
whatever	무엇이든지(= anything that)	무엇을 ~하더라도(= no matter what)
whichever	어느 것이든지(= anything which)	어떤 것을~하더라도(= no matter which)

복합관계부사	시간·장소·방법의 부사절	양보의 부사절
whenever	언제든지(= at any time when)	언제~하더라도(= no matter when)
wherever	어디든지(= at any place where)	어디서~하더라도(= no matter where)

however   어떻게 하든지(= how to do)   아무리~하더라도(= no matter how)

(1) **복합관계대명사**

복합관계대명사는 명사절이나 양보의 부사절을 이끈다.

You can invite whoever likes you. (명사절)

= You can invite anyone who likes you.

　너는 누구라도(누구든지) 초대해도 좋다/너를 좋아하는.

Whoever he is, I want to meet him once.

= No matter who he is, I want to meet him once.

　(양보의 부사절)

　그가 누구일지라도(누구라 하더라도) 나는 그를 한번 만나고 싶다.

(2) **복합관계부사**

복합관계부사는 시간, 장소, 방법, 양보의 부사절을 이끈다.

whenever ~할 때마다, 언제든지, 언제 ~하더라도

Whenever she may come back, I will be waiting for her.

(양보의 부사절)

= No matter when she may come back, I will be waiting for her.

　그녀가 언제 돌아올지라도 나는 그녀를 기다리고 있을 거다.

Whenever she is in trouble, she consults me. (시간의 부사절)

= At any time when she is in trouble, she consults me.

　그녀는 곤경에 처할 때마다(처할 때 언제든지) 나와 상담한다.

Exercises

A. 괄호 안에 관계대명사를 넣으시오. 생략 가능하면 생략하시오.

1. Anyone (   ) throws good money after bad is a fool.
2. The boy (   ) mother had had the accident also had to go to hospital.
3. The pop star, (   ) she had once seen on stage, was staying in the hotel.
4. The house (   ) roof was damaged by the storm is very old.
5. The number (   ) you have called is no longer in service.
6. He works in a stuffy little room (   ) walls are entirely papered with posters.
7. The town's 4,500 people had three doctors, two of (   ) were retiring.
8. The lady (   ) car was stolen went to the police at once.
9. He has failed the exam, (   ) is a pity.
10. David was the only one (   ) remembered the correct date.
11. My brother didn't help me, (   ) annoyed me a lot.
12. Your letters are the only things (   ) keep me going.
13. Is there a place (   ) does cars at that time of the day?
14. There are a lot of things (   ) she has to arrange.
15. Grammar, (   ) most students dislike, is very important.
16. The family next door, (   ) name I can't remember, are going to move.
17. All (   ) you need is love.
18. You're the only one (   )'s nice to me.

※ 1. who(that) 2. whose 3. who(m) 4. whose(of which) 5. — 6. whose(of which) 7. whom 8. whose 9. which 10. who(that) 11. which 12. that(which) 13. which(that) 14. — 15. which 16. whose 17. — 18. who(that)

B. 문장체인 「전치사＋관계대명사절」은 회화에서는 전치사가 관계대명사절 뒤로 가면서 목적격 관계대명사가 생략된다. 다음 문장체를 회화체로 바꾸시오.

1. The candidate must be a man with whom the people can identify.
2. The only person for whom he shows any respect is his father.
3. The Internet is a new world about which she knows little.
4. This is one of the points on which agreement has not yet been reached.
5. This is a kind of nonsense up with which I will not put.
6. Some misguided people think that a preposition is a word with which one should never end a sentence.

※ 1. ⋯ a man the people can identify with.
2. The only person he shows any respect for is his father.
3. ⋯ world she knows little about.
4. ⋯ points agreement has not yet been reached on.
5. ⋯ nonsense I won't put up with.
6. ⋯ a word one should never end a sentence with.

C. 다음 두 문장을 관계대명사로 연결하시오.

1. Yesterday we got a postcard. It had no stamp on it.
2. I've just talked to a boy. He knows Julia's telephone num-

ber.

3. Do you know the people? We are their guests tonight.
4. This morning Dad had to walk to work. This did not make him happy.
5. That coat belongs to my dad. I am wearing it at the moment.
6. Charlie works in a factory. It produces all kinds of paint.

※ 1. Yesterday we got a postcard that(which) had no stamp on it.
2. I've just talked to a (the) boy who(that) knows Julia's telephone number.
3. Do you know the people whose guests we are tonight?
4. This morning Dad had to walk to work, which did not make him happy.
5. The coat (that, which) I'm wearing at the moment belongs to my dad.
6. Charlie works in a factory that(which) produces all kinds of paint.

D. 다음 두 문장을 관계대명사 없이 연결하시오(목적격 관계대명사는 생략하시오).

1. What did you do with the money? Your parents gave it to you last week.
2. The girls didn't tell us their names. We met them at the disco yesterday.
3. 'Dr. Jekyll and Mr. Hyde' and 'The Time Machine' are among the best books. I have read them.
4. Please bring me the letter. I have put it on my desk.
5. The new house looks very nice. Chris and Linda have just

bought it.
6. Have you still got the book? You borrowed it from me before Christmas.

※ 1. What did you do with the money your parents gave you last week?
2. The girls we met at the disco yesterday didn't tell us their names.
3. 'Dr. Jekyll and Mr. Hyde' and 'The Time Machine' are among the best books I have read.
4. Please bring me the letter I have put on my desk.
5. The new house Chris and Linda have just bought looks very nice.
6. Have you still got the book you borrowed from me before Christmas?

제10장 수동태

능동태(能動態)는 주어가 동작을 하는 '주어가 ~하다'의 문장이고, 수동태(受動態)는 주어가 동작을 받는 '주어가 ~되다(받다, 당하다)'의 문장이다.
수동태는 능동태의 주어(행위자)를 모르거나 밝히기 어렵거나 밝힐 필요가 없거나 또는 글의 흐름상 수동태가 능동태보다 더 자연스러울 때 쓴다.

I was pleased with your advice. (이 경우 능동적 해석이 더 좋음)
나는 기뻐(만족)했다/너의 충고를 듣고(받고).
The concert was canceled due to rain.
콘서트는 취소되었다/비 때문에.
I was asked to finish the job.
나는 끝내도록 부탁(요청)을 받았다/그 일을.
He was refused entry into the country.
그는 거절당했다/그 나라 입국을.
Hope isn't achieved without effort.
소망(희망)은 성취되지 않는다/노력 없이.
English is spoken everywhere. 영어는 통용된다/어디에서나.

1. **수동태를 만드는 법 : be+과거분사+by**
   I love her. 나는 그녀를 사랑한다. (능동태)
   → She is loved by me. 그녀는 나의(나한테) 사랑을 받는다.

(수동태)
① 능동태의 목적어를 수동태의 주어로 바꾼다.
② 능동태의 동사를 「be + 과거분사」로 바꾼다.
be동사를 시제, 인칭, 수에 맞게 바꾼다.
③ 능동태의 주어를 「by + 목적격」으로 바꾼다.

☆ 「by 행위자」를 생략하는 경우
① 능동태의 주어가 일반인일 때
(they, one, people, somebody, anyone 등)
They speak English in Australia. 호주에서는 영어로 말한다.
→ English is spoken in Australia (by them).
② 능동태의 주어(행위자)가 명백하지 않거나 나타낼 필요가 없을 때
The building was built in 1970 (by somebody).
그 건물은 세워졌다/1970년에.
I was invited to Julia's party.
나는 초대되었다(초대받았다)/줄리아의 파티에.

2. 수동태의 시제

시제	능동태	수동태
현재	He write a letter.	A letter is written by him.
과거	He wrote a letter.	A letter was written by him.
미래	He will write a letter.	A letter will be written by him.
현재완료	He has written a letter.	A letter has been written by him.
과거완료	He had written a letter.	A letter had been written by him.
미래완료	He will have written a letter.	A letter will have been written by him.
현재진행	He is writing a letter.	A letter is being written by him.
과거진행	He was writing a letter.	A letter was being written by him.

* 현재완료진행형, 과거완료진행형, 미래완료진행형의 수동태는 쓰이지 않는다.
* will have written에서 will have는 조동사이고 마지막 written만 본동사이다.
* 조동사는 그대로, 본동사만 수동형으로 바뀐다.

3. **주의해야 할 수동태**

(1) **4형식 문장의 수동태**
4형식 문장은 간접목적어와 직접목적어를 주어로 하는 두 개의 수동태가 가능하다.
I gave her a book. 나는 그녀에게 책을 주었다.
→ She was given a book by me. 그녀는 책을 나한테 받았다.
→ A book was given her by me.
 책은 나로부터(나에 의해) 그녀에게 주어졌다.

* 간접목적어를 수동태의 주어로 할 경우, 만일 의미가 비논리적이면, 직접목적어만을 수동태의 주어로 만든다. 4형식 문장의 수여동사 중에서 buy, write, make, send, pass 등은 직접목적어만을 수동태의 주어로 한다.

Father bought me a bike. 아버지는 내게 자전거를 사 주었다.
→ I was bought a bike by father.
 나는 아버지에 의해 자전거를 사 주었다. (×, 비논리적)
→ A bike was bought for me by father.
 자전거는 아버지에 의해 내게 사 주었다. (○, 논리적)

(2) 5형식 문장에서 사역동사와 지각동사 뒤의 원형부정사는 수동태에서 「to부

133

정사」로 된다. 5형식 문장에서는 목적어만 수동태의 주어로 될 수 있고, 목적보어는 수동태의 주어가 될 수 없다. 능동태의 목적어만이 수동태의 주어로 되기 때문이다

I saw him play tennis. 나는 그가 테니스 치는 것을 보았다.

→ He was *seen play* tennis by me. (×)

　(seen play 본동사 두 개가 연거푸 올 수 없으므로 사이에 to가 옴)

→ He was *seen to play* tennis by me. (○)

(3) 조동사는 그대로, 본동사만 수동형으로 바뀐다

She can play the piano. 그녀는 피아노를 연주할 수 있다.

→ The piano can be played by her.

(4) 조동사 do는 조동사가 없는 문장을 부정문이나 의문문으로 만들 때 별도로 삽입된 조동사이므로 수동형으로 될 때는 없어진다

He didn't finish the work. 그는 그 일을 끝내지 않았다.

→ The work didn't was finished by him. (×)

→ The work was not finished by him. (○)

　그 일은 그에 의해 끝내지지 않았다.

He doesn't do the work. → The work is not done by him.

(5) 목적어가 없는 능동문도 수동문으로 되는 경우가 있다

Letters to the USA should send by airmail.

→ Letters to the USA should be sent by airmail.

Bicycles must not leave outside overnight.

→ Bicycles must not be left outside overnight.

(6) by 이외의 전치사를 쓰는 경우는 숙어적이다

Everyone knows his diligence. 누구나 그의 근면함을 안다.

→ His diligence *is known to* everyone.
그의 근면함은 누구에게든 알려졌다.

be married to ~와 결혼하다
be engaged to ~와 약혼한 사이이다.
be known to ~에게 알려지다
be known for ~으로 알려져 있다.
be annoyed at ~에 화가 나다
be surprised at ~에 놀라다.
be disappointed at ~에 실망하다
be surrounded with ~으로 둘러싸여 있다.
be satisfied with ~에 만족하다
be pleased with ~에 기뻐하다.
be interested in ~에 흥미가 있다
be tired of ~에 싫증나다.

(7) 전치사구, 부사구(절), 구동사(타동사구) 등은 한 덩어리처럼 취급한다
Our neighbors *look after* our house when we are on holiday.
→ Our house *is looked after* by our neighbors when we are on holiday.
우리 집은 우리 이웃들에 의해 돌보아진다/우리가 휴가 중일 때.
Jane *takes care of* the baby. 제인은 아기를 돌본다.
→ The baby is *taken care of* by Jane.
아기는 제인에 의해 돌봐진다.

(참고)

(8) 목적어가 명사절[접속사 that, whether(if)]인 문장의 수동태

일반인 주어가 say, think, believe, expect, suppose 등의 동사를 취하여 that절을 목적어로 취할 경우에, 수동태는 ① it을 가주어로 하는 경우와 ② that절 안의 주어를 주절의 주어로 하는 경우와 ③ that절을 수동태로 하는 경우 세 가지 형태가 가능하다.

They say that she is very beautiful. (2가지 경우)
= It is said that she is very beautiful. (①)
= She is said is very beautiful. (×)
= She is said to be very beautiful. (②)

People believe that they have killed the hostages. (3가지 경우)
= It is believed that they have killed the hostages. (①)
= They are believed to have killed the hostages. (②)
= It is believed that the hostages have been killed. (③)

(9) 수동태가 불가능한 동사들

① 기본적으로 목적어를 취할 수 있는 타동사만 수동태가 가능하다.
타동사일지라도 주어의 행위가 목적어에 영향을 미치지 못하는 일부 상태동사와 소유동사들은 수동태를 만들지 못한다.
become(suit, fit) 어울리다, escape 모면하다, have 가지다, lack 부족하다, own(possess) 소유하다, resemble 닮다 등

He had a car. 그는 차를 가지고 있었다.
→ A car was had by him. (×)
  차가 그에 의해 가지게 되었다.
Sarah resembles her mother. 사라는 그녀의 엄마를 닮았다.
→ Her mother is resembled by Sarah. (×)
  그녀의 엄마는 사라에 의해 닮아졌다.

② 목적어를 취할 수 없는 자동사일지라도 전치사와 함께 쓰여 타동사처럼 목적어를 취하는 구동사(타동사구)는 수동태가 가능하다.

「자동사 + 전치사 = 타동사 역할」

account for ~을 설명하다, agree to ~에 동의하다, deal with ~을 처리하다, laugh at ~을 비웃다, look for ~을 찾다, think of ~에 대해 생각하다, look at ~을 보다, wait for ~을 기다리다, return to ~으로 돌아가다 등

Sarah laughed at Peter. 사라는 피터를 비웃었다.
→ Peter was laughed at by Sarah. (O)
  피터는 사라의(사라에 의해) 비웃음을 받았다.

(10) 의문문의 수동태

① 의문사가 주어인 경우는 「by + 의문사」가 문두에 온다.
Who wrote the book?
→ By whom was the book written?
= Who(m) was the book written by?

② 의문사가 주어가 아닌 경우
When did he write the book?
→ When was the book written by him?

③ 의문사가 없는 의문문
Did he wash the car?
→ Was the car washed by him?

(11) 명령문의 수동태

① 긍정명령문(Let + 목적어 + be + p.p)
Know yourself. (네 자신을 알라) → Let yourself be known.

② 부정명령문
(Let + 목적어 + not + be + p.p/don't let + 목적어 + be + p.p)
Don't eat my chocolate. 내 초콜릿을 먹지 마라.
→ Let my chocolate not be eaten.
= Don't let my chocolate be eaten.

Exercises

A. 다음 능동문을 수동문으로 바꾸시오. 2가지 경우도 있음. 가능하면 행위자는 생략하시오.

1. We regard these people as antisocial and violent.
2. In Britain, cars should not park next to a yellow line.
3. The boys are repairing the bike.
4. In Australia the people speak English.
5. They paid us very well for our work.
6. His colleagues saw him as somewhat colorless and indecisive.
7. They told me that they had cancelled my reservation by mistake.
8. The grocer will send us the drinks tonight.
9. The nurse has told the children a good story

10. Police fear that they have killed the hostages.
11. He has described Russia as a rich country full of poor people.
12. They had never answered that letter.
13. We had to learn the poem by heart.
14. You can visit the Museum of London every day except Mondays.
15. Nobody has shown me the document.
16. I am sure that we can reach a compromise.
17. This is a problem that we must solve.
18. We should have supported her.

※ 1. These people are regarded as antisocial and violent. 2. In Britain, cars should not be parked next to a yellow line. 3. The bike is being repaired by the boys. 4. English is spoken in Australia. 5. We were paid very well for our work. 6. He was seen as somewhat colorless and indecisive by his colleagues. 7. They told me that my reservation had been cancelled by mistake. 8. The drinks will be sent to us by the grocer tonight./We will be sent the drinks by the grocer tonight. 9. The children have been told a good story by the nurse./A good story has been told to the children by the nurse. 10. It is feared that the hostages have been killed. 11. Russia has been described as a rich country full of poor people. 12. That letter had never been answered. 13. The poem had to be learned by heart. 14. The Museum of London can be visited every day except Mondays. 15. I haven't been shown the document./The document hasn't been shown to me. 16. I am sure that a compromise can be reached. 17. This is a problem that must be solved. 18. She should have been supported.

B. 다음 수동문을 능동문으로 바꾸시오.
   1. The door to the hidden room was broken down by the men.
   2. The concert has been put off because the pianist is ill.
   3. Will your dog be looked after when you are gone?
   4. After three hours the fire was put out.
   5. Shoes and hats must be taken off before you enter the temple.
   6. Look, all these things have been thrown away by tourists!

※ 1. The men broke down the door to the hidden room. 2. They have put off the concert because the pianist is ill. 3. Will somebody look after your dog when you are gone? 4. They put out the fire after three hours. 5. You must take off your shoes and hats before you enter the temple. 6. Look, tourists have thrown away all these things!

C. 다음 문장을 It is p.p(said, known, thought, expected, believed)형으로 바꾸시오.
   1. People believe that the asteroid will not hit the earth.
   2. You know very well that Kevin is the best skier in his group.
   3. They have reported that all passengers survived the crash.
   4. They say that chocolate is good for the brain.
   5. They think that the car was stolen by a young man.
   6. They expect Henry to go to Harvard one day.

※ 1. It is believed that the asteroid will not hit the earth.
2. It is very well known that Kevin is the best skier in his group.
3. It has been reported that all passengers survived the crash.
4. It is said that chocolate is good for the brain.
5. It is thought that the car was stolen by a young man.
6. It is expected that Henry will go to Harvard one day.

제11장 가정법

가정법(假定法)은 어떤 것을 가정하거나 상상할 때 쓴다. 가정법에는 가정법 현재, 가정법 과거, 가정법 과거완료, 가정법 미래가 있다.

1. **가정법 현재**

    해석은 현재-미래시제로 한다.
    현재 또는 미래에 대해 가정(상상, 소망)할 때 쓰인다.
    가정법 현재의 조건절은 직설법 현재의 조건절과 같다.
    (가정법 현재는 - 현실적인 경우 - 가능성이 있는 경우에 주로 쓰임)

    조건절(만일 ~한다면)   ,   주절(~할 것이다)
    If 현재동사   ,   will + 동사원형

    If you ask me, I will help you.
    (만일) 네가 내게 부탁하면 나는 너를 도울 것이다.
    = I will help you if you ask me.
    * 주절 뒤에 종속절이 오면 콤마는 안 찍는다.

2. **가정법 과거**

    해석은 현재시제로 한다. 현재 사실에 대해 가정(상상, 소망)할 때 쓰인다. 가정법 과거는 실현 가능한 경우와 불가능한 경우에 쓰인다.
    (가정법 과거는 - 현재에 대한 가정 - 가능성이 있는 경우에 주로 쓰임)

조건절(만일 ~한다면)   ,   주절(~할 텐데)
If 과거동사   ,   would(should, could, might) + 동사원형

If you asked me, I would help you.
네가 내게 부탁하면 나는 너를 도울 텐데.
 = You don't ask me, so I will not help you. (실현 가능한 경우)
If I were(was) a bird, I would fly to her.
내가 새라면 나는 그녀에게 날아갈 텐데.
 = I am not a bird, so I don't fly to her. (불가능한 경우)
* be동사의 가정법 과거동사는 인칭에 관계없이 were나 was를 쓴다.

3. **가정법 과거완료**

해석은 과거시제로 한다. 과거 사실에 대해 가정(상상, 소망, 아쉬움)할 때 쓰인다. 이미 지나간 과거에 대한 가정으로 실현 불가능하다.
(가정법 과거완료는-과거에 대한 가정-불가능한 경우에 주로 쓰임)

조건절(만일 ~하였다면)   ,   주절(~했을 텐데)
If had + p.p   ,   would + have + p.p

If you had asked me, I would have helped you.
네가 내게 부탁을 했다면 나는 너를 도왔을 텐데.
 = You didn't ask me, so I didn't help you.
If I had studied harder, I could have passed the exam.
내가 더 열심히 공부했더라면 나는 그 시험에 합격할 수 있었을 텐데.
 = I didn't study harder, so I didn't pass the exam.
* p.p = past participle 과거분사

4. **that절 속의 가정법 현재(동사원형, should+동사원형)**

　　ask, require, suggest, propose, advise, insist, demand, order 등과 같이 주장·제의·명령·요구 동사가 이끄는 that절 속에서나, desirable, important, necessary, essential 등과 같이 당연·필요·요구 등의 형용사가 이끄는 that절 속에서는 가까운 미래의 소망이나 당연함을 나타내므로 that절 속의 should는 대개 생략「(should)+동사원형」된다. (미식 영어) 이 경우 인칭에 관계없이 동사원형이 온다.

　　I demand that you (should) finish the work quickly.
　　나는 요청한다/당신이 그 일을 빨리 끝낼 것을(끝내야 한다고).
　　It is desirable that he (should) finish the work.
　　당연하다/그가 그 일을 끝내는(끝내야 하는) 것은.

5. **특별한 가정법 구문**

(1) 　I wish (that) + 과거동사 : 가정법 과거(~하면 좋을 텐데)
　　I wish(that) + had p.p : 가정법 과거완료(~했다면 좋았을 텐데)

　　I wish she came quickly. 그녀가 빨리 오면 좋을 텐데.
　　= I am sorry she doesn't come quickly.
　　　나는 유감이다/그녀가 빨리 안 와서.
　　I wish I had bought the house.
　　내가 그 집을 샀다면(샀더라면) 좋을 텐데.
　　= I am sorry I did not buy the house.
　　　나는 유감이다/내가 그 집을 사지 않아서.

(2) 　as if + 과거동사 : 가정법 과거(마치 ~인 것처럼)
　　as if + had p.p : 가정법 과거완료(마치 ~이었던 것처럼)

She speaks **as if (as though)** she was an American.
그녀는 말한다/마치 (그녀가) 미국인 것처럼.
= In fact she isn't an American.
사실은 그녀는 미국인이 아니다.
She talks as if she had read the book.
그녀는 이야기한다/마치 그 책을 읽었던 것처럼.
= In fact she didn't read the book.
She talked as if she had read the book.
그녀는 이야기했다/마치 그 책을 읽었던 것처럼.
= In fact she didn't read the book.
* It appears as if it's my fault. 그것은 내 잘못인 것처럼 보인다.

(3) It is time (that) + 과거동사(should 동사원형) : 가정법 과거
It is high(about) time : ~할 시간이다

It is time (that) we should go to bed.
= it is time (that) we went to bed. 우리는 잠 잘 시간이다.
= It is high(about) time we went to bed.
* It is time to go to bed. 잠 잘(잠자러 갈, 잠자리에 들) 시간이다.

6. If(조건절)의 대용어구
가정법 if절에서 접속사 if가 생략되면 조동사가 주어 앞에 오면서 무조건 도치가 발생한다.

(1) If it were(was) not for~ : ~이 없다면 : 가정법 과거
If it had not been for~ : ~이 없었다면 : 가정법 과거완료

If it were not for your help, we would be in trouble.

= *Were it not for* your help, we would be in trouble.
= *Without* your help, we would be in trouble.
= *But for* your help, we would be in trouble.
너의 도움이 없다면 우리는 곤경에 처할 텐데.

If it had not been for your help, we would have been in trouble.
= *Had it not been for* your help, we would have been in trouble.
= *Without* your help, we would have been in trouble.
= *But for* your help, we would have been in trouble.
너의 도움이 없었다면 우리는 곤경에 처했을 텐데.

(2) Unless = if ~ not : 만약 ~하지 않으면
Unless we are tired, let's finish the work.
= If we aren't tired, let's finish the work.
우리가 피곤하지 않으면 그 일을 끝내자.

(3) suppose(supposing) (that) : ~라고 가정하면, 만약 ~이라면
provided (that) : 만약 ~이라면
on condition (that) : 만약 ~이라면(if), ~이라는 조건으로

We will go on a picnic provided (that) it doesn't rain tomorrow.
우리는 소풍을 갈 거다/내일 비가 오지 않으면.
Suppose(supposing) I fail the exam, what should I do?
내가 시험에 떨어진다면(가정하면), 무엇을 나는 해야 하나?
I will do the job on condition (that) you help me.

나는 그 일을 할 거다/네가 나를 도와준다는 조건으로(도와준다면).

(참고)

7. 혼합가정법

I would help you, but I don't have time.
(가정법 과거 + 직설법 현재)
나는 당신을 도울 텐데, 그러나 나는 시간이 없다.
I'm busy right now, otherwise I would go with you.
(직설법 현재 + 가정법 과거)
나는 지금 바쁘다, 그렇지 않으면 나는 너와 함께 갈 텐데.
If she had taken the doctor's advice, she might still be alive.
(가정법 과거완료 + 가정법 과거)
그녀가 의사의 충고를 들었다면, 그녀는 아직 살아 있을지도 모른다.

8. 가정법 미래

가정법 미래는 미래에 대해 가정(상상, 소망)할 때 쓰인다.

조건절(만일 ~한다면) ,   주절(~할 것이다)
① If should + 원형 ,   would(will) + 원형
                         (should, shall/could, can/might, may)
② If were to + 원형 ,   would(should, could, might) + 원형

(1) 조건절에 should를 쓰는 경우 : 실현 가능할 때 인칭에 관계없이 should를 쓴다

If I should fail the driving test, I will try again.
= If I should fail the driving test, I would try again.
만일 내가 운전면허 시험에 떨어진다면 나는 다시 시도할 거다.

If it should be fine tomorrow, we will go mountain climbing.
= If it's fine tomorrow, we will go mountain climbing.
(가정법 현재) 내일 날씨가 좋으면 우리는 등산하러 갈 거다.

(2) 조건절에 were to를 쓰는 경우 : 실현 불가능할 때 인칭에 관계없이 were to를 쓴다

If I were to be born again, I would study harder.
내가 다시 태어난다면 나는 더 열심히 공부할 거다.
If the sun were to rise in the west, I would not change my mind.
해가 서쪽에서 뜬다 하더라도 나는 내 마음을 바꾸지 않을 것이다.

* 현대 영어는 조건절의 should와 were to를 혼용하기도 한다.
* 현대 영어는 가정법 미래 대신 대부분 가정법 현재를 쓰기 때문에 가정법 미래는 시험에도 거의 출제되지 않는다.

Exercises

A. 다음 문장을 가정법 현재로 고치시오.
(현실적인 경우-가능성이 있는 경우 → 가정법 현재)
1. If I (get) a better mark next time, my parents (buy) me a new laptop.
2. If John (not be) at home, we (go) to the movies without him.
3. If you (not leave) now, you (not catch) your train.
4. If Lucy (be) a little friendlier, people (like) her better.

5. If the wind (get) stronger, we (not go) sailing.

※ 1. If I get a better mark next time, my parents will buy me a new laptop.
   (조건과 시간의 부사절에서는 동사의 현재형이 미래를 대신한다.)
  2. If John is not at home, we'll(we will) go to the movies without him.
  3. If you don't leave now, you won't(will not) catch your train.
  4. If Lucy is a little friendlier, people will like her better.
  5. If the wind gets stronger, we will not go sailing.

B. 다음 문장을 가정법 과거로 고치시오.
   (현재에 대한 가정-가능성이 있는 경우 → 가정법 과거)
  1. If I (get) a better mark this time, my parents (buy) me a new laptop.
  2. If John (be) at home, we (go) to the movies together.
  3. If you (leave) now, you (not miss) your train.
  4. If Lucy (be) a little friendlier, people (like) her better.
  5. If the wind (get) stronger, we (not go) sailing.

※ 1. If I got a better mark this time, my parents would buy me a new laptop.
  2. If John were(was) at home, we would go to the movies together.
  3. If you left now, you would not miss your train.
  4. If Lucy were(was) a little friendlier, people would like her better.
  5. If the wind got stronger, we wouldn't go sailing.

C. 다음 문장을 가정법 과거완료로 고치시오.

(과거에 대한 가정-불가능한 경우 → 가정법 과거완료)

1. If I (get) a better mark last time, my parents (buy) me a new laptop.
2. If John (not be) at home, we (go) to the movies without him.
3. If you (leave) earlier, you (not miss) your train.
4. If Lucy (be) a little friendlier, people (like) her better.
5. If the wind (get) stronger, we (not go) sailing.

※ 1. If I had got a better mark last time, my parents would have bought me a new laptop.
2. If John had not been at home, we would have gone to the movies without him.
3. If you had left earlier, you would not have missed your train.
4. If Lucy had been a little friendlier, people would have liked her better.
5. If the wind had got stronger, we would not have gone sailing.

D. 다음 가정법 문장에서 괄호 안에 동사를 시제의 일치가 되도록 고치시오.

(주절의 시제를 기준으로 종속절의 시제를 맞추거나 또는 역으로 맞춘다.)

1. If you (lose) your way, you can call me on my mobile.
2. If the bottle had fallen a split second earlier, it (hit) me straight on the head.
3. I am sure if I (not pull) her out, she would have drowned.
4. What (you do) if you found a burglar in your home?

5. If he (go) into politics, he might have made it to the White House.
6. If there is a God, he (not punish) me for simply being wrong.
7. To be on the safe side, I think it (be) better if we bought a new lock.
8. If there is a war, there (can be) a high number of civilian casualties.
9. If Kennedy (not die), Lyndon Johnson would never have become President.
10. What (you save) if the house was on fire?
11. If we had a million dollars, we (can buy) ourselves a decent house.
12. If we'd had more money, we (can buy) a better house. (we'd had = we had had)
13. If you make that kind of mistake, you (be) out.
14. Maybe I wouldn't have dropped out of college if I (study) what I wanted to.

※ 1. lose 2. would have hit 3. had not(hadn't) pulled 4. would you do 5. had gone 6. will not punish 7. would be 8. could be ~할 거다(혼합가정법) 9. had not died 10. would you save 11. could buy 12. could have bought 13. you will be(you'll be, you're, you are) 14. I had studied(I'd studied)

제12장 일치와 화법

1. **주어와 동사의 수 일치**

    동사는 주어의 인칭과 수에 따라 문법적으로 일치해야 한다.
    단수주어 다음에는 대개 단수동사가 오고, 복수주어 다음에는 대개 복수동사가 오지만, 예외적인 경우도 있다.
    He plays the piano. They play tennis.
    The United States is a country in pursuit of peace and justice.
    미국은 평화와 정의를 추구하는 나라이다.

    (1) A and B, both A and B : A와 B 둘 다
    Peter and I are brothers. 피터와 나는 형제이다.
    Both animals and people need love.
    동물과 사람 둘 다 사랑을 필요로 한다.

    (2) A or B, either A or B, neither A nor B, not A but B,
    not only A but (also) B = B as well as A
    〈등위접속사 참조 → 165p〉

    as well as만 전자에 일치시키고 나머지는 모두 후자(B)에 일치시킨다. 주어일 경우 as well as를 제외하고 모두 동사에 가까운 명사(B)를 기준으로 동사의 수를 일치시킨다.

    (3) every A and B나 each는 단수 취급(단일개념으로 봄)

Every boy and girl in the class was invited to the party.
반에 있는 모든 소년 소녀가 파티에 초대되었다.
Slow and steady wins the race. (단일개념으로 봄)
천천히 그리고 꾸준한 것이 경주를 이긴다.
= Haste makes waste. 서두르면 일을 망친다(실패한다).
Each of the students studies hard. 학생들 각자 열심히 공부한다.
* 주어로 쓰이는 동명사도 단일개념으로 보아 단수 취급한다.
Watching new movies is very interesting.
새 영화를 보는 것은 매우 흥미롭다.

(4) 양을 나타내는 말들은 of 다음에 오는 명사에 의해 수가 결정된다
some of + 단수명사 → 단수동사, some of + 복수명사 → 복수동사
Some of student is diligent. Some of students are diligent.

주의 : one of(each of, every one of) + 복수명사 → 단수동사
One of my friends lives in the city. 내 친구 하나는 도시에 산다.
Each of my friends lives in the city. 내 친구 각자는 도시에 산다.
Every one of my friends lives in the city.
내 친구 모두는 도시에서 살고 있다.

(5) 일정한 양(정도)을 나타내는 시간, 거리, 가격, 무게 등은 복수형이라도 단일개념으로 보아 단수 취급한다
Twenty years is a long time. 20년은 긴 세월이다.
Ten thousand dollars is a lot of money.
Five miles is too far to walk.
* 분수(퍼센트)는 단수명사 뒤에는 단수동사가 복수명사 뒤에는 복수동사가 온다.
Two thirds(60 per cent) of the army is stationed there.

Two thirds of the officers are against the reforms.

(6) **There is 단수명사, There are 복수명사**
There is a book on the desk.
There are two books on the desk.
There's no place like home.

(7) **단수, 복수 취급하는 명사들**
〈단수/복수명사 참조 → 184p〉

2. 시제의 일치

주절과 종속절로 이루어진 복문에서 주절의 시제와 종속절의 시제를 사건의 흐름에 맞게 일치시키는 것을 시제의 일치라고 한다.
일반적으로 주절의 시제를 기준으로 종속절의 시제를 맞추지만, 경우에 따라서는 역으로 맞추기도 한다.

(1) **주절의 시제가 현재, 미래, 현재완료이면 종속절의 시제는 아무거나 가능하다**

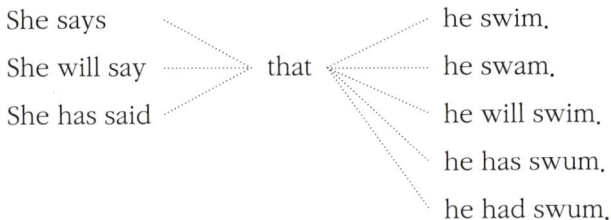

(2) **주절의 시제가 과거이면 종속절의 시제는 과거나 과거완료가 된다**
She thought that he came.
She thought that he had come.

(3) 주절의 시제가 현재에서 과거로 바뀌면 종속절의 시제는 다음과 같이 변한다.
즉 첫 번째 동사의 시제를 한 단계 낮춘다
현재, 미래 → 과거,
현재완료, 과거 → 과거완료

She thinks that he *comes*.
→ She thought that he *came*.
She thinks that he *will* come.
→ She thought that he *would* come.
She thinks that he *has* come.
→ She thought that he *had* come.
She thinks that he *came*.
→ She thought that he *had* come.

(4) 시제 일치의 예외
주절의 시제가 변해도 종속절의 시제가 변하지 않는 경우

① 종속절이 일반적 진리, 사실, 속담 등을 나타낼 때 → 항상 현재시제
He says, "The earth moves round the sun."
→ He said (that) the earth moves round the sun.
그는 말했다/지구가 태양 주위를 돈다고.
She says, "The world is round."
→ She said the world is round.

② 종속절이 현재의 습관을 나타낼 때 → 항상 현재시제
She says that he plays tennis every Saturday.
→ She said that he plays tennis every Saturday.
그녀는 말했다/그는 토요일마다 테니스를 친다고.

③ 종속절이 역사적 사실을 나타낼 때 → 항상 과거시제

We learn, "Columbus discovered America in 1492."

→ We learned Columbus discovered (had discovered) America in 1492.

우리는 배웠다/콜럼버스가 1492년에 아메리카를 발견했다고.

④ 종속절이 가정법을 나타낼 때 → 원래 시제 그대로

(가정법은 시제를 이미 한 단계 낮추었으므로)

She says, "If he were a bird, he would fly to me."

→ She said (that) if he were a bird, he would fly to her.

그녀는 말했다/그가 새라면 그는 그녀에게 날아올 텐데라고.

3. **화법**

말을 전달하는 법을 화법(話法)이라고 한다. 화법에는 남의 말을 그대로 전달하는 직접화법과 남이 말한 내용을 전달하는 사람의 입장에서 고쳐서 전달하는 간접화법이 있다.

She said to me, "I am a doctor." (직접화법)

그녀는 나에게 말했다/"나는 의사이다"라고.

전달동사와 피전달문 사이는 콤마를 찍고, 피전달문 앞뒤는 따옴표를 찍는다.

→ She told me (that) she was a doctor. (간접화법)

그녀는 내게 말했다/그녀는 의사라고.

간접화법에서는 콤마와 따옴표가 없어진다.

(1) **화법의 전환(직접화법 → 간접화법)**

① 콤마와 따옴표를 없앤다.

② 전달동사를 적당히 바꾼다. (said to → told)

that(목적절) 뒤에 주어 + 동사가 오므로 that은 생략할 수 있다.

③ 전달자의 입장에서 피전달문의 인칭, 시제를 바꾼다.
④ 전달자의 입장에서 주어, 형용사, 부사를 바꾼다.
we → they, now → then(at that time), this → that, here → there, bring → take, ago → before, today → that day, tonight → that night, this week → that week, next week → the following week(the next week), tomorrow → the next day(the following day), yesterday → the day before(the previous day), last night → the night before(the previous night), three days ago → three days before

(2) 화법의 시제
전달동사가 과거이면 피전달문의 시제를 한 단계 낮춘다.
피전달문의 첫 번째 동사만 한 단계 낮추면 된다.
have → had, have been → had been, will have → would have, will have gone → would have gone,
He went. → He had gone.
(과거동사의 한 단계 낮은 시제는 과거완료)
had gone → had gone
(과거완료보다 낮은 시제는 없으므로 그대로)

(3) 전달동사가 현재, 현재완료, 미래일 경우 피전달문의 동사는 변하지 않는다
She says, "I study English every day."
→ She says (that) she studies English every day.
She has said (that) she studies English every day.
She will say (that) she studies English every day.

직접화법
Tom says, "I am with my girlfriend on vacation in New York

now. We like New York very much. We have already seen many sights. We have talked with many people during this trip. On Sunday we went to Central Park. Today we are going to take a walk around the Onassis Reservoir. Tomorrow we will try to visit the Statue of Liberty. In two days we'll fly home again."

→ 간접화법

Tom said (that) he was with his girlfriend on vacation in New York then. (and that) They liked New York very much. They had already seen many sights. They had talked with many people during that trip. On Sunday they had gone to Central Park. That day they were going to take a walk around the Onassis Reservoir. The next day they would try to visit the Statue of Liberty. In two days they would fly home again.

탐은 말했다, 그는 그때 그의 여자 친구와 함께 뉴욕에서 휴가 중에 있다고. 그들은 뉴욕을 매우 많이 좋아한다고. 그들은 이미 많은 관광을 했다고. 그들은 그 여행 동안에 많은 사람들과 이야기 했다고. 일요일에 그들은 센트럴 공원에 갔었고. 그날 그들은 오나시스 저수지 둘레를 산책하려고 한다고. 그 다음날에 그들은 자유의 여신상을 방문할 거라고. 이틀 후에 그들은 다시 집으로 비행할 거라고.

(4) 의문문의 화법전환

① 의문사가 있는 의문문 : 전달동사를 ask로 바꾸고, 피전달문을 간접의문문인 「의문사 + 주어 + 동사」의 순서로 한다.
간접의문문은 평서문이므로 의문부호(의문표)가 없어진다.
She said to his son, "when do you return home?"
→ She asked his son when he returned home.

그녀는 그의 아들에게 물었다/언제 집에 돌아오느냐고.

She said to him, "who ate my apples?" (의문사가 주어인 경우)

→ She asked him who had eaten her apples.

그녀는 그에게 물었다/누가 그녀의 사과를 먹었냐고.

② 의문사가 없는 의문문 : 전달동사를 ask로 바꾸고, 피전달문을 「if(whether) + 주어 + 동사」의 순서로 한다. 의문표가 없어진다.

He said to me, "May I use your pen?"

→ He asked me if(whether) he might use my pen.

그는 내게 물었다/그가 내 펜을 사용해도 좋은지.

(5) 명령문의 화법전환

전달동사를 say 대신 ask(tell, order, beg, advise) 등으로 바꾸고, 명령문을 「to + 동사원형」으로 바꾼다. 피전달문의 시제는 변하지 않는다.

Mother said to us, "Be quiet in the room."

→ Mother told us to be quiet in the room.

Father said to me, "wash the car."

→ Father ordered me to wash the car.

아버지는 내게 명령했다/차를 씻으라고.

────────────────────────────────── (참고)

☆ 직설법의 명령문

① 직접명령문 : 일반적으로 you를 쓰지 않고 동사원형으로 시작한다.

You are quiet. → Be quiet. 조용히(들) 해라.

You never tell a lie. → Never tell a lie!

(강한 명령일 때는 감탄부호도 쓰인다)

You are quiet. 너(희)는 조용히 해라.

(상대방을 지적할 때는 you를 생략하지 않는다)
② 간접명령문 : 1인칭, 3인칭의 명령문으로 let을 사용한다.
Let us eat now. = Let's eat now.
자(지금) 먹읍시다. (Let's = Let us)
Let's go swim. 수영하러 가자. (let's 뒤에는 동사원형이 옴)

(6) 감탄문의 화법전환

전달동사를 say 대신 cry(shout, exclaim) 등으로 바꾸고 감탄문의 어순을 그대로 하거나, 부사 very를 써서 평서문으로 바꾼다. 감탄사가 없어진다.

He said, "what a crabby woman she is!"
= He cried out(said) what a crabby woman she was.
= He cried out that she was a very crabby woman.
　그는 외쳤다/그녀가 매우 심술궂은 여자라고.

☆ 직설법의 감탄문

① What a(an) + 형용사 + 명사 + 주어 + 동사!
It is a very beautiful flower. → What a beautiful flower it is!
그 꽃은 참(정말) 아름답구나! (얼마나 아름다운 꽃인가!)
② How + 형용사(부사) + 주어 + 동사!
That flower is very beautiful. → How beautiful that flower is!
The dog runs very fast. → How fast the dog runs!
저 개는 정말(참) 빨리 달리는구나!

Exercises

A. 다음 직접화법 문장을 간접화법 문장으로 바꾸시오.
   (전달동사가 과거이면 피전달문의 시제는 한 단계 낮춘다.)

   1. Bill said, "I'll meet her here after school tomorrow."
   2. Dad told us, "Uncle Simon and I have planted five trees since yesterday."
   3. Joe informed me, "I talked to your brother an hour ago."
   4. Mr. and Mrs. Albert said, "We've just come back from our camping trip."
   5. Grandma told Fred, "I'm getting nervous about your concert, Fred."
   6. Mrs. Smith said, "Mr. Smith will go on a business trip next week."
   7. The man complained, "I bought these scales last week but they don't work."
   8. The new secretary admitted, "I can't type very well but I can make good coffee."
   9. The headmaster told me, "Since you were elected, the school magazine has very much improved. I even enjoyed the article about myself."
   10. The Smith family told us, "Our holidays were terrible this year. We only got one hotel room instead of two we had booked."
   11. The interviewer wanted to know, "When did your pop career start and what are your plans for the future?"
   12. When I went to the interview for the new job I was asked,

"Why have you been out of work for 6 months? Are you not willing to work in a different job than the one you had before?"

13. The teacher asked us, "Put these 20 sentences into reported speech and learn the new words."
14. The receptionist asked, "Would you like a room with a bath or with a shower?"
15. Our teacher told us, "Next Monday we'll have a meeting for the parents. The headmaster wants to know how many of the parents will come."

※ 1. Bill said (that) he would meet her there after school the next day. 2. Dad told us (that) he and Uncle Simon had planted five trees since the day before. 3. Joe informed me (that) he had talked to my brother an hour before(ago). 4. Mr. and Mrs. Albert said (that) they had just come back from their camping trip. 5. Grandma told Fred (that) she was getting nervous about his concert. 6. Mrs. Smith said (that) Mr. Smith would go on a business trip the following week. 7. The man complained (that) he had bought the(those) scales the week before but (that) they didn't work. 8. The new secretary admitted (that) she couldn't type very well but (that) she could make good coffee. 9. ⋯ (that) since I had been elected, the school magazine had very much improved and (that) he had even enjoyed the article about himself. 10. (that) their holidays had been terrible that year and (that) they had only got one hotel room instead of the two they had booked. 11. when my pop career had started and what my plans was for the future. 12. why I had been out of work for 6 months and if(whether) I was not willing to work in a different job than the one I had had before. 13. to put those 20 sentences … and (to) learn the new words. 14. if(whether) I would like a room with a bath or with a shower. 15. (that) we would have a meeting for the parents the following Monday. The headmaster wanted to know how many of the parents would come.

B. 다음 직접화법을 간접화법으로 바꾸시오.
  (전달동사가 현재, 현재완료이면 피전달문의 시제는 변하지 않는다.)

1. The President says, "America will not give up the fight for freedom."
2. Our math teacher has told us, "I have never seen a better class."
3. At the end of the play Romeo thinks, "Juliet is dead."
4. Grandma remembers, "Life was hard when I was young."
5. Tina has explained, "I have tried to contact him, and now I'm waiting for an answer."
6. The newspaper reports, "Two hundred people saw the UFO yesterday."

※ 1. The President says (that) America will not give up the fight for freedom.
  2. Our math teacher has told us (that) he has never seen a better class.
  3. At the end of the play Romeo thinks (that) Juliet is dead.
  4. Grandma remembers (that) life was hard when she was

young.
5. Tina has explained (that) she has tried to contact him and that now she is waiting for an answer.
6. The newspaper reports (that) two hundred people saw the UFO yesterday.

제13장 접속사

접속사(接續詞)는 단어와 단어, 구와 구, 절과 절을 연결하는 품사이다. 접속사에는 등위접속사와 종속접속사가 있다.

1. **등위접속사**
   단어, 구, 절을 대등한 관계로 연결하는 접속사이다.
   and, but, or, for, so, nor, both 등

(1) and

① 대등연결

Homeless people are always cold, and hungry.
= Homeless people are always *cold* and *hungry*. (단어와 단어)
* 짧은 문장일 때 and 앞의 콤마는 생략할 수 있다.
Jack wants *to stay at home* and *(to) watch television*. (구와 구)
Today *I clean the rooms*, and *you go shopping*. (절과 절)
오늘 나는 방들을 청소하고 당신은 시장 보러 간다.

② 명령문 + and : ~하라, 그러면

Study hard, and you'll succeed.
열심히 공부해라, 그러면 너는 성공할 거다.
= If you study hard, you will succeed.

③ 동사 + and + 동사 = 동사 + to + 동사원형

go(come, be, try, sure, run, wait 등) + and + 동사원형에서 and는 to의 대용으로 쓰인다.

Come and help me. (회화체) = Come to help me. (격식체)

Let's go and play. = Let's go to play. = Let's go play.

Try and finish the job = Try to finish the job.

그 일을 끝내려고 노력하라.

(2) but

① 상반관계

I am tired, but I should the work.

= I am tired but should the work.

나는 피곤하나 그 일을 해야 한다.

He is weak, but I am strong. 그는 약하지만 나는 강하다.

Patience is bitter, but its fruit is sweet.

인내는 쓰다. 그러나 그 열매는 달다.

There had been warnings, **but** the authorities hadn't acted.

= There had been warnings, (but) **still** the authorities hadn't acted.

= There had been warnings, (and) **yet** the authorities hadn't acted.

경고가 있었다, 그런데도(그럼에도 불구하고) 당국은 실행하지 않았다.

② nothing but = only 오직, 단지

She does nothing but complain. 그녀는 오직 불평만 한다.

He is but a student. 그는 단지 학생이다. 그는 학생에 불과하다.

③ not A but B : A가 아니라 B이다
He is not a person, but a beast.
그는 사람이 아니라 짐승(동물)이다.

(3) or

Which do you like better, coffee or tea?
어느 것을 더 좋아하니/커피나 차(티) 중?
Rain or snow, I must go there.
비가 오든 눈이 오든 나는 거기에 꼭 가야 한다.

명령문 + or : ~하라, 그렇지 않으면
지금 가자, 그렇지 않으면 우리는 기차를 놓칠 거다.
Let's go now, or(or else) we'll miss the train.
= If we don't go now, we'll miss the train.
= Unless we go now, we'll miss the train.
Give me liberty, or give me death!
내게 자유를 달라, 그렇지 않으면 죽음을 달라!

(4) nor

nor 앞에 부정어가 있을 때 또 하나의 부정을 하기 위해 nor(~도 ~않다)를 쓴다.
부정어 nor 뒤의 문장은 도치된다.
nor = and neither = and not either.
She neither ate nor spoke. 그녀는 먹지도 말하지도 않았다.
= She did not either eat or speak.
= She didn't eat, nor did she speak.

(5) either A or B = A나 B 둘 중에 하나(동사는 B에 일치)
Either you or he has to do the work right now.
너나 그나 둘 중에 하나는 그 일을 해야 한다/지금 당장.

(6) neither A nor B = not ~either A or B = A도 B도 아니다.
I like neither alcohol nor tobacco.
나는 술도 담배도 좋아하지 않는다.
= I don't like either alcohol or tobacco.
Neither you nor he is diligent. 너나 그도 부지런하지 않다.
She is neither tall nor small. 그녀는 크지도 작지도 않다.

(7) not only A but (also) B = B as well as A = A뿐만 아니라 B도
She is not only a doctor but (also) a scientist.
= She is a scientist as well as a doctor.
그녀는 의사뿐만 아니라 과학자이다.
Not only you but (also) he is diligent. (동사는 후자에 일치)
= He as well as you is diligent. (동사는 전자에 일치)

* as well as '~만큼(같이)'
  may(might) as well as '~하는 편이 더 낫다'
I want to be rich as well as you. 나는 당신만큼 부자가 되고 싶다.
I may(might) as well go as stay. 나는 머무느니 가는 편이 더 낫다.

(8) for
for는 주로 전치사로 쓰이는데, 접속사로 쓰일 경우에는 항상 주절 뒤에 온다. 접속사 for 앞에는 콤마가 찍힌다. 접속사 for는 격식체로 사용빈도가 매우 낮고, 일상체로 since, as, because를 많이 쓴다.

For it is dark, it may rain. (×)   It may rain, for it is dark. (○)
Since(as) it is dark, it may rain.
= It may rain because it is dark.
* because 종속접속사는 대개 주절 뒤에 온다. 격식체에서 매우 드물게 강조할 때에만 주절 앞에 온다.

2. **종속접속사**

등위접속사를 제외한 모든 접속사가 종속접속사이다. 종속접속사에는 명사절을 이끄는 종속접속사와 부사절을 이끄는 종속접속사가 있다.

1) 명사절을 이끄는 종속접속사에는 접속사 that, whether(if), 의문사(wh-), 관계대명사(what, whoever 등)가 있다. 명사절을 이끄는 종속접속사절은 명사처럼 주어, 목적어, 보어로 쓰인다

(1) that 명사절 '~라는 것은, ~라는 것을' : 어느 정도 확실할 때 사용
That she can speak English is certain. (that절-주어)
It is certain *(that) she can speak English*.
(it은 가주어, that절은 진주어)
확실하다(틀림없다)/그녀가 영어를 말할 수 있다는 것은.
I know *(that) she can speak English*. (that절-목적어)
나는 안다/그녀가 영어를 말할 수 있다는 것을.
The truth is *that she can speak English*. (that절-보어)
사실은 그녀가 영어를 말할 수 있다는 것이다.

☆ 전치사 중 in과 except만 that절 앞에 놓여 that 명사절을 목적어로 취할 수 있다.
Men differ from animals in that they can think and speak.
사람은 동물과 다르다/생각하고 말할 수 있다는 점에서.

I know nothing *except* that she lives there.
나는 아무것도 모른다/그녀가 거기에서 산다는 것을 제외하고는.

(2) that으로 시작하는 명사절(두뇌동사와 두뇌형용사)

① 동사 + that절 : 두뇌동사(이성적 판단의 동사)
agree, feel, remember, believe, learn, decide, forget, notice, discover, hear, promise, think, know, explain, hope, read, understand, say 등

I think (that) Julia will come. 나는 생각한다/줄리아가 올 것을.
I know (that) Julia comes. 나는 안다/줄리아가 오는 것을.

② 사람 + be + 형용사 + that절 : 두뇌형용사(이성적 판단의 형용사)
certain, happy, sorry, amazed, confident, pleased, sure, angry, aware, disappointed, proud, surprised, worried, afraid, glad 등

I'm afraid (that) Julia comes.
나는 두려워한다/줄리아가 오는 것을.
I am glad (that) Julia comes.
나는 기뻐한다/줄리아가 오는 것을.

③ It + be + 형용사 + that절 : 두뇌형용사
amazing, good, important, lucky, interesting, likely, obvious, possible, surprising, strange, well, known, wonderful, nice, true 등

It's true (that) Julia comes. 사실이다/줄리아가 오는 것은.

It's important (that) Julia comes. 중요하다/줄리아가 오는 것은.

④ 주어로 쓰이는 that절

That Julia likes her new car is clear. (부자연스러운 문장)
= It is clear (that) Julia likes her new car. (자연스러운 문장)
분명하다/줄리아가 그녀의 새 차를 좋아하는 것은.

(3) whether(if) 명사절 '~인지 아닌지' : 불확실할 때 사용

Whether he is healthy (or not) is the question. (주어)
whether절은 주어, 목적어, 보어 자리에 오지만, if절은 목적어 자리에만 온다.
나는 그에게 물어보았다/건강한지(아닌지).
I asked him *if(whether) he is healthy (or not)*. (목적어)
종속절 끝에 있는 or not은 생략할 수 있다. whether 바로 뒤에는 or not이 올 수 있지만 if 뒤에는 바로 올 수 없다.
I asked him whether or not he is healthy. (○)
I asked him if or not he is healthy. (×)
The question is *whether he is healthy (or not)*. (보어)
의문은 그가 건강한지(아닌지) 이다.

(4) 관계대명사 what절도 명사절을 이끈다

I don't know what she wants.
나는 모른다/그녀가 원하는 것을.

2) 부사절을 이끄는 종속접속사

부사절은 부사처럼 시간, 이유, 목적, 결과, 조건, 양보 등을 나타낸다.

시간 : when ~할 때, ~하면, while~ 하는 동안, as soon as(soon

after) ~하자마자, after ~후에, since ~이래로, before ~전에, until(till) ~때까지, whenever ~할 때마다

장소 : where 어디에, wherever 어디든지

목적 : so(so that, in order that) ~하기 위해서, lest ~should ~하지 않기 위해서, ~하지 않도록

결과 : so(such) ~that 너무 ~해서 ~하다

이유 : because(as, since) ~때문에, now (that) ~이기 때문에, in that ~라는 점에서

조건 : if [provided (that)] ~라면, unless(if~ not) ~아니라면, in case (that) ~경우에 (대비해서), once 일단 ~하면, on condition (that) 만일 ~라면(if), ~라는 조건으로, as(so) long as(as far as) ~하는 한, as if(as though) 마치 ~인 것처럼

양보 : though(although, even though(if)) 비록 ~이지만, 비록 ~일지라도

(1) **시간을 나타내는 종속접속사**

Wait here *till(until)* I come back.
여기서 기다려/내가 돌아올 때까지.
I take a shower *before* I go to bed.
나는 샤워한다/잠자기 전에.
= Before I go to bed, I take a shower.
I arrived *after* Tim (had) left. (~후에)
We haven't seen Tony *since* he left Korea. (~이래로, ~이후로)
우리는 토니를 보지 못했다/그가 한국을 떠난 이후로.

When it's very cold, I put on a sweater. (~할 때, ~하면)
날씨가 매우 추우면(추울 때) 나는 스웨터를 입는다.
When it rains, I will stay (at) home.

비가 오면 나는 집에 머물거다.
When(If) Peter comes, you will see him.
피터가 오면 너는 그를 볼거다.
When he was a kid, he cried very much.
그는 어렸을(아이였을) 때 아주 많이 울었다.

While she has dinner, she watches TV. (동안에)
While most people like soccer, some don't like it. (반면에)
대부분의 사람들이 축구를 좋아하는 반면에, 몇몇은 그것을 좋아하지 않는다.

I will never forget your help *as(so) long as* I live. (~하는 한)
나는 당신의 도움을 결코 잊지 않을 겁니다/내가 살아있는 한.
As soon as he came home, he took a shower. (~하자마자)
그는 집에 오자마자 샤워를 했다.

(2) **장소를** 나타내는 종속접속사
    I want to live in the town where many my friends live.
    You can go wherever you like.
    너는 가도 좋다/네가 좋아하는 어디든지.

(3) **목적을** 나타내는 종속접속사 so와 so that은 '그래서, ~하기 위해서'의 두 가지 뜻이 있다.
    There were no chairs, *so (so that)* we had to stand.
    (계속적 용법)
    의자가 없었다, 그래서 우리는 서 있어야만 했다.
    Wear a sweater *so (so that, in order that)* you don't get cold.
    스웨터를 입어라/너는 감기에 걸리지 않도록(않기 위해서).

(4) **결과를 나타내는 종속접속사 : 너무 ~해서 ~하다**
so + 형용사(부사) + that
so + 형용사 + a(an) + 명사 + that
such + a(an) + 형용사 + 명사 + that

저 책은 너무 어려워서 나는 그것을 읽을 수 없다.
That book is so difficult that I can't read it.
= That is so difficult a book that I can't read it.
= That is such a difficult book that I can't read it.
= That book is too difficult for me to read.

(5) **이유(원인)를 나타내는 종속접속사**
Since(as) we don't have enough money, we can't buy a new car.
= We can't buy a new car because we don't have enough money.
우리는 새 차를 살 수 없다/우리는 충분한 돈을 가지고 있지 않기 때문에.
We couldn't wash because there was no water.
우리는 씻을 수 없었다/물이 없었기 때문에.
He was unlucky *in that* he had no friends. (~ 점에서)
그는 불행했다/친구가 없다는 점에서.
The weather is getting hotter *now that* the rainy season is over. (~이므로, ~이기 때문에)
날씨가 점점 더 더워지고 있다/장마철이 끝나서.

(6) **조건을 나타내는 종속접속사**
If I get home before 9, I'll phone you.

내가 9시 전에 집에 도착하면 네게 전화할게.

In case (that) you need money, I can lend you some. (~경우에)
네가 돈이 필요한 경우에 나는 네게 좀 빌려줄 수 있다.

Take an umbrella *in case* it rains. (~경우에 대비하여)
우산을 가져가라/비가 오는 경우를 대비해서.

I will do the work *on condition (that)* I am paid. (if, ~조건으로)
나는 그 일을 할 거다/돈을 준다면(주는 조건으로) .

As far as(as long as) I know, she will not come here.
(~하는 한)
내가 아는 한 그녀는 여기에 오지 않을 거다.

Once I start to read a book, I couldn't stop in the middle.
(일단 ~하면) 일단 내가 책을 읽기 시작하면, 나는 중지할 수 없다/중간에.

(7) **양보를 나타내는 종속접속사**

Though(although, even though(if)) she was very tired, she couldn't rest.
비록 그녀는 매우 피곤했을지라도, 휴식할 수 없었다.

Although we didn't have much money, we travelled a lot.
비록 우리는 많은 돈을 가지고 있지 않았지만 많은 여행을 했다.

(8) **as는 '~처럼, ~대로'의 의미로 종속접속사로 쓰이기도 한다**

Do to others as you would be done by (others).
다른 사람을 대우하라/네가 대우(대접)받고 싶은 대로.

She speaks English very well as if(as though) she was American.
그녀는 영어를 매우 잘 말한다/마치 그녀가 미국인 것처럼.

When (you are) in Rome, do as the Romans do.

로마에 있을 때는 로마인들이 하는 대로 하라.
(로마에서는 로마의 풍습을 따르라.)

(9) **like는** '~처럼, ~같이'의 의미로 상태를 나타내는 종속접속사로 쓰이기도 한다
Do like I do. 내가 하는 것처럼 하라.
She looks like she plays tennis very well.
그녀는 테니스를 매우 잘 치는 것처럼(것 같이) 보인다.

(10) 비교 종속접속사 than
My cold is better than (it was) two days ago.

Exercises

괄호 안에 적합한 접속사(드물게 전치사)를 넣으시오.
1. Do ( ) I say, not ( ) I do.
2. Have yourself extra time ( ) there are delays.
3. Dozens of reporters follow the president ( ) he goes.
4. You say you love her ( ) you never find time to be with her.
5. Wine won't do you any harm ( ) you drink it in moderation.
6. Her father died just ( ) she'd completed her first year at university.
7. You sound ( ) you're from London.
8. ( ) there's full moon, anything can happen.
9. It's nice walk ( ) you don't mind walking uphill.

10. Wear a sweater ( ) you don't get cold.
11. ( ) writing is a complex task; it can be learned and improved with practice.
12. We put towels on the chairs ( ) we didn't wet the seat cushions.
13. ( ) the war started I was 17 and not in the least interested in politics.
14. The electricity went off, ( ) there wasn't much we could do.
15. I didn't want to tell her the truth ( ) I didn't want to hurt her.
16. He couldn't come to the party ( ) he was ill.
17. ( ) he lives near me, we see each other often.
18. ( ) my little brother is ill, I have to stay at home.
19. The captain and crew didn't abandon ship ( ) all the passengers were safe.
20. We had plenty of laughs ( ) we sat in front of the fire and played board games.
21. ( ) it rained a lot, we had a good time.
22. ( ) you have a car, it's difficult to get there.
23. You can borrow my car ( ) you promise not to drive too fast.
24. Traveling by car is convenient ( ) you have somewhere to park.
25. A few years ago I worked ( ) a taxi driver.
26. I have no idea ( ) the story is true.
27. There were no chairs, ( ) we had to stand.
28. I went home ( ) I had dinner.

29. The dog always runs to the door (　) the bell rings.
30. I'll go on holiday next summer (　) I have time.
31. (　) we were in Italy we visited some friends.
32. (　) the last year we had a lot of work.
33. Simon sometimes behaves (　) a baby.
34. My car is (　) fast (　) yours.
35. My sister works (　) a secretary at Brown and Co.
36. She looks (　) her sister.

※ 1. as, as 2. in case 3. wherever 4. but(yet, and yet) 5. as(so) long as(as far as, if) 6. after 7. as if(as though) 8. When 9. if(provided) 10. so(so that, in order that) 11. Although(Though, Even though(if)) 12. so(so that, in order that) 13. When 14. so 15. because 16. because 17. As(Since) 18. Since(As) 19. until(till) 20. while 21. Although(Though, Even though(if)) 22. Unless 23. if(as long as, so long as, as far as)/on condition (that) 24. provided(that)/if 25. as 26. if(whether) 27. so(so that) 28. as soon as(soon after) 29. when 30. if 31. While 32. During 33. like 34. as, as 35. as 36. like

제14장 명사

명사(名詞)는 사물의 이름을 나타내는 품사이며 5종류가 있다.
가산명사(可算名詞, 셀 수 있는 명사)에는 보통명사, 집합명사가 있다.
불가산명사(不可算名詞, 셀 수 없는 명사)에는 물질명사, 추상명사, 고유명사가 있다.

★ 단수 가산명사 앞에는 한정사인 ① 관사, ② 지시대명사, ③ 소유격 대명사, ④ 부정대명사, ⑤ 의문대명사 중 하나가 반드시 붙는다.
불가산명사는 셀 수 없으므로 부정관사가 붙지 않고 복수형도 대개 없지만, 물질명사, 추상명사에는 가끔 복수형 어미가 붙기도 한다.
Korean food(foods), our effort(efforts, life, lives, hope, hopes)
복수 가산명사 어미에는 -s(-es)가 붙는다.
If you laugh, *blessings* will come your way.
웃으면 복이 온다(올거다).

1. **명사의 종류**

(1) **보통명사** : 모양을 가진 명사로 그 수가 많아서 셀 수 있는 명사이다
부정관사를 붙이고 복수형을 만들 수 있다.
a book, two books

(2) **집합명사** : 영국 영어에서는 집합체 전체를 하나로 간주할 때는 단수 취급하고, 집합체를 이루는 구성원으로 간주할 때는 군집명사로 복수 취급한다.

(audience, army, committee, crowd, nation 등)
My family is very large. 우리 가족은 대가족이다.
She has a large family. 그녀는 대가족이다.
My family are all well. 나의 가족(우리 가족)은 모두 잘 있다.
* 미국 영어는 집합명사를 구별 없이 단수 취급한다.

(3) 물질명사 : 물질은 일정한 모양을 갖추고 있지 않으므로 셀 수 없는 명사이다
(gold, sugar, gas, paper, wine 등)
Wine is good for health. 포도주는 건강에 좋다.

물질명사의 수량을 나타낼 때에는 다음과 같은 단위명사를 쓴다.
a piece of chalk, three pieces of chalk, a cup of coffee, a glass of water, two glasses of water, two pounds of sugar, two bottles of beer, two pieces of information, two bags of rice, two cups of coffee, 또는 two coffees라고도 함

(4) 추상명사 : 사물의 추상적인 개념을 나타내는 명사로, 셀 수 없는 명사이다
(life, death, kindness, beauty, health, art, happiness 등)
Art is long, life is short. 예술은 길고, 인생은 짧다.
Good and evil depends on the choice.
선과 악은 선택에 달려 있다.
Necessity is the mother of invention. 필요는 발명의 어머니다.
Health is much more important than wealth. (건강, 부)
Knowledge is power. 아는 것(지식)은 힘이다.

(5) 고유명사 : 하나밖에 없는 명사로 셀 수 없는 명사이다. 고유명사는 대문자로 시작하며, 원칙적으로 관사가 붙지 않지만, 정관사가 붙는 고유명사도 있다.

Korea, Tom, the United States of America, the Alps, the Pacific 등

2. 불가산명사 → 가산명사

(1) 물질명사가 → 보통명사화(a + 물질명사)

Wine is made of grapes. (wine 물질명사)
This is a good wine. 이것은 좋은 포도주이다. (a wine 보통명사)
Glass is colorless and transparent. (glass 물질명사)
유리는 무색 투명하다.
Bring me a glass of water. (a glass 보통명사)
She wears glasses. 그녀는 안경을 쓴다. (glasses 보통명사)

(2) 보통명사가 → 추상명사화

The pen is mightier than *the sword*.
문(文)은 무(武)보다 더 강하다.
She didn't severely scold his son in *the mother*.
그녀는 그의 아들을 심하게 야단치지 못했다/모정 때문에.

(3) 추상명사가 → 보통명사화(a + 추상명사)

She is a very beauty. 그녀는 매우 미인이다. (a beauty 보통명사)
She has done me a lot of kindnesses.
그녀는 내게 많은 친절을 베풀었다.

★ of + 추상명사 = 형용사

of value = valuable 귀중한, of importance = important 중요한
of beauty = beautiful 아름다운, of no use = useless 쓸모 없는
of use = useful, of ability = able, of any help = helpful

전치사 + 추상명사 = 부사

at will 마음대로, by luck 운좋게, by chance 우연히, in safety 안전하게, in haste 급히, on purpose 고의적으로, with kindness 친절히

all + 추상명사 = very 형용사

all beauty = very beautiful, all diligence = very diligent
all kindness = very kind, all confidence = very confident

(4) 고유명사가 → 보통명사화(a + 고유명사)

A Mr. Robert has come to meet you.
로버트 씨라는 분이 왔다/당신을 만나러.
I want to become a Newton.
나는 되고 싶다/뉴턴과 같은 과학자가.
He is a Lincoln. 그는 링컨 가문이다.
I have a Picasso. 나는 피카소 작품 한 점을 가지고 있다.

3. 명사의 수

단수명사를 복수명사로 만드는 법은 다음과 같다.

(1) 규칙 변화

어미에 -s나 -es를 붙인다.

① 어미에 -s를 붙인다.
book-books, tree-trees, girl-girls

② 어미가 s, x, z, ch, sh로 끝나면 -es를 붙인다.
box-boxes, bench-benches, dish-dishes
무성음(f, k, p, t)으로 끝나면 -s만 붙인다.
book-books, calf-calfs, desk-desks

③ 「자음 + y」로 끝나면 y대신 -ies를 붙인다.

city-cities, baby-babies, fly-flies
　④ 「모음 + y」로 끝나면 -s만 붙인다.
　　　boy-boys, day-days, key-keys
　⑤ 「자음 + o」로 끝나면 -es를 붙인다.
　　　potato-potatoes, tomato-tomatoes, hero-heroes
　　　예외 : piano-pianos, photo-photos, radio-radios
　⑥ 어미가 f, fe로 끝나면 대신 -ves를 붙인다.
　　　half-halves, wolf-wolves, wife-wives
　　　예외 : roof-roofs, safe-safes

★ -s, -es의 발음
　㉠ -s는 무성음 k, f, p, t 뒤에서 [s]로 발음된다.
　　seats[siːts]　ropes[roups]　backs[bæks]
　㉡ -s는 유성음 d, b, g, m, l… 뒤에서 [z]로 발음된다.
　　seeds[siːdz]　robes[rabz]　bags[bægz]
　㉢ 어미가 s, x, z, ch, sh로 끝나면 -es를 붙이고, 발음은 [iz]로 된다.
　　　dishes[diʃiz] catches[kætʃiz] mixes[miksiz] prizes[praiziz]

(2) 불규칙 변화

　① 단수/복수형이 다른 형태
　　man-men, woman-women, foot-feet, tooth-teeth, goose-geese,
　　mouse-mice, ox-oxen, child-children, brother-brethren

　② 단수/복수형이 같은 형태
　　deer 사슴, sheep 양, series 연속, swine 돼지, means 수단
　　fish 물고기, species 종, Chinese 중국인, Japanese 일본인

(3) 뜻이 다른 단수/복수형 명사들

advice 충고-advices 통지, air 공기-airs 태도, content 만족-contents 목차, authority 권위-authorities 당국, work 일-works 작품, cloth 천-clothes 옷, custom 습관-customs 관세, glass 유리-glasses 안경, good 선-goods 상품, letter 문자-letters 문학, look 봄-looks 용모, manner 방법-manners 예절, pain 고통-pains 수고, paper 종이-papers 서류, remain 나머지-remains 유해, respect 존경-respects 안부, sand 모래-sands 사막, saving 절약-savings 저축, time 시간-times 시대, water 물-waters 해역(수역), arm 팔-arms 무기, provision 준비-provisions 식량, damage 손해-damages 손해(배상)액, color 색깔-colors 깃발, honor 명예-honors 영예(우등, 명예상)

(4) 항상 복수 취급되는 명사들

The *police* have stopped my car. *Fish* live in water.
These *people* are tourist. *Cattle* are a plant-eating animal.
The *personnel* of this department are always diligent.
이 부서(과)의 직원들은 늘 근면하다.

(5) 항상 복수형으로 복수 취급되는 명사들

① scissors, glasses, jeans, shoes, gloves, pants 등 짝을 이루는 명사는 복수형으로만 쓰인다.
한 벌일 때는 a pair of, 두 벌일 때는 two pairs of로 표시한다.
two pairs of jeans, a pair of shoes,
Shoes are on display. 신발이 전시되어 있다.

② *Clothes* are quite expensive here. These *stairs* aren't very safe.
The city's *outskirts* are very beautiful.

(6) 복수형이지만 단수 취급되는 명사들

학과명 : economics 경제학, politics 정치학, mathematics 수학
  Mathematics is a subject I don't like.

놀이명 : bowls 볼링, billiards 당구, dominoes 도미노, cards 카드

병명 : measles 홍역, diabetes 당뇨병, the blues 우울증

기타 : news 소식, means 수단(방법)
  No news is good news. 무소식이 희소식이다.

나라명 : the United States (of America), the USA 미국, the Philippines 필리핀, the Netherlands 네델란드, Brussels 브뤼셀
  The Philippines has more than 7,000 islands.

(7) 단수 취급하는 명사들

물질명사, 추상명사, 집합명사들은 셀 수 없으므로 대개 단수 취급한다.
advice, counsel, manner, progress, hair, information, knowledge, wine, gas, staff, equipment, luggage, vocabulary, traffic 등

Much damage was caused by the flood.

This new furniture is very nice.

That's too much homework. I think Fred's hair is too long.

4. 명사의 격

명사의 격에는 주격, 목적격, 소유격이 있다.

(1) 주격(~은, 는, 이, 가)

명사가 주어, 주격보어, 호격, 동격으로 쓰일 때

The *woman* is very eager. (주어) 그녀는 매우 열심이다.

She is a good *pianist*. (주격보어) 그녀는 좋은 피아니스트이다.

That woman is Mrs. Braun, our music *teacher*. (동격)

저 여자분은 브라운 부인인데, 우리 음악선생이다.
Young *man*, take ambitions! (호격) 젊은이들이여, 야망을 가져라!

(2) 목적격(~을, 를, 에게)

명사가 목적어, 전치사의 목적어, 목적어의 동격, 목적격보어로 쓰일 때
She loves *music*. (타동사의 목적어) 그녀는 음악을 좋아한다.
She is interested in *music*. (전치사의 목적어)
그녀는 음악에 관심이 있다.
We call her *Julia*. (목적격보어) 우리는 그녀를 줄리아라고 부른다.
We met our music teacher, Mr. Kim. (목적어의 동격)
우리는 우리 음악 선생님을 만났다/김씨인.

(3) 소유격

① 생물의 소유격은 's로, 무생물의 소유격은 「of + 명사」로 나타낸다. s로 끝난 복수명사는 (')만 붙인다. s로 끝난 고유명사는 ('s)를 붙이기도 한다
girl → girl's, my wife → my wife's, Peter → Peter's,
girls → girls', wives → wives', my children → my children's
Julia's bicycle, Peter and Diane's house, the door of this room, the ladies' books, Thomas'(Thomas's)
* and로 연결된 두 사람 이상의 소유격은 마지막 사람만 소유격으로 나타낸다.
Tom, Sarah, Julia and Peter's house is by the river.

② 거리, 시간, 가격, 무게 등의 무생물 소유격은 's로 나타낸다
시간 : today's paper, summer's day, two hours' walk, two weeks' holiday, Saturday's defeat, moment's hesitation
거리, 지명, 천체 : four miles' distance, Europe's future, earth's sur-

face, school's history, church's traditions

무게 : one pound's weight(1파운드의 무게), two kilograms' weight

가격 : three dollars' worth of ice cream. (3달러어치 아이스크림)

인간의 활동과 관련된 것 : car's oil, brain's development, computer's memory, America's government, book's author

③ **이중소유격 = 명사 + of + -s소유격 = 명사 + of + 소유대명사**

이중소유격은 of-와 s-소유격의 결합이다. (a friend of Tim's)
한정사인 부정관사(a, an, the), 지시대명사(this, that, such), 부정대명사(some, each, every, any), 의문대명사(which, what, whose), 소유격 대명사(my, your, her) 등은 명사를 한정하거나 특정화시켜 주는 형용사 역할을 하므로 한정사(限定詞)라고 한다. 이들 한정사는 관사를 대신해 주는 역할을 한다. 한정사 두 개가 동시에 한 명사 앞에 올 수 없다. 그 때문에 소유격 대명사는 관사와 함께 쓸 수 없다. 이 경우 「명사 + of + -s소유격」 형태나 「명사 + of + 소유대명사」의 이중소유격을 쓴다. 즉 a friend of Tim's 형태나 a friend of mine 형태를 쓴다.

my a(the, this, that, such, some, every) book(×), this book of mine(○), Tom's some books(×), some books of Tom's(○), a(this) Tom's book(×), a(this) book of Tom's(○), a my father's friend(×), a friend of my father's(○), <u>my father's</u> friend(○), friends of hers(○), friends of Tim's = Tim's friends(○)

④ **소유격 뒤에 명사의 생략**

소유격과 함께 오는 명사가 앞에서 언급되었거나 문맥상 가리키는 것이 분명할 때 생략할 수 있다. 소유격 뒤에 house, shop, store, flat 등은 대개 생략된다.

The car is my father's (car). 명사의 반복을 피하기 위해서 생략

He stayed at his uncle's (house) during the summer vacation.

I have my hair cut at the barber's (shop).

나는 내 머리를 깎게 한다/이발소에서.

Exercises

A. 다음 괄호 안의 명사를 복수명사로 만드시오.

1. Although (woman) outnumber (man) in the population as a whole, in the prison population (man) outnumber (woman) by about 24 to 1.
2. My (foot) were aching, and I could feel a blister developing on my right heel.
3. I have my (tooth) checked twice a year.
4. It's not nice having (mouse) in the pantry.
5. To help prevent (louse), do not share personal (item) such as (comb), (brush), (hat), (scarf), and (towel).
6. There's free petting zoo that features (goat), (sheep), (calf), (donkey), (duck), (goose), and (rabbit).
7. The king had four (wife) and 24 (child).
8. The (leaf) on the (tree) have started to turn brown.
9. (Loaf) of freshly baked bread were cooling on (shelf) by the window.
10. These (aircraft) are capable of carrying up to 350 (passenger).

※ 1. women, men, men, women 2. feet 3. teeth 4. mice 5. lice, items, combs, brushes, hats, scarves, towels 6. goats, sheep, calves, donkeys, ducks, geese, rabbits 7. wives, children 8. leaves, trees 9. Loaves, shelves 10. aircraft, passengers

B. 괄호 안에 동사를 적합한 현재형으로 만드시오.

1. The United States (accept) more immigrants than all the other countries of the world combined.
2. The police (be) allowed to stop and search suspects in the street.
3. The contents of the book (be) as rich and attractive as (be) the binding and typography.
4. The news we are getting (be) not encouraging.
5. I believe it (be) these traditions that make our country great.
6. The American people (want) a government that (get) things done.
7. Electronics (be) a very interesting subject.
8. The government (have) a major interest in solving the problem.
9. The cattle (be) in the meadow.
10. We are a people that (love) to laugh and to celebrate.
11. All their furniture (be) made from rare materials such as rosewood, mahogany and walnut.
12. The acoustics of the new concert hall (be) far from perfect.
13. Fifty dollars (be) too much for a room in this dump of a hotel.
14. Ten miles (be) a long way if you're travelling under your own steam.

15. A large number of people (have) been involved in the creation of this website.
16. The number of people involved in the project (be) staggering.
17. (Be) Britain going to join the euro?

※ 1. accepts 2. are 3. are, are 4. is 5. is 6. want, gets 7. is 8. has 9. are 10. love(s) 11. is 12. are 13. is 14. is 15. have 16. is 17. Is

C. 다음 괄호 안의 명사를 알맞게 고치시오.
⟨불특정한 수 참조 → 61p⟩

1. We have two (dozen) eggs in the fridge at the moment.
2. (Dozen) of people are feared dead after a river of molten rock poured from the volcano.
3. Both Asian and African (elephant) are highly intelligent and peaceful (animal) whose continued existence is threatened.
4. Our son is ten (year) old.
5. We have a ten-(year)-old son.
6. She weighs two hundred and thirty (pound).
7. The club can't afford to spend a few (million) (euro) on new players just like that.
8. The club has spent (million) of (euro) on new players.
9. When the potatoes are tender, heat the cream and add two (spoonful) of parsley.
10. The industrial revolution of the 18th and 19th (century) saw a massive change in the way people lived and how this affected their (health).

11. You can find a lot of (information) on the internet.
12. The defendant was represented by two (counsel).
13. The robbers locked the cashier in the toilet and made off with the (content) of the safe.
14. The worm can cause all (manner) of problems in your computer.
15. We all looked at each other and shook our (head) in disbelief.
16. As many as ten thousand people lost their (life) in the fighting.
17. The flu is being blamed for the (death) of two more (people) in Colorado.
18. Babies go on putting things in their (mouth) well into their second (year).

※ 1. dozen 2. Dozens 3. elephants, animals 4. years 5. year 6. pounds 7. million, euros 8. millions, euros 9. spoonfuls 10. centuries, health 11. information 12. counsel 13. contents 14. manner 15. heads 16. lives 17. death(deaths), people 18. mouth(mouths), year

D. 괄호 안의 동사는 단수, 복수 중 어느 것이 적합한가?
1. The police (has, have) arrested two men.
2. Bad news (travel, travels) fast.
3. The United States (has, have) enormous power.
4. Mathematics (is, are) my best subject.
5. Twenty dollars (is, are) a lot for a 100 page paperback.
6. Most of the people here (is, are) extremely poor.

7. Three quarters of the surface of the earth (is, are) sea.

8. Two thirds of the people (lives, live) in poverty.

9. The contents of the parcel (was, were) easy to guess.

※ 1. have 2. travels 3. has 4. is 5. is 6. are 7. is 8. live 9. were

E. 다음을 소유격으로 만드시오.
　　1. (my cat) toys　　　　2. (my sister) birthday
　　3. (James) uniform　　　4. (America) government
　　5. (the students) room　　6. (the garden) wall
　　7. (Shakespeare) work　　8. (London) University
　　9. (the old man) coat　　10. (my friend) party

※ 1. my cat's toys 2. my sister's birthday 3. James'(James's) uniform 4. America's government 5. the students' room 6. the wall of the garden 7. Shakespeare's work 8. University of London 9. the old man's coat 10. my friend's party

제15장 관사

1. **부정관사의 용법**

   부정관사(不定冠詞)는 정해지지 않은 불특정한 막연한 것을 나타낸다.

   ☆ **부정관사의 발음**

   관사에는 정관사와 부정관사가 있다. 관사는 명사를 한정 수식하므로 형용사의 일종이다. 자음으로 발음이 시작되는 단어 앞에는 a가 오고, 모음으로 발음이 시작되는 단어 앞에는 an이 온다.

   a book[buk], a pencil[pénsəl], an apple[ǽpl], an hour[auər]

   * 주의 : a year[jiər], a word [wəːrd], a university[jùːnəvə́ːrsəti]

   ★ 단수 가산명사 앞에는 한정사인 ① 관사(a, an, the), ② 지시대명사(this, that), ③ 소유격 대명사(my, your, his, its), ④ 부정대명사(some, any, each, every, no, either, another), ⑤ 의문대명사(which, what, whose, whatever) 중 하나가 반드시 붙는다.

   I read a(the, this, my, some, every, no) book. (○)

   I read book. (×)

   what(whatever, which, whose, any, another) book do you read?

   ★ 부정관사는 여러 가지 의미를 나타낸다

   (1) one(하나의)의 뜻 : 시간, 측정, 양 등을 말할 때

These apples are only 80 cents a kilo. You don't say a word.
The work(job) does not finish in a week.
We sell 70 computers a month. My car runs 120 miles an hour.

(2) 단수 보통명사에 붙어 막연히 '하나의' 뜻을 나타내지만 한국어로 구태여 해석하지 않아도 된다

He is a teacher. 그는 선생이다. (직업)
This is a pen. 이것은 펜이다.
He is an Englishman. (국적)
= He is English(British). 그는 영국인이다.

(3) a certain(어떤, ~라는)의 뜻

A man called you. 어떤 남자가 너에게 전화했다.
A Mr. Kim came to meet you. 김 씨라는 사람이 왔다/너를 만나러.

(4) 처음 소개되는 단수 가산명사 앞에(새로운 정보일 때)는 부정관사가 붙고, 재차 언급되는 명사 앞에는 정관사가 붙는다

I had a problem yesterday. 나는 문제가 있었다/어제.
I have solved the problem today. 나는 그 문제를 해결했다/오늘.
I bought a book yesterday. 나는 책을 샀다/어제.
I'm reading the book now. 나는 그 책을 읽고 있다/지금.

(5) 어떤 사물을 총칭하는 경우

A dog is a faithful animal. 개는 충실한 동물이다.
= The dog is a faithful animal. = Dogs are faithful animals.
A friend in need is a friend indeed.
곤궁할(어려울) 때 친구가 참된(진정한) 친구다.
A healthy mind (dwells) in a healthy body.

건강한 신체에 건강한 정신이 깃든다.

(6) per(마다, 당, 각, 매)의 뜻

We eat three times a day. 우리는 먹는다/하루에 세 번.

I play tennis twice a week. 나는 테니스를 친다/일주일에 두 번.

(7) the same(같은)의 뜻

We are not of an age. = We are not the same age.

She is a swan of a girl. = She is a girl like a swan.

I want to be an Edison. 나는 되고 싶다/에디슨과 같은 과학자가.
 = I want to be a scientist like Edison.

(8) some(약간, 어느 정도)의 뜻

He is diligent *to a degree*. = He is quite diligent.

She didn't come for a time(for a while).

그녀는 오지 않았다/얼마 동안(한동안).

(9) 부정관사의 관용어구

as a doctor, have a temperature, in a hurry, take a seat, without a break, have a wash(bath, shower), come to an end, in a loud voice, a hundred people, in a moment, take a walk

2. 정관사의 용법

정관사(定冠詞)는 정해진 특정한 것을 나타낸다.

☆ 정관사의 발음

정관사 the는 자음으로 발음이 시작되는 단어 앞에서는 [ðə]로 발음하고, 모음으로 발음이 시작되는 단어 앞에서는 [ði]로 발음한다.

the[ðə] book[buk], the[ði] apple[ǽpl], the[ði] hour[auər]

★ 정관사는 다음과 같은 경우에 붙는다.

(1) **앞에 나온 명사를 다시 언급할 때**

I have a problem. I want to solve the problem.
나는 문제가 있다. 나는 그 문제를 해결하고 싶다.

(2) **화자나 청자가 서로 잘 알고 있는 것을 가리킬 때**

Please, open the door. 미안하지만, (그) 문 좀 열어.
Please, pass me the cup. 미안하지만, (그) 컵 좀 건네줘.

(3) **수식어구로 수식 받을 때**

The book *on the desk* is yours. (형용사구-전치사구)
This is the book *which I bought yesterday*. (형용사절-관계절)
This is the wine *my son bought for me*.
(형용사절-관계대명사절)
You may drink the water *in the bowl*. (형용사구-전치사구)
* 물질명사라도 수식어구에 의해 수식을 받으면 특정 명사화되므로 정관사 the가 붙는다.

(4) **형용사의 최상급, 서수**, only, any, same, very, next 등이 명사를 수식하는 경우 그 명사는 특정 명사화되므로 정관사 the가 붙는다.

the biggest man, the first prize, the same car

(5) **어떤 사물을 총칭하는 경우**

The dog is a smart(clever) animal.
= A dog is a smart animal.

= Dogs are smart animals.

(6) 세상에서 하나밖에 없는 유일한 것과 방향에 the가 붙음

the sun, the earth, the world, the sky, the ocean, the sea, the stars, the north, the west, the left, the right, the universe

(7) 신체의 일부를 나타낼 때 소유대명사 대신 the를 사용하기도 한다

She caught me by the hand. 그녀는 나의 손을 잡았다.
= She took my hand.
She hit me on the cheek. 그녀는 나의 뺨을 때렸다.
= She slapped my cheek.
She looked me in the eyes. 그녀는 내 눈을 쳐다보았다.
= She looked into my eyes.

(8) 악기나 발명품을 나타낼 때

She plays the piano.
The electric bulb was invented by Thomas Edison.
전구는 발명되었다/토마스 에디슨에 의해.

(9) 시간·거리·무게 등의 단위를 나타낼 때

by the day 일당으로, by the pound 파운드 단위로, by the kilo 킬로그램으로, by the meter 미터(기)에 따라, by the month 달 단위로, by the hour 시간당

(10) the + 형용사 = 복수 보통명사, the + 보통명사 = 추상명사

the dead 죽은 자들, the wounded 부상자들, the living 생존자들, the blind 맹인들, the poor 가난한 자들, the injured 다친 자들

the father(father's love) 부성애, the mother 모성애, the patriot(patriotism, patriotic) 애국심, the pen 글의 힘, the sword 무력의 힘

(11) 관용어구에

in the park, in the sky, on the farm, in the morning, in der dark, in the future, in the 1970s, on(at) the beach 등

(12) the가 붙는 고유명사

고유명사 앞에는 원칙적으로 정관사를 붙이지 않지만, 다음의 고유명사들에는 정관사가 붙는다.

① 누구에게나 잘 알려진 공공물 이름 앞에

(관공서, 공공건물, 신문, 잡지, 서적, 배, 선박, 열차, 비행기 등)
the White House 백악관, the NewYork Times 뉴욕 타임즈 신문, the National Museum 국립 박물관, the Digest 다이제스트 잡지, the Bible 성경, the KTX 케이티엑스호, the Titanic 타이타닉 호, the KAL 칼 기, the State Department 미 국무성

② 그러나 지명이 붙어있는 공공물 이름 앞에는 the가 붙지 않는다.

(역, 항구, 다리, 공원, 호수, 공항, 거리, 광장 등)
Seoul station, Namsan Park, Incheon Airport, Lake Michigan 미시간 호, Golden Gate Bridge 금문교, Oxford Street, Broadway, Trafalgar Square (런던의) 트라팔가 광장

③ 누구에게나 잘 알려진 대자연 이름 앞에

(바다, 강, 운하, 해협, 항만, 반도, 사막, 산맥 등)
the Pacific (Ocean) 태평양, the Han River 한강, the English Channel 영국 해협, the Gulf of Mexico 멕시코 만, the Korean Peninsula

한반도, the Sahara Desert 사하라 사막, the Alps 알프스 산맥, the Rocky Mountains 로키 산맥

* 주의 : Mount Everest 에베레스트 산, Mt. Baekdu 백두산

④ **복수형의 고유명사 앞에**

(국가, 국민, 군도, 산맥, 가족 등)

the United States of America 미합중국, the Williams 윌리암스 씨 가족, the Philippines 필리핀 군도, the Netherlands 네덜란드, the Koreans 한국 국민, the Alps 알프스 산맥, the Browns 브라운 씨 가족, the Americans 미국 국민

⑤ **단수형 나라 이름 앞에 the가 붙는 경우**

the United Kingdom(the UK) 영국, the Republic of Korea 대한민국

(13) **정관사를 붙여야 하나 부정관사를 붙여야 하나?**

① 처음 소개되는 단수 가산명사 앞에는 부정관사를 붙이고, 재차 언급되는 명사 앞에는 정관사를 붙인다.

② 명사에 '하나의, 한'을 붙여 말이 되면 부정관사를 붙이고, '그'를 붙여 말이 되면 정관사를 붙인다. I am a teacher. 나는 선생이다. teacher는 처음 소개되는 단수 가산명사이므로 부정관사가 붙는다. 나는 한 선생이다. 말이 된다. 나는 그 선생이다. 처음 소개되는 명사에 그는 어울리지 않으므로 정관사는 적합하지 않다.

3. **관사의 생략(관사가 붙지 않는 명사)**

(1) 불가산명사인 물질명사와 추상명사 앞에서

Give me *water(milk, wine)* to drink. (물질명사)

Effort is the mother of *success*. (추상명사)

Credit is better than *money*. 신용은 돈보다 낫다.

(2) 복수명사에는 대개 정관사가 붙지 않지만, 특정 복수명사를 가리킬 때는 정관사가 붙는다

Dogs are smart animals. 개는 영리한 동물이다.

The dogs (which, that) I have are very lovely.
내가 가지고 있는 개들은 매우 사랑스럽다.

(3) 수식어구에 의해 수식을 받는 명사는 가산명사이건 불가산명사이건 정관사가 붙는다. 막연한 선행사일 때는 부정관사가 붙기도 한다

I read about the life of Robin Hood.

The water in our town is clean.

The history of the Romans is fascinating.

The water which we use is valuable.

The books you gave me were boring.

I met a(the) man who(m) you know.

(4) 호칭할 때

Waiter, check, Please! 웨이터, 계산해요!

Edison, Tom, mother, father 등

(5) 관직·신분 명이 보어로 쓰일 때

They elected me president of their company.
그들은 나를 선출했다/그들 회사의 사장으로.

(6) 건물·기구가 본래의 목적(기능)으로 쓰일 때

School begins at 9 o'clock. 수업은 9시에 시작한다.

go to school (공부하러)학교에 가다, go to the school 학교에 가다

in school 재학중인, at school 수업중인

at(in) the school 학교(교내)에서

go to church 예배 보러 가다, go to the church 교회에 가다

go to hospital 입원하다, go to the hospital 병원에 가다

in hospital 입원중인, go to bed 잠자리에 들다

go to the bed 침대로 가다, in bed 취침중인

go to work 일하러 가다, go to the work 직장에 가다

(7) 식사, 운동경기, 질병, 학과 명 앞에서

I usually have dinner at 6:00. 나는 보통 6시에 저녁을 먹는다.

They play baseball now. I hate mathematics(math).

She died of cancer. 그녀는 암으로 죽었다.

* 가벼운 질병에는 부정관사가 붙는다.

a cold 감기, a fever 열병, a headache 두통, a toothache 치통

* 악기 이름 앞에는 정관사가 붙는다.

the violin, the piano, the guitar

(8) by + 교통수단(통신)을 나타낼 때

by mail 우편으로, by cellphone 휴대폰으로, by bus 버스로, by car 자동차로, on foot 걸어서, by train 기차로, by plane 비행기로, by letter 편지로

(9) 언어 명 앞에서

language 단어가 수반되는 언어 명에는 정관사가 붙는다.

She speaks English and Chinese.

201

그녀는 영어와 중국어를 구사한다.

She speaks the English language and the Chinese language.

(10) 계절 명 앞에서

　　Winter comes after autumn. 겨울은 가을 후에(뒤에) 온다.

(11) 대구를 이룰 때

　　arm in arm 서로 팔짱을 끼고, side by side 나란히

　　day and night 밤낮으로, rich and poor 빈부의

　　from place to place 여기저기, from door to door 집집마다

(12) 관용어구에서

　　at dawn 새벽에, at noon 정오에, at hand 가까이에, at home 집에서, from morning till night 아침부터 밤까지, at daybreak 새벽에, take care of ~을 돌보다, take part in ~에 참가하다

(13) 관사가 반복될 때

　　A white and red bag is hers.
　　하얗고 붉은 가방 하나는 그녀의 것이다.
　　A white and a red bag are hers.
　　하얀 가방 하나와 붉은 가방 하나는 그녀의 것이다.

4. 관사의 어순

(1) 관사의 위치는 관사 + 부사 + 형용사 + 명사(관부형명)가 원칙이다

　　a(the) very interesting book 매우 재미있는 책

　★ 그러나 아래 단어들이 오면 위치가 바뀐다.

(2) 전치한정사 : all, both, half, twice, most of, double + the + 명사
All (the, of the, my) children need toys.
Both (the, of the, his) children need love.
Take these pills twice a day.
It's about half a mile(a half mile) from here.
both books, twice my money, most (of the, of my) books

(3) too, so, as, how 등의 부사가 형용사를 수식하는 경우, 부정관사는 형용사 뒤에 온다
This is too difficult a book for me to read.
이것은 너무 어려운 책이다/내가 읽기에.
I have never seen so honest a man as James.
나는 결코 본 적이 없다/제임스만큼 정직한 남자를.

(4) such(quite, half, rather, what, whatever) + a(an) + 형용사 + 명사
Titanic was quite(rather) a good film
It was rather a difficult(a rather difficult) time.
I can't do the work in such a short time.
나는 그 일을 할 수 없다/그렇게 짧은 시간에.
What a beautiful garden it is! 얼마나 아름다운 정원인가!
= How beautiful a garden it is! (참 아름다운 정원이구나!)
What a pity! 참 유감이다! 불쌍해라! 애석한 일이다!

Exercises

A. 정관사를 필요한 경우에만 넣으시오.
1. We all know that (   ) public opinion is against it.
2. In (   ) opinion of most historians, Roosevelt ranks as one of America's greatest presidents.
3. She wrote a book about (   ) old age.
4. Most experts expect (   ) unemployment to rise.
5. What crimes are committed in (   ) name of (   ) liberty!
6. (   ) most important thing in (   ) life is (   ) love.
7. This is (   ) Switzerland.
8. This is (   ) Switzerland I love.
9. Sunburn isn't much of a problem in (   ) rainy Ireland.
10. When does (   ) school begin?
11. He works at (   ) hospital in (   ) Main Street.
12. (   ) lady over there is (   ) waitress.
13. A teacher told Einstein he wouldn't get very far in (   ) life.
14. What do you know about (   ) life of Mark Twain?
15. We had tea with (   ) queen in (   ) Buckingham Palace.
16. The workers are painting (   ) walls of (   ) prison.
17. (   ) bread is made from (   ) flour.
18. Many people spend their lunchtime at (   ) Hyde Park.
19. If you go by (   ) train, you'll arrive at (   ) Victoria Station.
20. If (   ) plane's on time, I arrive at (   ) New York Airport at 8.55.
21. There's a bank in (   ) High Street.

22. Lots of people have climbed (　) Mount Everest.
23. I always have (　) breakfast with my children before they go to (　) school.
24. He spent (　) most of his life in (　) jail.
25. Brian plays (　) piano, and Judy plays (　) flute.
26. John plays (　) tennis, and Mike plays (　) soccer.
27. My name is Martin in (　) town and Walter in (　) country.
28. Jack, if you're not in (　) bed by (　) time I come up, I'll be very angry.
29. (　) Museum of London shows (　) history of (　) town.
30. During (　) afternoon it got colder.
31. In (　) United States, (　) Election Day is (　) first Tuesday after (　) first Monday in (　) November.
32. It often rains here in (　) autumn.
33. My friends and I usually go to the movie on (　) Saturday.
34. School starts on (　) Monday after (　) first Sunday in (　) September.
35. (　) February is shorter than (　) January.
36. The next Olympic Games will be in (　) winter of 2018.
37. Thanksgiving Day is on (　) last Thursday in (　) November.

※ 1. - 2. the 3. - 4. - 5. the, - 6. The, -, - 7. - 8. the 9. - 10. - 11. the, - 12. The, the 13. - 14. the 15. the, - 16. the, the 17. -, - 18. - 19. -, - 20. the, - 21. the 22. - 23. -, - 24. -, - 25. the, the 26. -, - 27. -, the 28. -, the 29. The, the, the

30. the 31. the, -, the, the, - 32. - 33. - 34. the, the, - 35. -, - 36. the, 37. the, -

B. 부정관사를 필요한 경우에만 넣으시오.

1. Her father was (   ) photographer and she became (   ) journalist.
2. She was (   ) Marxist and (   ) member of the Socialist Party.
3. Roosevelt was elected (   ) president of the US in 1932.
4. In 1995 she visited Italy as (   ) tourist.
5. Laura serves as (   ) model for other states.
6. The farm is about (   ) hundred miles away.
7. Joe went out without (   ) umbrella.
8. I have (   ) terrible headache.
9. The next (   ) hundred miles will be more difficult.
10. We sell about (   ) hundred copies (   ) day.
11. It was certainly (   ) good advice.
12. That's (   ) good news.
13. We have (   ) very good police.
14. If you've got (   ) family, you've got to have (   ) life insurance.
15. She isn't feeling well and I'm sure she has (   ) temperature.
16. The country's isolation has finally come to (   ) end.
17. They live in (   ) bungalow at the seaside.
18. As (   ) coach he was (   ) great success.
19. He is not in (   ) good temper today.
20. I'll tell you more about it if you're not in (   ) hurry.

21. She answered slowly, but in ( ) loud, clear voice.
22. You can't ride ( ) bike here. It's too dangerous.
23. Why don't you say something nice for ( ) change?
24. What ( ) nonsense you're talking!
25. What ( ) wonderful surprise that was!
26. What ( ) nationality are you?

※ 1. a, a 2. a, a 3. - 4. a 5. a 6. a 7. an 8. a 9. - 10. a, a 11. - 12. - 13. - 14. (a), - 15. a 16. an 17. a 18. a, a 19. a 20. a 21. a 22. a 23. a 24. - 25. a 26. -

제16장 대명사

대명사(代名詞)는 명사의 반복을 피하기 위해 명사 대신 쓰는 품사이다. 대명사는 대부분 명사보다 짧고 대개 명사 앞쪽에 온다.
This child has lots of(a lot of, plenty of) toys.
→ He is my son.

1. **대명사의 종류**

   (1) 인칭대명사 : 사람을 나타낼 때 : I, you, he, she…
       재귀대명사 : myself, yourself, herself, itself…
   (2) 지시대명사 : 사람. 사물을 나타낼 때 : this(these), that(those)
   (3) 의문대명사 : 의문을 나타낼 때 : who, which, what
   (4) 부정대명사 : 막연한 사물을 나타낼 때 : one, none, some, any…
   (5) 관계대명사 : who, which, that, what

2. **인칭대명사**

   (1) 인칭대명사의 격변화

수	인칭	주격 (은,는,이,가)	소유격 (~의)	목적격 (을,를,에게)	소유대명사 (~의 것)	재귀대명사 (~자신)
단수	1인칭	I	my	me	mine	myself
	2인칭	you	your	you	yours	yourself

	3남성	he	his	him	his	himself
	3여성	she	her	her	hers	herself
	3중성	it	its	it	-	itself
복수 1인칭		we	our	us	ours	ourselves
2인칭		you	your	you	yours	yourselves
3인칭		they	their	them	theirs	themselves

(2) 대명사는 명사를 대신한 것으로 명사처럼 주격, 목적격, 소유격이 있다

She speaks English very well. (주격)

I gave *her* a book. (목적격)

This is *her* book. (소유격) → This is *hers*. (소유대명사)

소유격 + 명사 → 소유대명사

This is my computer. → This is mine.

(3) he, we, you, they는 막연히 일반인을 나타내기도 한다

They speak English in Australia. (they = Australians)

We have much rain in July. 7월에는 많은 비가 온다.

They(we, you, one, people) should always be polite.
사람은 늘 겸손해야 한다.

He who laughs last laughs best.
마지막에 웃는 자가 진짜(가장 좋게) 웃는 자다.

Com empty, return empty. 빈손으로 와서 빈손으로 돌아간다.

← (They, People, You, We) come empty (hands), return empty.

3. **대명사 it의 특별용법**

(1) 대명사 it은 앞에 나온 단어, 구, 절을 대신하여 '그것'으로 해석될 때 사용된다

I have bought *a book*. *It* is very interesting.
Look at *that cat*. *It* always comes to my window.
He tried to pass the exam, but he found *it* difficult.

(2) 비인칭 주어 it

날씨, 계절, 시각, 거리, 요일, 명암, 상황 등을 말할 때 it은 비인칭 주어로 쓰이며, 별도로 해석하지는 않는다.

It is very fine today. (날씨) = Today is a very good weather.
It blew very hard last night.
= The wind blew quite hard last night.
It was hard winter. (계절) = It was a bitterly(very) cold winter.
What time is it now? (시각) 지금 몇 시 입니까?
It is just eleven o'clock. 바로 11시입니다.
It is growing(getting) dark. (명암) 어두워지고 있다.
How far is it from here to the bus stop? (거리)
여기서부터 버스정거장까지는 얼마나 멉니까?
It is about two miles. 약 2마일 입니다.
What day is (it) today? (요일) = Today, what day of the week?
It is Saturday today. = Today is Saturday.
It's my birthday tomorrow. = Tomorrow is my birthday.
What's the date today? (날짜) = What date is (it) today?
= What's today?
It is April the 9th (today). 4월 9일이다.
= It is the 9(th) of April(today). = Today is April 9(th).

(3) 관용적으로 상황을 나타낼 때의 it

How is it going? = How is it with you? = How are you (doing)?
It is well with me. = I am well(fine). = fine. 나는 잘 있어.
It is all over with him. 그는 이제 끝장이다.
How do you like it here? 여기가 어떻게 마음에 드십니까?
That's it! 바로 그것이다! Fight it out! 최후까지 싸워라!
I couldn't help it 어쩔 수 없었어, I go it. 알았어.
Go for it 힘내, It's me. 나다, Take it easy. 쉬엄쉬엄 해

(4) **가주어와 가목적어 it**
 영어에서 「긴 것은 뒤로」의 습성 때문에, 주어나 목적어가 길면 뒤로 돌리고 그 자리에 가주어 it나 가목적어 it을 둔다.
 To learn English is easy. (to부정사구는 습성상 주어로 쓰지 않음)
 = It is easy *to learn English*. (it은 가주어, to부정사구는 진주어)
  쉽다/영어를 배우는 것은.

 That he married her is true.
 그가 그녀와 결혼했다는 것은 사실이다.
  = It is true *that he married her*. (it은 가주어, that절은 진주어)

 I know *it* easy *to learn English*.
 (it = 가목적어, to부정사구 = 진목적어)
 I found *it* difficult *to study science*. (5형식 문장)
 나는 알았다/과학을 공부하는 것이 어렵다는 것을.

(5) **It is ~ that 강조구문 : ~은 바로 ~이다**
 I saw Linda in the park yesterday.
 나는 린다를 보았다/어제 공원에서.
 It was I that(who) saw Linda in the park yesterday.

어제 공원에서 린다를 본 사람은 바로 나였다. (주어 강조)
It was Linda that(who, whom) I saw in the park yesterday.
내가 어제 공원에서 본 사람은 바로 린다였다. (목적어 강조)
It was in the park that(where) I saw Linda yesterday.
내가 린다를 어제 본 곳은 바로 공원이었다. (부사구 강조)
It was yesterday that(when) I saw Linda in the park.
내가 린다를 공원에서 본 것은 바로 어제였다. (부사 강조)

4. **재귀대명사**

재귀대명사(再歸代名詞)는 주어의 동작이 주어 자신에게로 되돌아가는 것을 나타내는 대명사이다.

(1) **재귀적 용법**

주어의 동작이 주어 자신에게 돌아가는 경우로 동사, 전치사의 목적어로 쓰인다. 목적어 자리에서 목적어로 쓰이므로 생략할 수 없다.
He killed himself. 그는 그 자신을 죽였다. (그는 자살했다)
She looks at herself in the mirror. 그녀는 자신을 본다/거울 속의.
God(Heaven) helps those who help themselves.
하늘은 돕는다/스스로 돕는 자를.
= God(Heaven) helps those who make an effort themselves.
　하늘은 돕는다/스스로 노력하는 자를.

(2) **강조 용법**

재귀대명사는 주어, 목적어, 보어를 강조하기 위하여 동격으로 강조하는 말 뒤에 오거나 문장 맨 끝에 온다. 동격 재귀대명사는 생략할 수 있다.
I myself had to prepare everything.
나는 스스로 모든 것을 준비해야만 했다.
= I had to prepare everything myself.

(3) 재귀대명사의 관용어구

by oneself 혼자서(홀로), of itself 저절로, 자연히, avail oneself of ~을 이용하다. for oneself 혼자 힘으로, 스스로, beside oneself 이성을 잃고, in itself 본질적으로, 그 자체가, come to oneself 제정신이 들다, between ourselves 우리끼리 얘기인데, in spite of oneself 자기도 모르게, help yourself 마음대로 드세요

5. 지시대명사

지시대명사는 사물을 가리킬 때 쓰이며, this(these)와 that(those)이 있다. 지시대명사 뒤에 명사가 오면 지시형용사가 된다.

This is my car, and that is yours. (지시대명사)

이것은 내 차이고 저것은 네 차다.

I love *this car*. (지시형용사)

(1) 명사의 반복을 피하기 위한 that

The weather of Korea is better than *that* of Europe.

한국의 날씨는 더 좋다/유럽의 날씨보다. (that = the weather)

The apartments in Seoul are more expensive than *those* in the country.

서울에 있는 아파트는 더 비싸다/시골의(시골에 있는) 아파트들보다.

(those = the apartments)

(2) 앞에 나온 구, 절, 문장 전체를 가리킬 때

I tried *to master English*, but I found *that* difficult.

(that = to master English)

나는 영어를 마스터하려고 노력했으나 그것이 어렵다는 것을 알았다.

To be or not to be, that is the question.

죽느냐 사느냐 그것이 문제로다. (that = to be or not to be)

She says nothing. That makes me angry. (that = 앞 문장 전체)

(3) 가까운 것은 this(후자), 먼 것은 that(전자)으로 가리킨다.
Both good and evil are good for the world, this gives us fear and hate, and that gives us peace and love. We are aware of peace and love only through fear and hate because the world was made with balace(harmony) of yin and yang. Therefore, love without evil can't exist and act, forever alone.
선과 악은 둘 다 좋다/세상을 위해, 후자(악)는 우리에게 불안과 미움을 주고 전자(선)는 우리에게 평안과 사랑을 준다. 우리는 평안과 사랑을 인식한다/오직 불안과 미움을 통해서만/왜냐하면 세상은 음양(양성자와 전자, 쌍 극, 좋고 나쁨)의 조화로 만들어졌기 때문이다. 그러므로(따라서), 악이 없는 사랑은 존재하고 행동(작용)할 수 없다/영원히 홀로.

6. 부정대명사

부정대명사(不定代名詞)는 정해져 있지 않은 막연한 사물을 나타내는 대명사이다. 부정대명사가 명사 앞에서 명사를 수식하면 부정형용사가 된다.
give me another(부정대명사), another problem(부정형용사)

(1) 부정대명사 one

주격	소유격	목적격	재귀대명사	복수
one	one's	one	oneself	ones

① 일반 사람을 나타낼 때
One should keep his(their) promise.
사람은 자신의 약속을 지켜야만 한다.

One should always respect for his parents.
사람은 자신의 부모님을 늘 공경해야 한다.
In order to love others, one must first learn to love oneself.
다른 사람을 사랑하기 위해서, 사람은 먼저 배워야 한다/자신을 사랑하는 것을.

② 앞에 나온 명사의 반복을 피하기 위해
If you need a pen, I will lend you one. (같은 종류의 펜)
I bought a pen, but I lost it. (똑같은 펜)
Two heads are better than one.
두 머리는 낫다/한 머리보다. (백지장도 맞들면 낫다.)

③ no one은 단수, none + of + 단수(복수)명사 → 단수(복수)취급
No one handles the machine. 아무도 그 기계를 다루지 못한다.
None of us handle the machine.
None of the information is useful.

(2) other(다른), others(다른 것들), another(다른 하나)

① 둘 중 하나는 one이고, 다른 하나는 the other
I have two sons, one is a doctor and the other is an economist.
나는 두 아들이 있는데, 하나는 의사이고 다른 하나는 경제학자이다.

② others가 단독으로 쓰이면 other people(다른 사람들)을 뜻함
Some like soccer in der class, and others like volleyball.
반에서 몇몇 사람들은 축구를 좋아하고 다른 사람들은 배구를 좋아한다.

③ '다른 하나, 또 하나, 다른'을 말할 때는 another = an + other를 쓴다.
This bike isn't to my taste. Show me another.
이 자전거는 내 취향에 맞지 않소. 다른(다른 하나) 것을 보여 주시오.
I won't make another mistake. 나는 다른 실수를 하지 않을 거다.
I will not make other mistakes.
나는 다른 실수들을 하지 않을 거다.
I want to read another book. I want to read other books.
* another + **단수(불)가산명사**, other + **복수가산명사, 불가산명사**

④ other than = except (for) ~을 제외하고
No one knows the secret other than Peter.
= No one knows the secret except (for) Peter.
아무도 그 비밀을 알지 못한다/피터를 제외하고.

(3) some과 any

some은 주로 긍정문에, any는 의문문, 부정문, 조건문에 쓰인다.
Some of the students want to go to the movies. (긍정문)
If you have any money, lend me some. (조건문)
Would you like to eat anything else? (의문문)
No, I don't eat any more. (부정문)

① 권유하거나 긍정의 대답을 예상하는 의문문에 some을 쓸 수 있다.
Will you have some coffee? 커피 좀 드시겠어요?
Can I use your pen some time?
내가 네 펜을 사용해도 되니/당분간?

② some + 단수 보통명사이면, '어떤'의 뜻이 된다.
Some child wants to play. 어떤 아이는 놀기를 원한다.

Some children want to play. 몇몇 아이들은 놀기를 원한다.

③ any가 긍정문에 쓰이면 '어떤 ~라도'의 뜻이 된다.
Any child can solve such a question.
어떤 아이라도 그런 문제는 풀 수 있다.
You can eat any food in the kitchen.
너는 어떤 음식이라도 먹어도 좋다/부엌에 있는.

④ some(any) + 단수(복수)명사 : some(any) book, some(any) books

(4) each, every, both
each와 every 다음에는 단수명사가 오므로 단수 취급한다.
Each room was cleaned well. 각 방은 잘 청소되었다.
Every room is in use. 모든 방은 사용 중이다.
= All rooms are in use.
Every one of the children is crying. 아이들 모두 울고 있다.
Both of them(They both) arrived at the same time.
Both (the, of the) students have done their own homework.
학생 둘 다 그들 자신의 숙제를 했다.
Each of the students has his own book.
학생들 각자 자신의 책을 갖고 있다.
All (the, of the) children need safe toys.

(5) all
all 단독으로 사람을 나타내면 복수 취급, 사물을 나타내면 단수 취급한다.
all + 복수명사 → 복수동사, all + 단수명사 → 단수동사

All were present. 모두 참석(출석)했다.
All was stolen. 모두 도난당했다.
All the people were present. 모든 사람들이 참석했다.
All the money was stolen. 모든 돈은 도난당했다.

* every + **단수(불)가산명사**, all + **복수가산명사, 불가산명사**
We make every effort to satisfy customers.
우리는 모든 노력을 한다/고객을 만족시키기 위해.
Almost every country is interested in atomic energy.
거의 모든 나라는 원자력에 관심이 있다.
All students have to learn hard.
모든 학생들은 열심히 배워야 한다.
All violence has to be avoided. 모든 폭력은 피해져야만 한다.
All mistakes have to be avoided. 모든 실수들은 피해져야만 한다.

* My jeans were all dirty. (all + 형용사) 내 바지는 모두 더럽다.
I worked all day yesterday. She plays the piano every day.
He comes to see me every two days.
그는 나를 보러 온다/이틀마다.

(6) **Both(둘 다), either(둘 중 하나), neither(둘 중 어느 것도 아니다)**
Both the sons are very diligent. 아들 둘 다 매우 근면하다.
There's tea or coffee. You can drink either.
차 또는 커피가 있다. 너는 둘 중 하나를 마실 수 있다.
Would you like tea or coffee? Neither, thanks.
차나 커피 마실래요? 둘 다 아니에요, 감사해요.

(7) **부분부정과 전체부정**

not + all(both, every, whole) = 부분부정 : 모두 ~인 것은 아니다

not + any(either) = 전체부정, 또는 none, no one, neither, nothing, nobody 등으로 나타내는 경우 전체부정이 된다.

She doesn't like everyone. (부분부정)
그녀는 모든 사람을 좋아하는 것은 아니다.
She doesn't like anyone. (전체부정)
그녀는 어떤 사람도 좋아하지 않는다.
He did not talk with all of them. (부분부정)
그는 그들 모두와는 이야기하지 않았다.
He did not talk with any of them. (전체부정)
그는 그들 중 어느 누구와도 이야기 하지 않았다.
I don't like both of them. (부분부정)
나는 그들 둘 다 좋아하는 것은 아니다.
I don't like either of them. (전체부정)
나는 그들 둘 중 하나도 좋아하지 않는다.
Neither(none, no one, nobody) of them likes me. (전체부정)

7. 의문대명사

용도	주격	소유격	목적격
사람	who	whose	whom
사물·동물	which	—	which
사람·사물·동물	what	—	what

(1) who, which, what의 용법

Who are you? What's your job? What's your name? (주격)
Who is older, he or she? 누가 더 나이가 많으니/그와 그 여자 중?

219

Whose schoolbag is this? Whose fault is it? (소유격)

What do you mean? 무슨 말씀이신지요? (목적격)

Which would you like, wine or beer? (목적격)

What are you (doing)? (주격) 너 무엇 하니?

What do you do? 무슨 일을 하니? (직업이 무엇이니?)

(2) 의문대명사의 위치

① 의문대명사가 주어이면, 주어 앞에 조동사가 오지 않는다.
Did who eat my chocolate? (×)
Who ate my chocolate? (○)

② 의문대명사가 전치사의 목적어일 경우, 전치사는 문두나 문미(문장 끝)에 온다.
Who(m) are you waiting for? = For whom are you waiting?
What do they talk about? = About what do they talk?

③ 의문문이 명사절일 때 간접의문문이라고 하고, 어순은 평서문의 어순이다.
의문사[의문대명사(who, what, which), 의문부사(where, when)] + 주어 + 동사 …
Where does she live? 그녀는 어디에 사니? (직접의문문)
Do you know *where she lives*? (간접의문문)
너는 아니/그녀가 사는 곳을(그녀가 어디에 사는지)?
Who is she? 그녀는 누구니?
Who **do you think** she is? 그녀가 누구라고 너는 생각하니?

(3) 의문형용사

명사를 수식하는 의문사(의문대명사)를 의문형용사라고 한다.
What hat is that? = What kind of hat is that?
Which subjects do you like best? I like music best.
Whose schoolbag is this? = Whose is this schoolbag?
이것은 누구의 책가방이니? = 이 책가방은 누구의 것이니?

Exercises

A. 괄호 안에 적합한 주격 인칭대명사를 넣으시오.

1. Look, there's a spider in the corner! Is ( ) dead? I hate spiders.
2. Is Brian at home, Mrs. Johnsons? Yes, Kevin, ( ) is in his room.
3. Look, there are Frank and Mike. I think ( ) are very good friends.
4. My brother and I are in the same school, but ( ) do not have the same teachers.
5. Do you like Elizabeth? No, I don't. I think ( ) is arrogant.
6. Thank you for the ice cream, Mr. Nelson. ( ) was very good.
7. Is this your sweater, Jack? No, sir, ( ) have a blue sweater, not a green one.
8. Frank and Joe, can ( ) answer my question? No, sir, ( ) can't!

※ 1. it 2. he 3. they 4. we 5. she 6. It 7. I 8. you, we

B. 괄호 안에 적합한 목적격 인칭대명사를 넣으시오.

1. Paul is hiding in the tree. Can you see ( )?
2. I read a book. ( ) was very good.
3. I read some books. ( ) were very good.
4. I don't like Harry very much. Please don't tell ( ) my address.
5. Look, there is Mrs. Stevens. Let's ask ( ) about the exam.
6. Why do you ask ( )? I have no idea where Barry is.
7. Did you see the photos? Yes, I saw ( ).
8. Children, where are ( )? Please shout "Here we are!".
9. We can't open this door! Can you help ( ), please?

※ 1. him 2. It 3. They 4. him 5. her 6. me 7. them 8. you 9. us

C. 괄호 안에 적합한 소유격 대명사를 넣으시오.

1. I like Linda and ( ) sister, but I don't like ( ) brother. He's a bully.
2. My dad is okay. He sometimes lets me ride ( ) motorbike.
3. Mr. Johnson says we have to do ( ) homework at home and not here.
4. Jack, is this ( ) pen? No, ( ) pen is blue, not grey.
5. Tom and James are my neighbors. I often go to ( ) place to play video games.
6. The capital of Austria is Vienna. ( ) German name is "Wien".
7. Peter and Paul, show me ( ) hands! They are dirty again!
8. Barry and Brian are my brother. We live in a nice house to-

gether with ( ) parents and ( ) grandma.

9. The boy has got a room of ( ) own.

10. The boys painted ( ) faces red.

※ 1. her, her 2. his 3. our 4. your, my 5. their 6. Its 7. your 8. our, our 9. his 10. their

D. 괄호 안에 적합한 소유대명사를 넣으시오.

1. Is this Sylvia's picture album? Yes, it's ( ).

2. George, is this your bus pass?
   Let me see! No, it isn't ( ).

3. Look, Robert, I have found a bunch of keys.
   You have lost ( ), haven't you?

4. This looks like the children's football! Yes, it's ( ).

5. Brian and Frank, is this your car over there? Yes, it's ( ).

6. These are your brother's shoes, aren't they?
   Yes, I think they are ( ).

7. Boys, look here! There are some clothes on the floor.
   I think they are ( ).

8. Get off this bike! It's ( ), not ( )!

※ 1. hers 2. mine 3. yours 4. theirs 5. ours 6. his 7. yours 8. mine, yours

E. 괄호 안에 적합한 재귀대명사를 넣으시오.

1. Frank, don't always look at ( ) in the mirror! We all know you look good!

2. Your cold will not cure ( ). You'll have to see a doctor.

3. Angela is very selfish. She thinks only of (　), never of others.
4. Girls, did you make these dresses (　)? Yes, and we are very proud!
5. I introduced (　) to our new neighbor.
6. She made (　) a pullover.
7. The father decided to repair the car (　).
8. You play very well, Tim. I (　) could not do it better.
9. What are you doing here by (　) Veronica?
10. The problem will not go away by (　). You'll have to drive it away!

※ 1. yourself 2. itself 3. herself 4. yourselves 5. myself 6. herself 7. himself 8. myself 9. yourself 10. itself

F. 괄호 안에 보기의 적합한 부정대명사를 넣으시오.

every, all, some, none, each, anybody(anyone), something, anything, somewhere, anywhere, any, everyone(everybody), everything

1. Fred and Tony play tennis (　) Wednesday. They play (　) afternoon.
2. I have taken (　) my medicine. I need a new bottle.
3. Not (　) boys like football; (　) prefer tennis or volleyball.
4. (　) of my friends wanted to go to the movie, so I stayed at home, too, and did (　) of my homework for next week.
5. Look at this mess! (　) the books are where they should

be!
6. (　) woman likes fashion magazines. No, (　) find them boring.
7. (　) jeans in this shop are now cheaper.
8. (　) people like sports and (　) don't.
9. It snowed (　) day yesterday, so (　) of the trains did not run.
10. Can I have (　) milk, please? I'm sorry, but (　) the bottles in the fridge are empty. Do you want (　) apple juice instead?
11. (　) day has 24 hours, and (　) week has seven days.
12. Last week was terrible! We had tests on (　) day of the week.
13. Does (　) mind if I open the window? Yes! (　) of us have a cold.
14. Would you like (　) to drink, Joe? No, thanks. I've just had (　) juice.
15. The old man is sleeping (　) under a bridge, I think. That's because he hasn't got (　) to go. He is homeless.
16. Can I have (　) paper for my typewriter, please? Sure! Take (　)! It's (　) over there on the desk.
17. Have you seen (　) of these films? No, I haven't, but Angela has seen (　) of them.
18. Would you like (　) more tea? Yes, please. And could I have (　) cookies,　too, please?
19. (　) of us has received an equal share.
20. He has read (　) book on the list.
21. (　) loves a good joke.

22. The first thing you learn as a politician is that ( ) you say has to be worded carefully.

23. ( ) good things come from heaven.

※ 1. every, all 2. all 3. all, some 4. None, some 5. None 6. Every, some 7. All 8. Some, some 9. all, some 10. some, all, some 11. Every, every 12. each 13. anybody(anyone), Some 14. something(anything), some 15. somewhere, anywhere 16. some, some, somewhere 17. any, some 18. some, some 19. Each 20. every 21. Everyone/Everybody 22. everything(anything) 23. All

G. 괄호 안에 적합한 단어를 고르시오.

1. We have written too (many, much) sentences today.
2. They have got so (many, much) children.
3. There wasn't (many, much) dirt in the hall.
4. How (many, much) wine did you drink?
5. You can go along (both, either) street.
6. (Both, Either) buses go to the station.
7. (Both, Either) of us were invited.
8. (Both, Either) of the teams may win.
9. He did (no, not) come.
10. (No, None) of the boys complained.
11. These results are (no, not) too bad.
12. There were (no, not) pictures in the room.
13. (No, Not) a single car was sold.
14. (None, Nobody) answered the phone.

※ 1. many 2. many 3. much 4. much 5. either 6. Both 7. Both 8. Either 9. not 10. None 11. not 12. no 13. Not 14. Nobody

제17장 전치사

전치사(前置詞)는 명사(대명사) 앞에 놓여 전치사구를 만든다. 전치사구에는 형용사구, 부사구가 있으므로 전치사구는 문장에서 형용사, 부사처럼 쓰인다. 형용사구는 앞에 있는 명사를 수식하고, 부사구는 앞에 있는 동사, 형용사, 부사, 문장전체를 수식한다.

1. 전치사의 용법

(1) 전치사구는 문장에서 형용사나 부사처럼 쓰인다
The book *on the desk* is yours. (형용사구)
책상 위에 있는 책은 네 것이다.
She has studied music *in Seoul for three years*. (부사구)
그녀는 음악을 공부했다(공부해왔다)/서울에서 3년 동안.

(2) 전치사의 목적어는 목적격이어야 한다
Look at I. (×) Look at me. (○)
Wait for her here. I talk with him.

(3) 전치사의 목적어로 동사를 쓸 때에는 동명사를 써야 한다
Before go to school, I feed the dog. (×)
Before going to school, I feed the dog. (○)

★ 전치사의 목적어로는 명사상당어구[명사, 대명사, 동명사(구), 부정사(구), 명

사구, 명사절]가 쓰인다.

① He goes to *school*. (명사) 그는 간다/학교에.

② Listen to *me* carefully. (대명사) 내 말을 들어라/주의 깊게.

③ Thank you for *helping* me. (동명사)

감사합니다/나를 도를 도운 것에 대해.

④ I am glad of *your success*. (명사구)

나는 기뻐한다/너의 성공을.

⑤ Look for *what you can do*. (명사절)

찾아보아라/네가 할 수 있는 것을.

People differ from animals in *that they can think and talk*. (명사절)

사람은 동물과 다르다/(사람은) 생각하고 말할 수 있다는 점에서.

He does nothing except *that he eats and drinks*. (명사절)

그는 아무것도 안 한다/먹고 마시는 것 이외에는.

* 전치사 in과 except만 목적격 that절(명사절)을 이끈다.

⑥ He does nothing except *eat and drink*. (부정사구)

Nothing remains but *(to) go home*. (부정사구)

집에 갈 수밖에 없다.

* 전치사 but과 except만 부정사구를 이끈다.

(4) **전치사가 부사나 접속사로 쓰이기도 한다**

I saw her before. (부사) 나는 그녀를 보았다/전에.

Before I have a meal, I wash my hands. (접속사)

Before a meal I wash my hands. (전치사)

식사 전에 나는 내 손을 씻는다.

2. **전치사의 어순(숙어적)**

(1) 전치사 + 명사(대명사)

We wept *for joy*. 우리는 울었다/기뻐서.

We met *by chance*. 우리는 만났다/우연히.

I did it for *you*. 나는 그것을 했다/너를 위해.

(2) 명사 + 전치사

a *cheque for* 200 dollar, 200달러짜리 수표

There's no *reason for* concern. 걱정할 이유가 없다.

(3) 동사 + 전치사

She *looks at* me. 그녀는 나를 쳐다본다.

She *asked* me *for* advice.

그녀는 내게 충고를 요청했다. (동 + 목 + 전)

구동사 : have to, be able to, be about to, be going to, be willing to

(4) be + 형용사(분사) + 전치사

She is *different from* me. 그녀는 나와 다르다.

We *were surprised at* the result. 우리는 그 결과에 놀랐다.

(5) 전치사 + 형용사

I *regard* it *as* important. 나는 그것을 중요하다고 간주한다.

Things *went from* bad *to* worse. 상황(일)은 더욱 악화되었다.

(6) 전치사 + 부사

till recently 최근까지, since then 그 이후, from here 여기로부터, for always 영구히, from abroad 해외로부터

(7) 전치사구(형용사구, 부사구)는 연거푸 올 수 있다

The house at the top of the hill at the back of the village is ours.

마을 뒤에 언덕 꼭대기에 있는 집은 우리 것이다.

3. 전치사의 후치

전치사는 전치사의 목적어 앞에 오는 것이 원칙이지만, 다음과 같은 경우에는 전치사의 목적어 앞이나 문미(문장 끝)에 온다.

(1) 전치사의 목적어가 의문사일 때

What is he talking about? (일상체)

= About what is he talking? (격식체)

Which house does he live in?

= In which house does he live?

(2) 전치사의 목적어가 관계사절일 때

This is the house (which) he is staying at. (일상체)

= This is the house at which he is staying. (격식체)

　이것은 집이다/그가 머물고 있는.

(3) 부정사구가 전치사의 목적어를 수식할 때

She has no friends to play with. 그녀는 친구들이 없다/함께 놀.

(4) 감탄문에서

What a trouble he got into! 그가 그런 곤경에 빠지다니!

(5) 수동문에서

The Children are well taken care of.

그 아이들은 잘 보살펴지고 있다.

4. **전치사의 생략**

(1) 서술적 용법에서

나이(age), 크기(size), 모양(shape), 색채(color), 가격(price) 등을 나타내는 형용사구(전치사구)의 전치사 of는 생략할 수 있다.

The old machine is (of) no use. 그 오래된 기계는 쓸모 없다.
We are (of) the same age. 우리는 같은 나이이다.
The car is (of) dark blue. 그 차는 짙은 청색이다.
(Of) what price is this? 이것은 가격이 얼마입니까?

(2) 시간(시각), 거리, 정도(상태), 방법 등의 부사구(전치사구)에서 본연의 의미를 나타내는 전치사는 생략할 수 있다

He had trouble (in) catching a taxi. (방법)
그는 어려웠다/택시를 잡는 데.
He plays tennis (in) the way I like. (방법)
그는 테니스를 친다/내가 좋아하는 방식으로.
He travels to USA (by) first class. (방법)
그는 미국으로 여행한다/일등석으로.
He sent the letter (by) air mail. (방법)
그는 그 편지를 보냈다/항공우편으로.
We have studied English (for) an hour. (시간)
우리는 영어를 공부했다/한 시간 동안.
I waited for her (for) a long time. (시간)
나는 그녀를 기다렸다/오랫동안.
(For) How long have you lived this house? (시간)

얼마나 오랫동안 이 집에서 살았니?
We will meet (on) Saturday. (요일) 우리는 토요일에 만날 거다.
(At) What time does tennis game begin? (시각)
몇 시에 테니스 시합이 시작하니?
By now(this) is the time to arrive (at). (시각)
지금쯤 도착할 시간이다.
We walked (for) three miles. (정도) 우리는 3마일을 걸었다.
I have no money to buy the car (with). (상태)
나는 돈이 없다/그 차를 살.

(3) 전치사의 목적어가 last, next, some, every, this, that 등의 수식을 받을 때 시간을 나타내는 전치사(in, on, at)는 반드시 생략된다
그러나 last나 next가 명사 뒤에 오면 전치사는 생략되지 않는다.
I saw her last (on) Saturday. 나는 그녀를 보았다/지난 토요일에.
He works hard (in) this year. 그는 열심히 일한다/금년에.
He always is at home (at) that time. 그는 늘 집에 있다/그 시간에.
Our family goes camping every (in) summer.
우리 가족은 캠핑하러 간다/여름마다.
(on) Next time I'll take the better test.
다음 번에 나는 더 나은 시험을 치를 거다.
We will meet again in June next.
우리는 다시 만날 거다/내년 6월에.
We met in April last. 우리는 만났다/지난 4월에.

(4) 관계대명사 that의 선행사가 시간을 나타낼 때, 절 뒤에 오는 전치사는 생략할 수 있다
By this is the time (that) she arrives (at).

233

5. 유사한 전치사와 접속사

	전치사 + 명사 상당어구	접속사 + 주어 + 동사
~때문에	because of(due to, owing to)	because(as, since)
~에도 불구하고	despite(in spite of, for all)	although(though, even though)
~경우에	in case of	in case, in case (that)
~을 제외하고	except(excepting)	except(excepting) that
~동안에	during, for	while
~뒤(후)에	after(following)	after
~전에	before(prior to, ago)	before
~하기 위해	for	so(so that, in order that)

6. 전치사의 종류

(1) 시간의 전치사

① at, on, in

at : 하루 미만의 짧은 시간. (시, 분, 정오 등)

on : 요일, 날짜, 주말

in : 월 이상의 긴 시간

at 6:45, at midnight, at lunchtime, at sunset, at night, at Christmas (크리스마스 때), at this time(이 맘 때), at the moment(지금), at the same time(동시에), at the beginning(end), at the age of 15, at once(즉시), at first(last), on Monday, on April 15, 2003. on Christmas Day, on my birthday, on Sunday morning, on Friday night, on the weekend = on weekends, on a rainy day(비 오는 날에), in the Middle Ages(중세에), in October, in 1998, in the 16th century, in the future, in the past, in (the) Winter, in (the)

1960s(1960년대에), in (my) life, in my school days(학창 시절에), in the morning, in the afternoon, in the end(마침내), He arrived at 4:00(on Saturday, in November, in 2008, in der morning).

② until(till) : ~까지(동작의 계속), by : ~까지(동작의 완료)
I will wait here till seven. The café is open till(until) 5 o'clock.
Can you repair the bike by tomorrow?

③ from ~로부터(출발점), since ~이래로(과거부터 현재까지 계속)
The game lasts from 8.30 till 9.30.
I have lived here since last year.
나는 여기서 살아왔다/지난해 이래로.

④ for ~동안, during ~동안, over ~에 걸쳐, through(out) ~동안 내내
for 다음에는 대개 숫자를 포함한 시간명사가 온다.
We've been here for three hours.
우리는 여기에 있었다/세 시간 동안.
I lived in the country during the summer vacation.
나는 시골에서 살았다/여름 휴가 동안.
She wept for days over.
그녀는 울었다/며칠 동안 내내.
The baby cried through(out) last night.
그 아기는 울었다/어젯밤 내내.

⑤ before(~전에), ago(~전에), after(~후에)
「시간명사+ago」는 현재를 기준으로 하여 '~전'이란 뜻으로 쓰이고, before는 과거의 어떤 시점을 기준으로 하여 '~전'이란 뜻이다.
Paul usually goes to bed before ten.

파울은 잠잔다/보통 10시 전에.
The subway left five minutes ago. 지하철은 출발했다/5분 전에.
The subway comes after five minutes again.
지하철은 온다/5분 후에 다시.
Finish your homework before dinner.
네 숙제를 끝내라/저녁식사 전에.

⑥ in(~지나서, ~후에), within(~안에)
The train will be arriving at Seoul Station in two hours.
그 기차는 도착할 거다/서울역에/2시간 후에.
I should finish the work within two days.
I'll be there within an hour.
My birthday is in June. My birthday is on June 15th.

(2) 장소의 전치사

① at(~에) : 좁은 장소
in(~안에) : 넓은 장소
on : (표면에 접촉된) 위에
at the bus stop, at the door, at the front desk, at the church, at the table, at(in) a party, at a front, at the school, at work(일하는 중), at the traffic light(신호등에서), in the room, in a building, in a garden, in a town(city), in the field, in the picture, in a(the) country, in a(the) pool, in a river, in your mouth, in Chile, in the sky, in a small village in the mountains(산속에 작은 마을에서), on the wall(벽에), on the ceiling, on the door, on the floor, on the left, on the bus, on the table, on a page, on an island, on the ground, on a chair, on the grass, on the beach, on your

shirt(너의 옷에)

Peter is not at home at the moment.

She works as a guide at(in) a zoo in Seoul.

The people had to stay in their houses because of the rain.

② in(~안에), into(~안으로), out of(~밖으로)

She is in the room. 그녀는 방안에 있다.

He comes into the room. 그는 방 안으로 간다(온다).

He goes out of the room. 그는 방 밖으로 나간다.

* The goods(item) is *out of stock*. 그 상품은 품절이다.

③ on(표면) 위에 ↔ beneath(표면) 밑에

over(바로) 위에 ↔ under(바로) 밑에

above(떨어져) 위에 ↔ below(떨어져) 아래에

up 위로 ↔ down 아래로

My book is on the desk. 내 책은 있다/책상 위에.

A climber found the body buried beneath a pile of leaves.
한 등반자가 발견했다/낙엽더미 밑에 묻혀 있는 시체를.

The lamp hangs over the table. 전등이 걸려 있다/테이블 위에.

The dog is lying under the table. 개는 누워 있다/테이블 밑에.

Our plane is above the clouds. 우리 비행기는 있다/구름 위에.

The sun has sunk below the horizon.
태양이 침몰했다/수평선 아래로.

He went down the hill. 그는 갔다/언덕 아래로 (언덕을 내려갔다).

* The shirt costs over $10. 그 셔츠는 가격이 10불 이상이다.

④ before(~ 앞에), behind(~ 뒤에), after(~의 뒤를 쫓아)

He stands before her. (= in front of) 그는 서 있다/그녀 앞에.

There is a high hill behind the house. (= at the back of)
높은 언덕이 있다/그 집 뒤에.
He went after the thief. 그는 도둑 뒤를 쫓아갔다.

⑤ between(둘) 사이에, among(셋 이상) 사이에, 가끔 셋 이상 사이에도 between이 쓰인다.
I am standing between Tim and Susan.
나는 서 있다/팀과 수산 사이에.
I am standing among many people.
All the delicious Korean foods are becoming popular among foreigners.
온갖 맛있는 한국 음식은 인기를 끌고 있다/외국인들 사이에.
I am standing among(between) Tim, Susan and Sandra.
I am standing among(between) six friends.
* 뒤에 기수 + 복수명사가 오거나 분명한 대상이 올 때는 셋 이상이더라도 between을 쓰기도 한다.

⑥ across ~을 건너서, ~을 가로질러서, along ~을 따라서, through ~통하여, ~사이로, ~을 지나, round(around) ~주위에, ~둘레에
We walked along the street for a while.
우리는 그 길을 따라 걸었다/한동안.
He ran fast across the street. 그는 빨리 뛰어갔다/길을 가로질러.
We took a walk through a forest. 우리는 산책했다/숲 사이로.
I saw her through the window. 나는 그녀를 보았다/창문을 통해.
The earth moves round(around) the sun.
지구는 이동한다/태양 주위를.

⑦ by, beside(~ 옆에, 곁에), near (to), close (to) ~가까이에

His desk is by the window. I want to sit beside her.
We live near the river. 우리는 산다/강 가까이에.
A few close relatives live near L.A.
몇몇 가까운 친척이 사신다/L.A. 인근에.
* We learn by listening. 우리는 배운다/들으면서(듣고).

(3) **방향의 전치사**

to(~로) : 도착 지점을 나타냄(go, come, return 등과 함께 쓰임)
for(~향하여) : 방향을 나타냄(leave, start, make, head, depart 등과 함께 쓰임)
toward(s)(~쪽으로) : 운동의 방향을 나타냄
from(~로부터) : 출발점을 나타냄
out of(~로부터) : 공간에서 분리, 이탈을 나타냄
off(~로부터) : 선·면에서 분리, 이탈을 나타냄
He went to school. 그는 갔다/학교에.
He left for Seoul. 그는 떠났다/서울로(서울을 향하여 떠났다).
He ran toward the school. 그는 뛰어갔다/학교 쪽으로.
He took a wallet out of his pocket.
그는 지갑을 꺼냈다/그의 호주머니에서.
The girl proudly said she was off the drugs.
그 소녀는 자랑스럽게 말했다/그녀가 마약을 끊었다고.

(4) **원인·이유의 전치사**

because of(due to) ~때문에, for 찬성하는, against 반대하는
be famous for ~로 유명하다, be known for ~로 알려져 있다
die of ~으로 죽다(직접적인 원인)
die from ~으로 죽다(간접적인 원인)
The train was delayed because of(due to) bad weather.

열차가 연착되었다/날씨가 나빠서.
I am for(against) the plan. 나는 그 계획에 찬성(반대)한다.
He jumped for joy. 그는 기뻐서 날뛰었다.
France is famous for its wine. 프랑스는 포도주로 유명하다.
She died of lung cancer. 그녀는 폐암으로 죽었다.
He died from the plane accident. 그는 비행기 사고로 죽었다.

(5) 수단·도구의 전치사

with(~을 가지고, ~으로)

by ~로(수단), ~에 의하여(행위자)

Write with a pencil. 연필로 써라.
The book was written by Mr. Lee. 그 책은 쓰여졌다/이 씨에 의해.
She comes home by bus. 그녀는 집에 온다/버스로.
The window was broken by(with) a ball.
그 창문은 부서졌다/공에 의해.
She is in bed with a cold. 그녀는 침대에 있다/감기로.
Her face was red with anger. 그녀의 얼굴은 붉어 있었다/분노로.

(6) 재료의 전치사

be made of ~로 이루어지다(만들어지다) : 물리적 변화(형태만 바뀜)

be made from ~로 이루어지다(만들어지다) : 화학적 변화(성질이 바뀜)

in(~로), make~ into ~으로 ~을 만들다.

The desk is made of wood. 책상은 나무로 만들어진다.
Wine is made from grapes. 포도주는 포도로 만들어진다.
Write a letter in black ink in place of red.
검정색 잉크로 편지를 써라/빨간색 대신에.
The baker makes flour into bread.
제빵사는 밀가루로 빵을 만든다.

(7) 예외의 전치사

except (for) ~을 제외하고, ~외에는

* but이 전치사로 쓰이면 except (for)의 의미가 있다.

We work every day except (for) Sunday and Saturday.
우리는 매일 일한다/일요일과 토요일을 제외하고.
= Except for Sunday and Saturday, we work every day.
Everyone had a good time but John.
모든 사람들이 즐거운 시간을 가졌다(보냈다)/존을 제외하고.

(8) 양보의 전치사 : ~임에도 불구하고

despite = in spite of = with all = for all

Despite his old age, he is still in good health.
그의 많은 나이에도 불구하고 그는 여전히 좋은 건강이다.
Many people came here in spite of the bad weather.
많은 사람들이 여기에 왔다/나쁜 날씨에도 불구하고.
For all(with all) his wealth, he is not happy at all.
그의 부유함에도 불구하고 그는 전혀 행복하지 않다.

(9) 목적(의도)의 전치사

for ~하기 위해, to ~하러(~하기 위해), on ~하러(용무),
after ~을 추구하여, ~을 쫓아서, at ~으로(에게, 을)

The house is for sale. 그 집은 팔 거다(팔기 위한 거다).
She came to see me. 그녀는 왔다/나를 보러(보기 위해).
I sent him on a business(on an errand).
나는 그를 사업차 보냈다(심부름 보냈다).
I ran after the thief, but I didn't catch him.
나는 도둑을 뒤쫓아 뛰어갔으나, 나는 그를 잡지 못했다.
They threw stones at us. 그들은 우리에게 돌들을 던졌다.

(10) 테마의 전치사

about, on, concerning, regarding, of ~에 관해서(대해서)
a book about(on) English grammar 영문법에 관한 책.
We're thinking of going to America for our holidays.
우리는 미국으로 가는 것에 관해 생각하고 있다/우리 휴가 동안에.
I'm a little worried(concerned) about(regarding) your health.
나는 좀 걱정스럽다/네 건강에 대해.
We argue about(on) environmental pollution.
우리는 논쟁한다/환경오염에 관해(대해).

Exercises

★ 전치사는 명사(대명사), 동사, 형용사(현재분사, 과거분사) 등과 결합하여 전치사구(형용사구, 부사구), 구동사(동사구)를 만들어 숙어(관용어구)로 쓰인다. 그 때문에 전치사구를 사전에서 찾으려면 어구의 생김새에 따라 전치사 왼쪽으로 또는 오른쪽으로 또는 전치사 좌우로 찾아야 한다.

A. 괄호 안에 적합한 전치사를 넣으시오.

1. As a child she suffered (   ) asthma.
2. Do you believe (   ) life after death?
3. Her interest (   ) politics was sparked by the civil rights movement.
4. Just think (   ) the money you'd save.
5. Russia is rich (   ) natural gas.
6. There were some Picasso prints (   ) the wall.

7. This reminds me ( ) a story I once heard.
8. A friend of mine has a deep hatred ( ) computers.
9. Her parents were waiting ( ) her at the airport.
10. The two newly-weds say it was love ( ) first sight.
11. There are still millions of slaves ( ) the world.
12. There is very little natural wilderness left ( ) the British Isles.
13. We paid extra for a room with a view ( ) the mountains.
14. You have every reason to be proud ( ) your accomplishments.
15. He still went bowling ( ) the age of 102.
16. How many hours do you sleep ( ) average?
17. She can't cook but she's extremely good ( ) her job.
18. She interviewed the president during his visit ( ) Japan.
19. The manager personally welcomed us ( ) the hotel.
20. The pilots are ( ) strike ( ) the moment.
21. Three of the club's players are ( ) the national team.
22. When I heard the news ( ) the radio I couldn't believe it.
23. "I suppose I was wrong," he said ( ) a low voice.
24. He makes calls on his mobile while driving ( ) 100 mph.
25. I like travelling ( ) train because it's relaxing.
26. I'm sure she ignored me ( ) purpose.
27. She's married ( ) a guy she met in college.
28. There are situations when paying ( ) credit card is a bit risky.
29. What do you mean ( ) "traditional values?"
30. I sometimes wonder what would have become ( ) me if I hadn't met you.

31. Indonesia consists (　) thousands of islands.
32. Like the queen, she never had any money (　) her.
33. The building is typical (　) early rural church architecture.
34. The wine tasted (　) dark cherries.
35. Two of the city's main homeless shelters are closing (　) lack of money.

※ 1. from 2. in 3. in 4. of 5. in 6. in 7. of 8. of 9. for 10. at 11. in 12. in 13. of 14. of 15. at 16. on 17. at 18. to 19. to 20. on, at 21. on 22. on 23. in 24. at 25. by 26. on 27. to 28. by 29. by 30. of 31. of 32. on 33. of 34. of 35. for

※ 1. suffer from ~로 고통받다, 시달리다 2. believe in ~을 믿다 3. be interest in ~에 관심이 있다 4. think of ~을 생각하다 5. rich in ~이 풍부하다 6. print in ~로 인쇄하다, ~의 자국이 있다 7. remind of ~을 생각나게 하다 8. hatred of ~을 증오하다 9. wait for ~을 기다리다 10. love at ~에 반하다 11. in the world 이 세상에(서) 12. in the British Isles 영국제도에서 13. a view of ~의 풍경(전망)이 14. be proud of ~을 자랑스러워하다 15. at the age of ~의 나이로 16. on average 평균적으로 17. be good at ~에 능숙하다 18. visit to ~로의 방문 19. welcome to ~에의 환영 20. on strike 파업중, at the moment 지금 21. on the national team 국가대표 팀(선수)에 22. on the radio 라디오에서 23. in a low voice 낮은 목소리로 24. at 100 mph. 시속 100마일로 25. by train 기차로 26. on purpose 고의로(일부러) 27. be married to ~와 결혼하다 28. pay by credit card 신용카드로 지불하다 29. What do you mean by this? 이것은 무슨 뜻이죠? 30. become of ~은 어떻게 되다 31. consist of ~으로 구성되다(이루어지다) 32. money on her 그녀 수중의 돈 33. typical of ~을 대표하는 34. taste of ~의 맛이 나다 35. for lack of ~이 부족하기 때문에(부족하여)

B. 괄호 안에 적합한 전치사를 넣으시오.

1. (　) the time we arrived (　) the station the last train was gone.
2. She arrived late (　) the appointment.
3. She was scheduled to arrive (　) home (　) the morning of September 11, 2001.
4. Her only son died (　) suicide (　) 2004.
5. Jack learns that his wife has died (　) her own hand.
6. Each year thousands (　) people die (　) fire-related injuries.
7. They lived (　) selling vegetables from their garden.
8. He has never worked a day (　) his life and lives (　) his parents.
9. Astronomers say that the moon is made (　) green cheese.
10. Cheese and yoghurt are made (　) milk.
11. (　) torture people will confess (　) crimes they never committed.
12. We are a specialty shop and deal (　) things that are not always easy to find (　) the larger stores.
13. If we don't deal (　) this problem now, it will come back to haunt us.
14. Nobody laughed (　) the jokes.
15. We left the dog (　) a neighbor when we went (　) holiday.
16. All efforts to prolong human life with animal organ trans-

plants have met ( ) failure.

17. She was rushed ( ) hospital, where she was immediately operated ( ).
18. What if I have paid ( ) the goods, but the seller doesn't send them?
19. A creative person can never be replaced ( ) a computer.
20. The wounded man was screaming ( ) pain.
21. This shop specializes ( ) large sizes.
22. She spends most of her spare money ( ) books.
23. I wrote a cheque ( ) $1,500 but there was only $1,450 ( ) my account.
24. We offer our customers a discount of 10 percent ( ) condition that they pay within four weeks.
25. My parents' neighbors will not go out together ( ) fear of being burgled if the house is empty.
26. When she heard that her husband was alive, she wept ( ) joy.
27. The children cried ( ) joy and excitement.
28. Everyone is in such a hurry ( ) the morning.
29. He said that he did not know anyone ( ) the name of Steve Williams.
30. She wrote a number of books ( ) the name of Patricia Holden.
31. It may seem a good idea, but ( ) my opinion it won't work in the present situation.

※ 1. By, at 2. for 3. -, on 4. by, in 5. by 6. of, from 7. by 8. in, off 9. of 10. from 11. Under, to 12. in, in 13. with 14.

at 15. with, on 16. with 17. to, on 18. for 19. by(with) 20. in(with) 21. in 22. on 23. for, in 24. on 25. for 26. for(with) 27. with 28. in 29. by 30. under 31. in

1. by the time 그때까지(그 무렵에), at the station 역에(서) 2. late for the appointment 약속에 늦게 3. on the morning (정해진 날짜의) 아침에 4. by suicide 자살로 5. by her own hand 그녀의 자신의 손으로 6. thousands of people 수천의 사람들이 7. live by ~로 먹고 살다 8. live off ~에 의지해서(도움으로) 살다 9. make of (물리적) ~로 만들다 10. make from (화학적) ~로 만들다 11. under torture 고문을 당하여, confess to a crime 범행을 자백하다 12. deal in (물품을) 취급하다, in the store 가게에서 13. deal with (일을) 다루다 14. laugh at ~을 비웃다 15. leave with ~에게 맡기다, on holiday 휴가중에 16. meet with failure 실패로 끝나다 17. rush to hospital 급히 병원으로 보내다, operate on ~을 수술하다 18. pay for 대금을 지불하다(빚을 갚다) 19. be replaced by(with) ~의해 대체되다(~로 교체하다) 20. in(with) pain 아파서(고통으로) 21. specialize in ~을 전문으로 하다 22. spend on ~에 쓰다 23. cheque for $100 100달러짜리 수표, in my account 내 계좌에 24. on condition (that) ~라는 조건으로 25. for fear of ~할까봐(두려워하여) 26. for(with) joy 기뻐서 27. cry with joy 기뻐서 외치다 28. in the morning 아침에 29. by the name of ~라는 이름의 30. under the name (of) ~라는 이름으로 31. in my opinion 내 견해로는(내 생각으로는)

제18장 조동사

조동사(助動詞)는 본동사를 도와 본동사가 나타내기 어려운 문장의 형식과 의미를 나타내 주는 보조동사이다.
본동사(本動詞)는 문장의 의미를 나타내 주는 주동사이다. 맨 마지막 동사가 본동사이다.
I play tennis. (play는 본동사)
I have played tennis. (have는 조동사, played는 본동사)
I will have finished my homework by tomorrow.
(will, have는 조동사, finished는 본동사)

1. 특수 조동사

조동사에는 일반 조동사와 특수 조동사(be, have, do)가 있다.

be동사 : ① 진행형 = be + -ing
          ② 수동태 = be + p.p
have동사 : 완료시제 = have(had) + p.p
do동사   : 부정문, 의문문, 강조에 쓰임
           * p.p = past participle 과거분사

(1) do(does)

① do는 조동사로도 본동사(~하다)로도 쓰인다.
I did the work. 내가 그 일을 했다. (did는 본동사)

② 의문문, 부정문을 만들 때 조동사로 쓰인다.

의문문은 주어 앞에 조동사가 온다.

What did you do yesterday? (did는 조동사, do는 본동사)

Do you speak English? (do는 조동사, speak는 본동사)

I don't like to eat anything. (do는 조동사, like는 본동사)

③ 본동사 앞에서 본동사의 의미를 강조한다.

He does love her. 그는 정말 그녀를 사랑한다.

Do be careful. 제발 조심해!

④ 대동사로 쓰일 때

대동사(代動詞)는 동사의 반복을 피하기 위해 동사 대신 쓰는 동사이다.

Did you play tennis yesterday?

Yes, I did. (= Yes, I played tennis yesterday.)

"I went to a party yesterday." So did I.

(= I also went to a party yesterday.)

(2) be(am, is, are)

① be동사는 진행형(be + ing)과 수동형(be + 과거분사)에서 조동사로 쓰인다.

② be동사는 늘 조동사와 본동사로 쓰이므로 의문문과 부정문을 만들 때는 일반 조동사처럼 쓰인다.

He is a teacher. (is는 본동사)

Is he a teacher? He isn't a teacher. (is는 조동사이며 본동사)

Who's your favorite singer? (Who's = Who is)

(3) have(has)

① have동사는 완료시제(have + p.p)에서 조동사로 쓰인다.
He has finished his homework.
(has는 조동사, finished는 본동사)
Has he finished his homework?

② have동사가 본동사(가지다, 먹다)일 경우 부정문과 의문문을 만들기 위해서는 do 조동사가 필요하다.
I have a pen. (have는 본동사)
Do you have a pen? (의문문)
I don't have a pen. (부정문)

* 영국 영어에서는 have가 '갖는다'의 뜻을 가질 때 현재형에서만 의문문과 부정문을 만드는 데 do 조동사를 필요로 하지 않는다.
Have you a pen? = Have you got a pen? I haven't a pen.

2. **일반 조동사**

일반 조동사에는 can, may, must, will, shall, ought to, used to, need, dare 등이 있다. 일반 조동사 뒤에는 동사원형이 오고, 두 개 이상의 조동사가 연거푸 올 수 없다.

1) can(could) = be able to ~할 수 있다

(1) 능력(가능) : ~할 수 있다
He can speak English fluently.
그는 영어를 유창하게 말할 수 있다.
= He is able to speak English fluently.

Anybody can make mistakes. 누구나 실수를 할 수 있다. (가능성)
When I was young, I could run very fast. (can의 과거)
내가 어렸을 때 나는 매우 빨리 달릴 수 있었다.

(2) 허락 : ~해도 좋다

Can I borrow your book for a minute? Yes, you can.
네 책을 빌려도 되니(좋으니)/잠깐? 그래 좋아.
Can(May) I smoke in this room? No, you cannot(may not).

(3) 부정적 추측 : ~일 리가 없다

He can't fail (in) the exam. 그는 시험에 떨어질 리가 없다.
Can the news be true? 그 소식은 사실일 수 있니?
The news can't be true.
그 소식은 사실일 수 없다(사실일 리가 없다).

(4) 대용어 : can = be able to ~할 수 있다

You will be able to help him tomorrow. (○)
너는 그를 도울 수 있을 거다/내일.
You will can help him tomorrow. (×)
이 경우 일반 조동사는 연거푸 올 수 없기 때문에 대용어를 쓴다.

(5) could의 용법

① 제의(제안)

Could you come now and help me? 지금 와서 나를 도울 수 있니?
When you go to Seoul tomorrow, you could stay by(at) uncle's (house).
네가 내일 서울에 가면 삼촌 집에 머물 수 있을 거다.

② 정중한 부탁(요청)

여기에서 could는 과거의 의미가 아니라 현재, 미래의 의미로 쓰인다.
would you나 could you는 거의 똑같은 정중한 부탁의 표현이다.
Could(Would) you help me a short time?
저를 도와주실 수 있나요/잠깐?
Can you help me a short time? (could보다 덜 공손함)
Can I have some more bread, please?
빵 좀 더 주시겠어요/미안하지만?

③ **could는 추측을 나타내기도 한다.** (~일 거다, ~일지도 모른다)
Laura could be in the library. 로라는 도서관에 있을 거다(거야).
When(if) I go to Seoul, I could get a new job.
내가 서울에 가면 나는 새 직장을 얻을 수 있을 거야.

④ **could have + p.p : ~할 수 있었는데**
should have + p.p : ~했어야 하는데
would have + p.p : ~하려고 했었는데
must have + p.p : ~했음이 틀림없다
cannot have + p.p : ~했을 리가 없다
may(might) have + p.p : ~했을는지도 모른다

I could have married her. 나는 그녀와 결혼할 수 있었는데.
I should have married her. 나는 그녀와 결혼 했어야 하는데.
He cannot have married her. 그는 그녀와 결혼했을 리가 없다.
He may(might) have married her.
그는 그녀와 결혼했을는지도 모른다.

(6) can의 관용어구

① cannot but do(동사원형) : ~하지 않을 수 없다
　= cannot choose but do
　= have no choice but to do
　= cannot help ~ing

　I cannot but think about her.
　= I cannot help thinking about her.
　= I have no choice but to think about her.
　= I have no alternative but to think about her.
　　나는 그녀에 관하여 생각하지 않을 수 없다.

② cannot ~ too much = cannot ~enough : 아무리 ~해도 지나치지 않다
　I can't thank you too much. = I can't thank you too enough.
　나는 아무리 당신에게 감사해도 지나치지 않다.

③ cannot~ without ~ing : ~할 때마다 반드시 ~하다(2중 부정 = 긍정)
　I cannot see him without thinking of his sister.
　= Whenever I see him, I think of his sister.
　　나는 그를 볼 때마다 반드시 그의 여동생을 생각한다.

2)　may(might)

　(1) 허가 : ~해도 좋다
　　May(Can) I sit here? Yes, you may(can).

　(2) 대용어 : 허락 : may ~해도 좋다 = be allowed to ~허용(허락)되다
　　You may stay in our house tonight.

= You are allowed to stay in our house tonight.
너(희)는 허락된다/우리 집에 머무는 것이/오늘밤에.

(3) 불확실한 추측 : (아마, 혹시) ~일지도 모른다
She may not come. 그녀는 (혹시) 안 올지도 모른다.
He may be rich. = He is possibly rich.
= It is possible that he is rich.
I'll be late this evening. 나는 늦을 거야/오늘 저녁에. (확실성)
I may(might) be late this evening. (불확실성)
나는 늦을지도 모른다/오늘 저녁에.

(4) might는 may보다 더 불확실한 추측을 나타냄
I may(might) go to Pusan tomorrow.
나는 부산에 갈지도 모른다/내일.
You may(might) have left your book at school.
너는 네 책을 놓아두었을지도 모른다/학교에.

☆ 불확실 → 확실한 추측
다음 확실성의 순서는 절대적이지는 않지만 대략적이다.
(불확실)might, may, could, can, should, would, will, must(확실)
Jane is sick. (100%) 제인은 아프다.
Jane must be sick. (90% 이상) 제인은 아픈 것이 틀림없다.
Jane can(could, should, may, might) be sick. (70% 이하)
제인은 아플 거다.

(5) 정중한 제의(요청)
Might I turn the TV on? 제가 TV를 켜도 될까요?
May I turn the TV on? (might는 may보다 더 공손함)

(6) 기원문(may + 주어 + 동사원형) : ~하소서

　　May you succeed! 부디 성공하소서!

　　May God bless you! 부디 당신에게 신의 은총이 함께하길!

(7) may의 관용어구

① may well + do(동사원형) : ~하는 것도(것은) 당연하다

　　She may well hate me. 그녀가 나를 미워하는 것도 당연하다.

　　= She has a good reason to hate me.

　　= It is natural that she (should) hate me.

② may as well(had better) + do : ~ 하는 것이(편이) 더 낫다

　　You may as well go home right now.

　　= You had better go home right now.

　　너는 집에 가는 것이 더 낫다/지금 당장.

3) must(have to)

(1) 의무 : (꼭) ~해야 한다

　　I must do the work within today.

　　나는 그 일을 (꼭) 해야 한다/오늘 안에.

　　You must come back by nine o'clock.

　　너는 (꼭) 돌아와야 한다/9시까지.

(2) 강한 추측 : ~임에 틀림없다

　　He must be an Australian. 그는 호주인임에 틀림없다.

　　= I'm sure (that) he is an Australian.

　　Our new neighbor's children must be very noisy.

There's nobody at home. They must have gone out.
= It is certain (that) they have gone out.
틀림없다(확실하다)/그들은 외출했음이.
= They have gone out certainly.

(3) must not : 금지, ~해서는 안된다
You must not sleep in class. 너(너희)는 자면 안된다/수업 중에.
You must not tell anybody about it.
너는 어느 누구에게도 말해서는 안된다/그것에 관해.

(4) must의 부정은 need not이거나 don't have to이다
I must finish my homework today.
나는 내 숙제를 끝내야 한다/오늘.
I need not finish my homework today.
= I don't have to finish my homework today.
= It is not necessary to finish my homework today.
끝낼 필요가 없다/내 숙제를 오늘.

(5) 대용어 : must = have to = have got to
must(꼭 ~해야 한다)는 너무 강한 의미의 단어이므로 일상어에서는 대부분 have to가 쓰이고, must는 잘 쓰이지 않는다. 즉 have to는 일상체(회화체)이고, must는 격식체(문장체)이다.
I must visit my uncle today. = I have to visit my uncle today.
= I have got to visit my uncle today.

* I must finish the work yesterday. (×)
I had to finish the work yesterday. (○)
I will must work harder next week. (×)

I will have to work harder next week. (O)

4) will

(1) 단순미래를 나타냄
I will go to the park tomorrow. 나는 공원에 갈 거다/내일.
It'll get(it's getting) warmer soon. 더 따듯해질 거다/곧.

(2) 주어의 강한 의지(고집)를 나타냄
He will see her now. 그는 그녀를 보려고 한다/지금.
I can see you're busy, so I won't stay long.
나는 당신이 바쁜 걸 볼 수 있으니 나는 오래 머물지 않을 거다.
I will not go there. 나는 가지 않을 거다/거기에.

(3) 가벼운 명령 : ~해 주시오
You will wait here till I return.
여기서 기다리시오/내가 돌아올 때까지.
All people will leave the building at once.
모든 사람들은 건물을 떠나주시오/즉시.

(4) 현재의 습관 : ~하곤 한다
He will often stay at uncle's. 그는 자주 삼촌 집에 머물곤 한다.
He will often be late. 그는 자주 늦곤 한다.

(5) 자연적인 습성 : ~하기 마련이다
Accidents will happen. 사고는 일어나기 마련이다.
Children will be noisy. 아이들은 떠들기 마련이다.

(6) would의 용법

① 과거의 반복적 습관 : ~하곤 하였다
    I would often get up late on Sunday morning.
    나는 자주 늦게 일어나곤 했다/일요일 아침에.
    Every morning she would go for a walk.
    = Every morning she used to go for a walk.

② 가정, 추측을 나타냄(would의 약 80% 이상)
    Somebody's at the door. That would be a postman.
    누군가 문에 있다. 그 사람은 우편배달부일 거다.
    It would be nice to buy a new car.
    좋을(멋질) 거다(좋을 텐데)/새 차를 사는 것은.
    * I would love(like) to live by the ocean. (I'd = I would)
    = I want to live by the ocean.

③ 정중한 부탁 : ~해 주시겠습니까?
    Would(could, will, can) you close the door, please?
    = Would you mind shutting the door, please?
    문 좀 닫아 주시겠어요/죄송하지만? (will은 would보다 덜 공손함)

④ 소망 : ~하고 싶다
    I would like to see my parents. 나는 내 부모님을 뵙고 싶다.
    I would like a cup of coffee. 나는 한 잔의 커피를 원한다.
    = I want a cup of coffee.

⑤ 가정법
    I would call Julia if I had her number.

나는 줄리아에게 전화할 텐데/내가 그녀의 번호를 가지고 있다면.

⑥ would rather do : 차라리 ~하는 게 더 낫다(~하고 싶다)
I'd rather stay home. = I would rather stay home.
= I would prefer to stay home.
I'd rather walk than take a bus.
나는 차라리 걷는 게 더 낫다(나을 텐데)/버스를 타는 것보다.
(나는 차라리 걷고 싶다/버스를 타는 것보다.)

* had better do : ~하는 것이 더 좋다(낫다), ~해야 한다
I'd better go now. = I had better go now.
= I better go now. (회화에서 had는 자주 생략된다)

부정 : You had better not go now.

5) shall(should)

(1) shall의 용법
shall과 will은 정중한 제의(제안)를 할 때 쓰인다.
Shall(Will) I(we)…? (정중한 제의)
Shall(will) I open the door? 제가 문을 열까요?
When shall we meet again? 우리는 언제 다시 만날까요?
When will we meet again? 우리는 언제 다시 만나게 될까요?
Shall we dance? 우리 춤 출까요?
Shall we go to the movies? 우리 영화 보러 갈까요?
* 현대 영어는 영국에서만 shall(미래)을 사용한다. 미국에서 shall은 매우 국한적으로 쓰이고, will(미래)이 주로 쓰인다.

(2) should의 용법

① 대용어 : should = ought to : (마땅히) ~해야 한다(충고, 의무)
　부정 : should not(shouldn't) = ought not to : ~해서는 안된다.
　be supposed to : (규칙, 관습에 따라) ~해야 한다, ~하기로 되어 있다,
　　　　　　　　~할 예정이다

People should love their neighbors.
= People ought to love their neighbors.
사람은 자신의 이웃을 사랑해야 한다.
You should not lie. 너는 거짓말을 해서는 안된다.
= You ought not to lie. (not은 to부정사 앞에 옴)
Ought I to go there? (의문문인 경우 ought만 주어 앞으로)
She is supposed to do the work.
그녀는 그 일을 하기로 되어 있다. 그녀는 그 일을 해야 한다.
Mum said we are supposed to come home before 9 p.m.
엄마는 말했다/우리가 집에 와야 한다고/저녁 9시 전에.

② 기대에 어긋날 때
Mary should be here by now.
메리는 여기에 있어야 하는데/지금쯤.
She isn't here yet. That is not normal.
That man shouldn't go to the red light.
저 남자는 가서는 안되는데/빨간 불에.

③ 기대(추측)할 때
린다는 열심히 공부했다. 그래서 그녀는 시험에 합격할 거다.
Linda has studied hard, so she should pass the exam.

= She passes probably the exam.
= it is probable that she passes the exam

많은 호텔들이 있다/서울에는. 어렵지 않을 거다/머무를 곳을 찾는 데.
There are plenty of hotels in Seoul.
It shouldn't be hard to find a place to stay.
= I don't expect it to be hard. (5형식 문장)

④ should have + p.p : ~했어야 하는데(후회나 아쉬움을 나타냄)
I should have made her girlfriend.
나는 그녀를 여자친구로 만들었어야 하는데.
You missed a great party last night. You should have come.
너는 큰 파티를 놓쳤다/지난밤에. 네가 왔어야 하는데.

(3) that종속절 속에서 should가 생략되는 경우(미국식 영어)

① **주절에 두뇌형용사(이성적 판단의 형용사)가** 쓰인 that절에서 주절의 형용사 자체가 소망, 당위성을 나타내므로 that절 속의 should는 대개 생략된다. 이 경우 인칭에 관계없이 동사원형이 온다.
(wrong, well, essential, fair, good, important, necessary, right 등)
It is important that you (should) not make a noise.
중요하다/너희들이 시끄럽게 하지 않는(않아야 하는) 것이.

② **주절에 두뇌동사가** 쓰인 that절에서 주절의 동사 자체가 소망, 당위성을 나타내므로 that절 속의 should는 대개 생략된다.
(insist, require, wish, order, decide, suggest, demand, ask 등)
She suggests that he (should) finish the work.

그녀는 제의한다/그가 그 일을 끝내는 것을(끝내야 한다고).

③ lest 절에서 : ~할까봐, ~하지 않도록

I am anxious lest he (should) fail.

나는 걱정이다/그가 실패할까봐.

Be careful lest you (should) fall from the cliff.

조심해라/네가 절벽에서 떨어지지 않도록.

6) used to

(1) 과거의 습관 : ~하곤 했다

I used to play tennis a lot(much), but I don't often play now.

나는 테니스를 많이 치곤 했지만, 지금은 자주 치지 않는다.

I used to like candy when I was young.

나는 사탕을 좋아하곤 했다/내가 어렸을 때.

I used to get up early except Sunday.

나는 일찍 일어나곤 했다/일요일을 제외하고.

(2) 과거의 상태 : 한때 ~했다

We used to live in Pusan. 우리는 한때 부산에 살았다.

He used to drink wine too much.

그는 한때 술을 너무 많이 마셨다.

(3) be used to + 동명사(명사) ~하는 데 익숙하다

be used to + do : ~하는데(하기 위해) 사용되다

She is used to swimming. 그녀는 수영하는 데 익숙하다.

We are used to French custom.

우리는 프랑스의 관습(풍습)에 익숙하다.

The book can be used to understand the computer.
그 책은 사용될 수 있다/컴퓨터를 이해하는데.

7) need와 dare

need(~을 필요로 하다)와 dare(감히~ 하다, ~할 용기가 있다)는 의문문, 부정문에서는 조동사로 쓰이므로 어미변화를 안한다. **긍정문에서는 본동사로 쓰이므로 어미변화를 하며, 그 뒤에 to부정사가 따라 온다.**

He need not come here. 그는 여기에 올 필요가 없다.
Need he come here? 그는 여기에 올 필요가 있니?
No, he needn't. 아니, 그는 여기에 올 필요가 없다.
He needs to come here. 그는 여기에 올 필요가 있다.

* 미국 회화에서는 need, dare가 본동사로 쓰이기도 한다. 이 경우 본동사 두 개가 올 수 없으므로 to부정사가 온다.

He doesn't need to come here.
Does he need to come here?
He needs to go there.

* He needs going there. (동명사) He needs money. (명사)

Exercises

A. can(could)을 「be able to」형으로 바꾸시오.

1. I am very sorry but I cannot tell you Tim's address.
2. We can show you the way to the castle if you really want to know it.
3. Can anyone stop that train?

4. Uncle Andrea could not walk after his accident.

5. Mr. Jones could answer all our questions.

6. Could Tony help you with the cooking?

※ 1. but I'm not able to tell… 2. We are able to show… 3. Is anyone able to stop that train? 4. Uncle Andrea was not able to walk… 5. Mr. Jones was able to answer… 6. Was Tony able to help…

B. 밑줄 친 부분을 have to 형으로 바꾸시오.

1. Where's Gina? I think she <u>went</u> to the dentist.

2. Look at this! You've made a mess and I <u>will clean</u> it up again.

3. Grandma doesn't feel well. We'<u>ve called</u> the ambulance.

4. I <u>don't</u> get up so early in summer because there's no school.

5. Tina came to the station with me, so I <u>didn't</u> walk alone.

6. Look at Martin! He <u>doesn't</u> work today because it's his birthday.

※ 1. had to go to the dentist 2. will have to clean… 3. we've had to call… 4. don't have to get… 5. didn't have to walk… 6. doesn't have to work…

C. 괄호 안에 조동사를 대용어나 적합한 문형으로 만드시오.

1. Jane (can) play the piano when she was 5.

2. The Bill (must) get up very early tomorrow.

3. Maria (may not) go out when she was 16.

4. I (need not) go to the office yesterday.

5. You (should not) lie.

6. We (must) move because my father got a new job.

7. If you go on learning, you (can) go to university next year.

8. Brian (may not) go to the party next weekend.

9. In India some women (may not) to leave the house.

10. I'm sorry, I (cannot) visit you next month.

※ 1. was able to(could) 2. will have to 3. wasn't allowed to 4. didn't have to 5. ought not to 6. had to 7. will be able to 8. will not be allowed to go 9. are not allowed to 10. will not be able to

D. 괄호 안에 적합한 사역동사 (let, allow, keep, make)를 넣으시오.

1. Did Paul (   ) you see his hamster? Yes, It's lovely, isn't it?

2. Most people in my class don't like music because the teacher always (   ) us write so much, but we never sing.

3. Don't (   ) Linda use your pen! She will break it.

4. Mum will be very angry if you (   ) her wait with lunch again.

5. Mum will be very angry if you (   ) her waiting again.

6. Will you (   ) us to stay out until midnight, Mum?

7. They will not (   ) you into the house with those dirty shoes.

8. They will (   ) you take off your shoes before you can enter the house.

※ 1. let 2. makes 3. let 4. make 5. keep 6. allow 7. let(allow) 8. make

E. 괄호 안을 「have+목적어+과거분사」형으로 만드시오.

사역동사+목적어+과거분사[목적어(사물)와 뒤의 동사가 수동관계일 때]

1. During my last visit to London I (my picture, paint) by a street artist.
2. Our school (install, new computers) next year.
3. President Clinton always (his picture, take) by the same photographer.
4. We (repair, our car) if it wasn't so old and rusty.
5. Dad (never, his shirts, iron) by Mother. He always does it himself.
6. During the holidays we (breakfast, serve) in our room every morning.

※ 1. During my last visit to London I had my picture painted by a street artist.
2. Our school will have new computers installed next year.
3. President Clinton always has his picture taken by the same photographer.
4. We would have our car repaired if it wasn't so old and rusty.
5. Dad has never his shirts ironed by Mother. He always does it himself.
6. During the holidays we had breakfast served in our room every morning.

제19장 동사의 시제

1. **동사의 변형**

   동사는 원형, 과거, 과거분사의 세 형태로 변한다.
   변하는 형태에 따라 규칙동사와 불규칙동사로 나뉜다.

(1) 규칙동사

   ① 원형에 -(e)d를 붙여 과거, 과거분사를 만든다.

원형	과거	과거분사
want	wanted	wanted
play	played	played
pass	passed	passed

   ② -e로 끝나는 동사는 -d만 붙인다.

like	liked	liked
escape	escaped	escaped

   ③ 「자음 + y」로 끝나는 동사는 y를 i로 고쳐 -ed를 붙인다.

study	studied	studied
carry	carried	carried

   ④ 「단모음 + 자음」으로 끝나는 단음절 동사는 자음을 겹쳐 -ed를 붙인다.

stop	stopped	stopped
plan	planned	planned
handicap	handicapped	handicapped

⑤ -ic로 끝나는 동사는 k를 첨가한다.

traffic	trafficked	trafficked
panic	panicked	panicked

★ -ed의 발음

① 무성음 k, f, p, s, ch, sh로 끝나는 말은 [t]로 발음된다. 무성음은 공기를 밀어낼 때 울림이 없는 음이다. 목구멍으로부터 나오는 무성음은 없다.

looked [lukt], finished[fíniʃt], laughed[læft]

② d, t로 끝나는 말은 [id]로 발음된다.

decided[disáidid], invited[inváitid], wanted[wɔ́:ntid]

③ 유성음으로 끝나는 말은 [d]로 발음된다.

유성음은 목을 만지면 후두가 떨리는 음이다.

유성음은 무성음 이외의 자음과 모든 모음이다.

smelled[smeld], cleaned[kli:nd], robbed[rabd]

(2) 불규칙동사

(불규칙 동사표 참조할 것 → 332p)

see	saw	seen	
lie	lay	lain	눕다, ~에 있다 (자동사)
lie	lied	lied	거짓말하다 (자동사)
lay	laid	laid	~을 놓다, 두다 (타동사)

(3) 현재분사나 동명사를 만드는 법

① 동사원형 + ing

　study → studying, look → looking, say → saying

② -e로 끝나는 동사는 e를 없애고 ing를 붙인다.

　like → liking, write → writing　* agree → agreeing

③ -ie로 끝나는 동사는 ie를 y로 고쳐 ing를 붙인다.

　die → dying, lie → lying

④ 「단모음 + 자음」으로 끝나는 단음절 동사는 자음을 겹쳐 ing를 붙인다.

　swim → swimming, run → running, bar → barring

⑤ 「단모음 + 자음」으로 끝나는 2음절 이상의 동사에서 마지막 음절에 악센트가 있으면 자음을 겹쳐 ing를 붙인다.

　begin → beginning, commit → committing

　* 첫 음절에 악센트가 있으면 자음을 겹치지 않는다.

　　offer → offering, focus → focusing

2. **동사의 시제**

시제(時制)는 동사를 통해 때를 나타내는 것을 말한다.
기본시제에는 현재, 미래, 과거가 있으며, 총 12시제가 있다.

시제	직설법	동사형
현재	He *writes* a letter.	현재형
과거	He *wrote* a letter.	과거형
미래	He *will write* a letter.	will + 동사원형
현재완료	He *has written* a letter.	have + p.p
과거완료	He *had written* a letter.	had + p.p

미래완료	He *will have written* a letter.	will have + p.p
현재진행	He *is writing* a letter.	be(현재) + -ing
과거진행	He *was writing* a letter.	be(과거) + -ing
미래진행	He *will be writing* a letter.	will be + -ing
현재완료진행	He *has been writing* a letter.	have been + -ing
과거완료진행	He *had been writing* a letter.	had been + -ing
미래완료진행	He *will have been writing* a letter.	will have been + -ing

3. 기본시제

1) 현재시제를 쓰는 경우

   (1) 현재의 사실, 동작, 상태, 규칙적인 것, 자주 일어나는(않는) 것 등
   We love each other. We learn from our mistakes.
   He is married to a musician. The book sells quite well.
   I get up at 6:00 every morning. We often play tennis.
   What does this word mean? He never goes to school by bus.
   * 현재시제는 be동사를 제외하고 동사의 원형으로 나타내며, 주어가 3인칭 단수인 경우에 한해서 동사 어미에 -(e)s를 붙인다.

   (2) 불변의 진리, 사실, 격언을 말할 때
   Light travels faster than sound. 빛은 소리보다 더 빨리 이동한다.
   Honesty is the best policy. 정직은 최선의 방책이다.
   Good begets good and evil begets evil.
   선은 선을 낳고 악은 악을 낳는다.

   (3) 왕래발착 동사(go, come, start, begin, leave, arrive, reach, end 등)의 현재형은 미래부사(구)와 함께 쓰여 미래를 대신한다

He comes tomorrow afternoon.
Soccer game(match) begins on Friday morning.

(4) 스케줄 미래나 확정된 미래는 현재시제로 나타낸다

Tomorrow is Sunday. (확정된 미래)
What time does the movie begin? (스케줄 미래)
The bus leaves at 8:30 tomorrow morning.
I start my new job on Monday.
What time do you finish your work tomorrow?
I have an appointment with a doctor on Wednesday.
나는 의사와 약속이 있다/수요일에.

(5) 시간과 조건의 부사절에서는 현재형이 미래시제를 대신한다

시간과 조건의 부사절에서 의미가 미래일 때는 현재형이 쓰이지만, will, be going to, be + -ing 등의 미래형은 쓰이지 않는다.
이 경우 주절은 대개 will미래를 쓴다.
I will phone you if(when) I get home.
나는 네게 전화할 거다/내가 집에 도착하면.
I'll study together if(when) he comes tomorrow.

★ 그러나 명사절과 형용사절에서는 미래시제일 경우 미래형을 쓰기도 한다.
I don't know when she will come home tomorrow. (올건지, 명사절)
I don't know when she comes home tomorrow. (오는지, 명사절)
나는 모른다/언제 그녀가 내일 집에 오는지.
I don't know the day when she comes back. (돌아오는, 형용사절)
I don't know the day when she will come back. (돌아올, 형용사절)
나는 모른다/그녀가 돌아올 날을.

2) 과거시제를 쓰는 경우

(1) 과거의 사실, 동작, 상태 등을 나타낼 때
I met Julia yesterday. I last saw her three days ago.
When did you phone home? What time did he arrive?
I did the shopping and the cooking.

(2) 역사적 사실, 사건을 나타낼 때
World War II broke out in 1939.
제2차 세계대전이 일어났다/1939년에.
The world's first subway was built in London.

(3) 현재완료 시제를 대신하는 과거시제
Did you ever read the book?
≒ Have you ever read the book?
당신은 그 책을 읽어본 적이 있나요?

(4) 과거완료 시제를 대신하는 과거시제
The bus left before I got to the bus stop.
≒ The bus had left before I got to the bus stop.
버스는 출발했다/내가 버스 정거장에 도착하기 전에.

3) 영어에서 미래시제를 표현하는 방법

(1) will + 동사원형 : (자연히) ~할 거다
① 자연적인 미래; 화자가 영향을 미칠 수 없는 자연적인 미래
It will rain tomorrow.
② 사전에 생각함이 없이 즉흥적으로 미래의 일을 말할 때

"Sandra is in the hospital." "Oh really? I'll go and(to) visit her."

③ 조건절(if절)의 주절에서

If it rains, I'll stay at home.

④ 미래의 일을 추측할 때(아마, 혹시 ~할 거다)

I think Tim will arrive late. 나는 생각한다/팀이 늦게 도착할 것을.

She will probably come tomorrow. 그녀는 아마 내일 올 거다.

(2) **미래진행형** = will be + -ing : ~하게 될 거다

① 미래의 일을 예상할 때

I will be working soon. 나는 곧 일하게 될 거다.

She will be arriving at the house tomorrow.

그녀는 집에 도착할 거다/내일.

② 예정된(계획된) 미래를 나타낼 때

I'll be seeing Tina tomorrow at the office. (긴 것이 뒤로)

= I'll be seeing Tina at the office tomorrow.

(3) **be going to** : ~하려고 하다, ~할 셈이다

① 화자의 의도적 미래를 나타낼 때

I am going to bring you the book tonight.

I'm going to go to doctor tomorrow.

나는 내일 의사한테 가려고 한다.

What are you going to do tomorrow?

너는 내일 무엇을 하려고 하니?

② 논리적 결과로 오는 미래

Kevin is coughing. He is going to be ill tomorrow.

케빈은 기침을 하고 있다. 그는 내일 아플 거다.

* be about to + do : 막 ~하려고 하다, 막 ~하려던 참이다

We are about to have dinner.

우리는 막 저녁식사를 하려던 참이다.
* be supposed to + do : ~하기로 되어 있다, ~할 예정이다
What time are we supposed to meet tomorrow?
우리는 몇 시에 만나기로 되어 있니/내일?

(4) 현재시제 ← 스케줄 미래(차 시간표, 프로그램)와 확정된 미래
The bus leaves at 8:30 tomorrow. Tomorrow is Monday.
The new film starts next Saturday.
I have an appointment with Julia on Saturday.

(5) 시간과 조건 부사절에서는 현재시제가 미래시제를 대신함
When she comes, you will see her.
그녀가 오면 너는 그녀를 볼 거다.
If it's fine tomorrow, we will go fishing.
내일 날씨가 좋으면 우리는 낚시질하러 갈 거다.

(6) 현재진행형 = be + -ing : ~할 것이다(~할 거다)
현재진행형은 주로 계획된(약정된) 미래의 일에 쓰인다.
I'm having dinner with Julia on Saturday. (I'm = I am)
나는 줄리아와 함께 저녁식사를 할 거다/토요일에.
He's moving to Seoul. 그는 이사할 거다/서울로.
Tim and Lisa are getting(will get) married next week.
팀과 리사는 결혼할 거다/다음 주에.

(7) 미래완료형 = will have p.p : ~해버릴 거다
미래완료형은 미래의 어느 시점에 일이 완료될 것을 나타낼 때 쓰인다.
By tomorrow I will have done the work.
내일까지 나는 그 일을 끝내버릴 거다.

I will have left here by this time tomorrow.
나는 여기를 떠나버릴(떠났을) 거다/내일 이맘 때.

4. 완료시제

(1) **현재완료 = have + p.p**

현재완료는 과거에 일어난 동작이나 상태가 현재에 완료된 것을 나타낸다. 그 때문에 뚜렷한 과거부사(구) yesterday, last week, a week ago 등과 함께 쓸 수 없다. 완료시제는 동작의 완료, 경험, 계속, 결과를 나타낸다.

I have bought the book yesterday. (×)
I bought the book yesterday. (o)
I have bought the book today. (o)

① **완료 : 막 ~했다**

(just, yet, now, today, already, now 등의 부사와 함께 사용됨)
He has just come back home. 그는 방금(막) 집에 돌아왔다.
He's(He has) already left. 그는 벌써 떠났다.

② **경험 : ~한 적이 있다**

(ever, never, before, twice, once 등의 부사와 함께 사용됨)
He has ever been to Brazil. 그는 브라질에 가본 적이 있다.
He has gone to Brazil. 그는 브라질로 갔다. (결과)
I have ever seen a tiger. 나는 호랑이를 본 적이 있다.

③ **계속 : ~ 해오고 있다**

(for three hours, since last Friday 등의 부사구와 함께 사용됨)
We have lived in the same house for five years.

우리는 똑같은 집에서 살아왔다(살았다)/5년 동안.
He has been sick since last Saturday.
그는 아파 왔다/지난 토요일부터(이후).

④ 결과 : ~했다, ~해 버렸다
I have lost a great deal of money. 나는 많은 돈을 잃어버렸다.
She has brought up three children. 그녀는 세 아이를 길렀다.

★ have와 have got
① have(US) ≒ have got(UK)
I have a book = I have got a book.
I have to go. = I have got to go = I've got to go.
② 의문문, 부정문에서
Do you have any question? Have you got any question?
I don't have any question. I haven't got any question.

(2) 과거완료 = had + p.p
과거완료는 어떤 동작이나 상태가 대과거에 일어나서 과거에 완료된 것을 나타낸다.

① 완료
He had already finished his breakfast when I called him.
그는 이미 그의 아침식사를 끝냈다(끝냈었다)/내가 그에게 전화했을 때.

② 경험
I could recognize her at once, for I had seen her before.
나는 그녀를 즉시 알아볼 수 있었다. 왜냐하면 내가 전에 그녀를 본 적이 있었기 때문이다.

③ 계속

　　The house had been empty for ages.
　　그 집은 비어 있었다/오랫동안.
　　I had learned English for five years.
　　나는 영어를 배워 왔었다(왔다)/5년 동안.
　　No sooner had I hung up *than* the phone rang again.
　　내가 전화를 끊자마자 전화가 다시 울렸다. (~하자마자 ~하다)
　　Scarcely had I started, when it rained.
　　= As soon as I started, it rained. 내가 출발하자마자 비가 왔다.

④ 결과

　　The bus had already left before I reached the station.
　　버스는 이미 출발했다(했었다)/내가 정거장에 도착하기 전에.
　　She had lost her job and couldn't earn money.
　　그녀는 그녀의 직업을 잃어서 돈을 벌 수 없었다.

　　* 종속절에서 내가 정거장에 도착한 것보다 주절에서 버스가 출발한 것이 더 먼저 일어난 시제이므로 종속절의 시제 과거보다 주절의 시제는 더 이른 시제 과거완료(대과거)를 사용했다.

★ 선후 관계의 두 가지 다른 과거사건이더라도 그 사건들을 발생한 순서대로 말하거나, 또는 글의 흐름상 선후 관계의 순서가 명확할 때는 굳이 과거시제와 과거완료시제로 따로 구분하지 않고 둘 다 과거시제로 표현할 수 있다. 과거시제와 과거완료시제의 의미상의 차이는 거의 없기 때문이다.
　　She had lost her job and couldn't earn money.
　　≒ She lost her job and couldn't earn money.
　　　그녀는 그녀의 직업을 잃어서 돈을 벌 수 없었다.
　　I lost the book which I had bought yesterday.

≒ I bought a book yesterday and lost it.
　　나는 어제 책을 사서 그것을 잃어버렸다.
The bus had already left before I reached the station.
≒ The bus already left before I reached the station.
　　버스는 이미 떠났다/내가 정거장에 도착하기 전에.

(3) **미래완료 = will have + p.p : ~했을 것이다**
미래완료는 어떤 동작이나 상태가 미래 어느 때에 완료될 것을 나타낸다.

① 완료
I will have finished the work by six o'clock.
나는 그 일을 끝냈을 것이다(끝내버릴 것이다)/6시까지.

② 경험
If I read this book once more, I will have read it three times.
내가 이 책을 한 번 더 읽으면 그것을 세 번 읽은 것(셈)이 될 거다.

③ 계속
I will have studied English for five years by next month.
나는 영어를 공부한 것이 될 거다/5년 동안 다음달까지.

④ 결과
I will have left America by this time next year.
나는 미국을 떠나버렸을 거다/내년 이맘때쯤.

5. **진행시제**

(1) 현재진행형 = be + -ing(현재분사)

　① 현재(이 순간)에 동작이 진행되고 있는 것을 나타냄
　　I am studying now. 나는 지금 공부하고 있다.
　　I'm not feeling well today. 나는 오늘 몸 상태가 안 좋다.

　② 미래의 대용
　　She is coming back tomorrow. 그녀는 내일 돌아올 거다.
　　= She will come back tomorrow.
　　She is arriving home tonight. 그녀는 오늘 밤에 집에 도착할 거다.
　　= She will arrive(get) home tonight.

　③ 현재진행형은 일시적인 상태에 쓰이고, 현재형은 오래 지속되는 상태에 쓰인다. 늘 반복되는 상태에는 현재형과 현재진행형이 모두 쓰인다.
　　I'm living in(at) my relative's until I find my own house.
　　나는 내 친척집에서 살고 있다/내 자신의 집을 찾을 때까지.
　　I live in Seoul. 나는 서울에서 산다.
　　He is always watching television. 그는 늘 TV를 보고 있다.
　　He always watches television. 그는 늘 TV를 본다.

(2) 과거진행형 = was(were) + -ing
　　She was watching TV when I visited her.
　　그녀는 TV를 보고 있었다/내가 그녀를 방문했을 때.
　　This time last year I was living on(in) Jeju Island.
　　작년 이맘때 나는 제주도에서 살고 있었다.

(3) 미래진행형 = will be + -ing : ~하게 될 거다, ~하고 있을 거다
　　I will be working soon. 나는 곧 일하게 될 거다.

I'll be living in the country this time next year.
나는 시골에서 살고 있을 거다/내년 이맘때.
Don't call me between 7and 8. We'll be having dinner.
7시와 8시 사이에는 내게 전화하지 마라. 우리는 저녁을 먹고 있을 거다.

(4) 현재완료진행형 = have been + -ing
현재완료형은 어떤 동작이 현재에 끝난 것이고, 현재완료진행형은 어떤 동작이 현재에도 진행되고 있어 끝나지 않은 상태이다.

He has studied all day today. (현재완료)
그는 공부했다/오늘 하루 종일. (지금은 공부하지 않는다)
He has been studying all day today. (현재완료진행형)
그는 공부해 오고 있었다/오늘 하루 종일. (지금도 공부하는 중이다)
I have been studying English for five years.
나는 영어를 공부해 오고 있었다/5년 동안. (지금도 공부하는 중이다)
Have you been waiting for him for a long time?
너는 그를 기다리고 있었니/오랫동안? (지금도 기다리는 중이다)

(5) 과거완료진행형 = had been + -ing
We'd been playing tennis for about two hours when it started to rain hard. (We'd = we had)
우리는 약 2시간 동안 테니스를 치고 있었다/비가 심하게 오기 시작했을 때.

(6) 미래완료진행형 = will have been + -ing
미래완료진행형은 미래완료형과 같은 의미이나 단지 과정이 아직 끝나지 않았을 때 쓰인다.

It will have been raining for six days by today.
비가 오고 있는 것이 될 거다/6일 동안 오늘까지.

By the end of April I will have been working in this firm for 3 years.
4월 말까지 나는 일한 것이(일한 셈이) 될 거다/이 회사에서 3년 동안.

(7) 진행형으로 쓰이는 동사들은 동작동사들이다

감정, 지각, 소유를 나타내는 상태동사들은 그 속에 이미 진행의 상태가 포함되어 있기 때문에 진행형에 쓰이지 않는다.

love, want, fear, hate, like, hope, envy, hear, see, taste, feel, know, remember, smell, sound, have, possess, belong to, own, be, exist, differ, resemble, understand, agree, believe 등

He is loving his baby. (×)   He loves his baby. (○)
He is having two sons. (×)   He has two sons. (○)
He is having dinner now. (○)

Exercises

A. I를 she로 바꾸시오.

1. I spend most of my time in the country(countryside).
2. I read the papers before I start doing the housework.
3. I finish working at about five.
4. I often go out with friends.
5. I do what I like.
6. What time do I have to check in for my flight?

7. I miss being at home but I feel that my job gives me a great opportunity to travel to places I couldn't afford otherwise.

8. I pity any man who is married to a woman like me.

※ 1. She spends most of her time 2. She reads the papers before she starts 3. She finishes working 4. She often goes out 5. She does what she likes. 6. does she have to check in for her 7. She misses being at home but she feels that her job gives her a great opportunity to travel to places she couldn't 8. She pities any man who is married to a woman like her.

B. 괄호 안을 적합한 현재형이나 현재진행형으로 만드시오.

1. Where (you usually stay) when you're in London?
2. We (just have) dinner. Would you mind calling again in about an hour?
3. What (you normally do) in the evening, (watch) TV?
4. I (visit) my grandmother about once every two weeks.
5. It (get) late. Shall we go home?
6. What (you do) here? Oh, I (look) for a knife and fork. Where (you keep) them?
7. My boss (speak) English and French fluently.
   I (not know) if he also (speak) Spanish.
8. (You love) me? Of course I (love) you. Why (you ask)?
9. We (exchange) emails at least once a day.
10. I think you (look) wonderful tonight.
11. We (think) about opening a branch in Brighton.
12. What (you usually do) with your weekends?
    Oh, I (shop), (go) to a film, (see) friends.

13. The trouble is, I (never know) when you (be) serious.
14. What (you read) these days? Jane Eyre by Charlotte Bronte. I (enjoy) it enormously.

※ 1. do you usually stay 2. We're just having 3. do you normally do, watch 4. visit 5. It's getting late 6. are you doing, I'm looking, do you keep 7. speaks, don't know, speaks 8. Do you love, love, do you ask(are you asking) 9. exchange 10. you're looking(you look) 11. We're thinking 12. do you usually do, shop, go, see 13. never know, you're (you're being) 14. are you reading, I'm enjoying

C. 괄호 안의 동사를 적합한 과거, 현재완료, 과거완료형, 완료진행형으로 만드시오. 동시에 시제의 일치도 생각하시오.

1. We (just come) back from Italy when we got the news.
2. We (come) back from Italy yesterday.
3. He noticed she (look) tired and (ask) her where she (be).
4. Don't you ever go to movies? No, I don't. I (not be) to a movie in months.
5. I love chess. I (play) it for years. Good mental training.
6. Before he (become) a lawyer, Lincoln (try) his hand at a variety of occupations.
7. We (live) here for years. Yes, we (move) into this house nine years ago.
8. Mr. Jones is your brother-in-law, isn't he? Yes. How long (you know) him?
9. You (be) together less than an hour and already you're quarrelling.

10. She began to think a mistake (be) made.

11. I (search) my wallet high and low last half hour.

12. It's time we (go) to sleep.

13. I wish I (know) what you're thinking right now.

※ 1. had just come 2. came 3. looked(was looking), asked, had been 4. haven't been 5. have played 6. became, (had) tried 7. have lived(have been living), moved 8. have you known 9. have been 10. had been 11. have been searching (have searched) 12. went 13. knew

D. 괄호 안의 동사를 적합한 미래형으로 만드시오.

1. I (probably see) you at Friday's meeting, then.

2. Wait here. I (not be) long.

3. How long (you stay)?

4. There are a lot of clouds. It (rain) soon.

5. The train to London (leave) at 6 p.m.

6. There's one thing I'm absolutely sure about; I (not marry) him.

7. We (watch) a film on TV tonight.

8. It's a very good question, very direct, and I (not answer) it.

9. Excuse me, sir, the bar (close) in a few minutes.

10. Sandra (be) late today. There has been such heavy traffic on the M 15.

11. In 10 years from now we (probably, be) rich.

12. My daughter (get) married in January.

13. I imagine you (celebrate) tonight.

14. The headmistress (retire) next July.

15. The museum (open) to the public on Thursday.

※ 1. I'll(I will) probably see 2. won't be 3. are you staying(are you going to stay, will you be staying) 4. It's going to rain 5. leaves 6. I'm not going to marry(I'm not marrying) 7. We're watching(we're going to watch, we'll be watching) 8. I won't answer(I'm not going to answer) 9. is closing(closes, will be closing) 10. is going to be 11. will probably be 12. is getting (will be getting) married 13. you'll be celebrating 14. will be retiring (is retiring, retires) 15. will open (is opening, opens, will be opening)

제20장 특수구문

1. **강조**
   단어, 구 등을 이용하여 특정 문장 성분을 강조한다.

   (1) **동사의 강조**
   긍정문에서 조동사 do를 본동사 앞에 써주면 '정말, 진정으로, 제발, 어서'의 뜻이 추가되어 동사가 강조된다. 이 경우 시제변화는 조동사 do가 하고 본동사는 동사원형으로 머문다.
   He does like tennis. 그는 정말(진정으로) 테니스를 좋아한다.
   Be quiet! → Do be quiet! 제발 조용히 해!

   (2) **명사의 강조**
   명사 앞에 the very를 써주면 '바로 그'라는 뜻이 추가된다.
   She is the very woman I want to meet.
   그녀는 내가 만나기를 원한 바로 그 여자이다.

   (3) **재귀대명사에 의한 강조**
   I myself have done the work. 나 스스로 그 일을 했다.
   = I have done the work myself.

   (4) **반복을 통한 강조**
   We waited for hours and for hours.
   우리는 몇 시간이고 몇 시간이고 기다렸다.

(5) 도치에 의한 강조

I have never felt better. Never have I felt better.
나는 기분이 더 좋았던(결코 더 좋게 느껴본) 적이 없었다.

(6) 의문문의 강조

의문문에 ever, at all, whatever, in the world, on earth, the hell 등을 쓰면 '도대체'라는 뜻이 추가된다.
Who on earth broke my bike?
도대체 누가 내 자전거를 망가뜨렸어?

(7) 부정문의 강조

부정문에 at all, whatever, in the least, on earth, for the world 등을 쓰면 '결코, 전혀'의 뜻이 추가된다.
He received no help in the least. 그는 도움을 받지 않았다/전혀.
I don't like him at all. 나는 그를 좋아하지 않는다/전혀.

(8) 비교급과 최상급의 강조

비교급 앞에 : even, much, far, by far, still, a lot : 훨씬, 더욱
최상급 앞에 : even, much, far, by far, the very : 바로, 단연코, 정말
He is much older than me. 그는 나보다 훨씬 더 연상이다.
The car is much the highest price in this shop.
= The car is the very highest price in this shop.
 그 차는 단연코 가장 비싼 가격이다/이 상점에서.

2. 도치

문장의 특정 요소를 강조하기 위하여 특정 요소를 문장 맨 앞에 위치시키고, 주어와 동사의 위치를 바꾸는 것을 도치라고 한다.

(1) 목적어의 도치

① 목적어가 문두에 오면 주어(대명사)와 동사의 위치가 변하지 않으므로 도치는 일어나지 않는다.
Nobody knows *what she wants*.
아무도 모른다/그녀가 원하는 것을.
→ *What she wants* nobody knows.
I love Jane. → Jane, I love.

② 그러나 부정목적어가 문두에 오면 무조건 도치된다.
They liked *none of these things*.
= *None of these things* did they like.

③ 목적어가 문두에 올 때 혼돈되는지 주의해야 한다. 혼돈이 되는 경우 목적어는 문두에 올 수 없다.
The dog bit the cat. 개가 고양이를 물었다.
≠ The cat bit the dog. 고양이가 개를 물었다.

(2) 형용사 보어의 도치

형용사 보어가 문두에 오면 무조건 도치된다.
I'm happy whenever I see her. 나는 행복하다/그녀를 볼 때마다.
→ Happy am I whenever I see her.

(3) 부사어구의 도치

① 관용적 도치 : 부사어구가 문두에 올 때 일반명사가 주어이면 도치되고, 대명사가 주어이면 도치되지 않는다.
He comes here. → Here he comes.

My bus comes here. → Here comes my bus.

② **부정 부사어구**가 문두에 오면 무조건 도치된다. **무조건 도치**는 조동사가 주어 앞에 온다.

I have never seen such a kind man.
→ Never have I seen such a kind man.
　나는 결코 본 적이 없다/그런 친절한 사람을.
I had seldom seen such a thing. (좀처럼(거의)~ 않다)
→ Seldom had I seen such a thing.
　나는 좀처럼(거의) 본 적이 없다/그런 것을.
No sooner had Peter seen her *than* he turned away.
피터는 그녀를 보자마자 고개를 돌렸다. (~하자마자 ~하다)

③ 한정 부사어구의 도치
한정 부사어구가 문두에 오면 무조건 도치된다.
He plays tennis only Sunday.
그는 테니스를 친다/오직 일요일에만.
→ Only Sunday does he play tennis.
He is very tired now. So am I.
그는 지금 매우 피곤하다. 나도 그래.
He doesn't play baseball. Neither do I.
그는 야구를 하지 않는다. 나도 하지 않는다.

(4) **가정법 if의 생략**

if가 생략되면 무조건 도치되어 조동사가 주어 앞에 온다.
If I had a lot of money, I could buy a new house.
→ Did I have a lot of money, I could buy a new house.
If I were a bird, I could fly to her.

→ Were I a bird, I could fly to her.
If I had studied harder, I could have passed the exam.
→ Had I studied harder, I could have passed the exam.

3. **생략**

   영어는 간결성을 매우 중시하므로 문장에서 불필요한 말이나 반복되는 말은 가능한 생략된다.

(1) 반복어구의 생략

   One of us lives in Seoul and the other (lives) in Jeju Island.
   우리들 중 하나는 서울에서 살고, 다른 하나는 제주도에서 산다.
   Buy what you want to (buy). 네가 사기를 원하는 것을 사라.
   Peter only eats and (Peter only) drinks all day.
   피터는 오직 먹고 마신다/하루 종일.

(2) 부정사 다음의 반복어구(대부정사)

   You can go home if you want to (go home).
   너는 집에 가도 좋다/네가 집에 가기 원하면.

(3) 조동사 다음의 반복어구

   Is he an American? Yes, he is. (= He is an American.)
   Should you tell her it? I should. (= I should tell her it.)
   너는 그녀에게 그것을 말해야만 하니?

(4) 비교구문 than 다음의 반복어구

   He is richer than I (am rich). 그는 나보다 더 부유하다.
   I love you more than (I love) him.
   나는 너를 더 사랑한다/그보다.

(5) 관용어구

No parking! = No parking is allowed. 주차금지
Closed. = This store is closed today.
Thank you! = I thank you.
Glad to see you! = I'm glad to see you.

4. **삽입**

단어, 구, 절 등을 끼워 넣어 추가적인 정보를 제공하는 것을 삽입이라고 한다. 삽입어구는 생략해도 문장 구조에는 영향을 미치지 않는다. 삽입어구는 구, 절, 동격어구(명사상당어구) 등으로 되어 있다.

(1) 명사의 동격어구

My friend, *Paul*, studies in America.
내 친구 파울은 미국에서 공부한다.

(2) 명사구의 동격어구

My hobby, playing tennis, is very interesting.
내 취미인 테니스 치는 것은 매우 흥미롭다.

(3) 구나 절의 삽입

She failed again, *I am afraid*. 그녀는 또 실패했다/안 됐지만.
He will come, *I will say*, here on weekends.
그는 여기에 주말에 올 거라고 나는 말하겠네.
Peter, *the eldest brother*, got a new job.
큰형인 피터는 새 직장을 얻었다.
Who **do you think** he is? 그가 누구라고 너는 생각하니?

(4) 관용어구의 삽입

The economy of Korea, *I think(I believe),* is in good shape now.
내가 생각하기(내가 믿기)에는 한국경제가 지금 좋은 편이다.
He is, so to speak, a bear. 말하자면 그는 곰이다.

5. 의문문과 부정문

의문문과 부정문은 특히 회화(일상어)에서 많이 쓰인다.
〈의문대명사 219p, 특수 조동사 248p. 참조〉

부정문은 not이 조동사(be) 뒤에, 본동사 앞에 온다.
조동사가 여러 개이면 첫 번째 조동사 뒤에 온다.
의문문은 조동사(be)가 주어 앞에 온다.

You have a pen. (have는 본동사)
Do you have a pen? You don't have a pen.
Don't you have a pen?
I will have finished the job by tomorrow.
(will과 have는 조동사, finished는 본동사)

의문문	부정문
1. You work on Saturday.	You don't work on Saturday.
2. Do you work on Saturday?	Don't you work on Saturday?
3. Yes, I do.	No, I don't.
4. Can you speak English?	Can't you speak English?
5. Did he sell his car?	Didn't he sell his car?
6. Is he a teacher?	Isn't he a teacher?
7. Does she have a car?	Doesn't she have a car?
8. Have you ever been to Canada?	Haven't you ever been to Canada?

9. What did you do yesterday?
10. Where are you from? (Where do you come from?)

    What nationality are you?

    What(which) country are you from?
11. What does this word mean?
12. How much does this pen cost(How much is this pen)?
13. How much time do you have?
14. How many people came?
15. How old is she?
16. How cold is it today?
17. How long have you been studying English?
18. How often do you play tennis in a week?
19. Can I meet Mary, if I go to Seoul?
20. Could you tell me how to get to station?
21. What(Which) bus goes to school?   What bus doesn't go to school?
22. What(which) countries did you visit? What countries didn't you visit?
23. What(which) class are you in?
24. What color is your car?
25. Which bag is yours?
26. Which is your bag?
27. Which would you like, tea or coffee?
28. What is the population of Korea?
29. What is the weather like today(How's today's weather)?
30. What happened to her last night?
31. Will Paul be here tomorrow?   Won't Paul be here tomorrow?
32. What time does the game begin?
33. What made her angry?
34. Who lives there?

35. Who can answer that question?   Who can't answer that question?
36. What kind of car did you buy?
37. Who did you meet yesterday?
38. Who(m) should I talk to?   Who shouldn't I talk to?
39. To whom should I talk?   To whom shouldn't I talk?
    = Who should I talk to?   = Who shouldn't I talk to?
40. To whom do you wish to speak?   To whom don't you wish to speak?
    = Who do you wish to speak to?   = Who don't you wish to speak to?
41. Whose book is this?
42. Whose is this?
43. Until what time are you studying?
44. When and where were you born?
45. Why do we go out for dinner?   Why don't we go out for dinner?
46. Do you know when he has gone?   Don't you know when he has gone?
47. Do you know why she didn't come?   Don't you know why she didn't come?
48. Do you know where he is now?   Don't you know where he is now?
49. Did you ask if(whether) she comes?   Didn't you ask if(whether) she comes?
50. She has come, hasn't she?   She hasn't come, has she?
51. Yes, she has. (= Yes, she has come.)   No, she hasn't. (= No, she hasn't come.)

※ 2. Don't you work on Saturday?라고 대부분 질문하지, 매우 격식체인 Do you not work on Saturday?라고 일상어에서는 잘 쓰지 않는다.

6. be동사 홀로는 본동사이며 조동사이므로, be동사는 단독으로 쓰여도, 주어 앞에 올 수 있다.

7. have동사는 단독으로 쓰이면 본동사이므로, 의문문을 만들려면 조동사 do가 주어 앞에 온다.

8. 너는 캐나다에 가본 적이 있니? have been에서 have는 시제를 나타

내는 조동사로 쓰였기 때문에, 의문문을 만들려면 have조동사가 주어 앞에 온다.

12. how much는 단독으로 쓰이기도 함.

13~14. how much(many) + 명사.

15~18. How + 형용사(부사).

17. 너는 얼마나 오랫동안 영어를 공부해 오고 있었니?

20. 어떻게 역에 가는지, 내게 말해 줄 수 있니?

21~23. 어느(어떤)의 질문에는 의문사 what이나 which를 두루 씀.

24. What + 명사

28. 한국의 인구는 얼마입니까?

31. won't = will not

33~35. 의문사 자신이 주어인 경우에는, **의문사(S) + 동사(V)**의 순으로 된다.

36~40. 주어 앞에 조동사가 있으므로 의문사는 목적격으로 쓰였음.

37. 너는 어제 누구를 만났니?

46~49. 간접의문문 : 의문사(의문부사, 의문대명사) + 주어 + 동사

50. 부가의문문.

Exercises

비스듬하게 쓰여진 문장 부분을 질문하시오.

1. I usually go to bed *at 9 o'clock*.
2. I haven't spoken to him *for one week*.
3. *2 weeks ago* the famous actor died.
4. *My sister* moved last month.
5. We stayed at home because *Sarah was ill*.

6. Lucy learned typing *at school*.

7. He drinks *a glass of wine* every evening.

8. He invited *Peter and Maria*.

9. They're talking about *Ronny*.

10. He gave it to *the boss*.

11. Canberra is the capital of *Australia*.

12. *The black* umbrella is mine.

13. I prefer *the brown one*.

14. That's *Jack Palmer's* dog.

15. She's on *Smith's* side.

16. I went in *Peter's* car.

※ 1. When do you usually go to bed? 2. How long haven't you spoken to him? 3. When did the famous actor die? 4. Who moved last month? 5. Why did you stay at home? 6. Where did Lucy learn typing? 7. What does he drink every evening? 8. Who(m) did he invite? 9. Who are they talking about? 10. Who did he give it to? 11. What is Canberra the capital of? 12. Which umbrella is yours? 13. Which do you prefer? 14. Whose dog is that? 15. Whose side is she on? 16. Whose car did you go in?

부록 I. 악센트 규칙

영어의 악센트 규칙을 많이 터득하면 할수록 영어 발음을 더 정확히 낼 수 있으므로 영어 회화나 영어 단어 암기에 큰 도움이 된다.

영어의 어원은 헬라어(그리스어)와 라틴어(이탤릭어파)이므로 영어 단어는 접두어(접두사, 어두)와 어근과 접미어(접미사, 어미)로 되어 있다. 그 때문에 영어의 어두와 어미의 관계를 살펴보면 영어 단어의 악센트 위치와 밀접한 관계가 있음을 알게 된다.

- 어두(prefix) + 어근(root) + 어미(suffix)
  In + vestm + ent[invéstmənt], Re + cogn + ize[rékəgnàiz]
- 어두 + 어근 : dis + tract[distrǽkt]
- 어근 + 어미 : work + er[wə́:rkər]
- 어근 : work[wə:rk]

접두어(접두사, 어두)에는 다음 것들이 있다.
ab, ac, an, as, at, ad, ant, be, con, com, de, di, dis, es, en, em, ex, for, over, ob, op, im, in, mal, mis, ob, op, pre, pro, per, re, sur, sub, un 등

★ **악센트 규칙**

1. 다음 어미로 끝나는 단어는 어미 앞 음절에 악센트가 찍힌다
   ion, ian, ial, ish, ic, ican(ical), ious, ient(ience), sive(sure), sory(sary), ity(ify), dual(tual), tal

* 어미 tual과 tal은 드물게 어미 둘째 음절에도 악센트가 찍힌다.

2. **다음 어미로 끝나는 단어는 대개 어미 둘째(두 번째) 음절에 악센트가 찍힌다**
able, ate, ent(ant), ence(ance), ment, tive(ture), ist, age, al(cal), ful, less(ness), ute, try, ty(cy, fy), ing, ous, graph 등

어근 생김새에 따라 어미 첫째 음절에도 악센트가 찍히는 경우가 있다.
current[kə́:rənt]에서 어미 ent는 악센트가 둘째 음절에 찍히는 어미이지만, 어근의 생김새에 따라 2음절 단어이므로 어미 첫 음절에 악센트가 찍힐 수밖에 없다.
intelligent[intéləd3ənt]에서는 4음절 단어이므로 규칙대로 어미 ent의 둘째 음절에 악센트가 찍힌다. (e>i)
2음절 단어 saying[séiiŋ]에서 악센트는 어미 ing의 첫 음절에 찍힐 수밖에 없다.
4음절 단어 accompanying[əkʌ́mpəniiŋ]에서 악센트는 규칙대로 어미 ing의 둘째 음절에 악센트가 찍힐 수 있다. 그 이유는 음절에 여유가 있고, 강모음 [ʌ]이 있기 때문에 단어의 강-약-강 리듬에 잘 맞아 들어가기 때문이다.
preventable[privéntəbl]에서 악센트는 어두 pre나 어근 vent에 찍히는데, pre는 어두로 힘들고 vent의 [e]는 강모음이므로 어미 첫 음절인 [e]음에 악센트가 찍힌다. inevitable[inévətəbl]에서는 강모음 [e]에 악센트가 찍히므로 여기서는 규칙대로 어미 able의 둘째 음절에 악센트가 찍힌다. (e>i)
ly가 부사의 어미일 때 가끔 어미 3째 음절에도 악센트가 찍히는 것처럼 보인다. 그러나 악센트가 어미 ly 앞에 다른 어미의 영향을 받았기 때문이다.
eminently[émənəntli]에서는 어미 두 개가 나란히 있는데, 첫 번째 어미 ent의 영향을 받아 ent 두 번째 음절인 e에 악센트가 찍힌다.

passionately[pǽʃənətli]에서는 어미 세 개가 나란히 있는데, 첫 번째 어미 ion의 영향을 받아 ion 앞 음절인 a에 악센트가 찍힌다.

3. 접두어(어두)에는 원래 악센트가 잘 안 찍히지만, 어미(접미어)의 영향으로 악센트가 접두어로 밀려가서 접두어에 악센트가 찍히는 경우도 있다
incident[ínsədənt]에서 어미 ent는 대개 어미 둘째 음절에 악센트가 찍히므로 어두 in에 악센트가 찍힌다.
compromise[kάmprəmàiz], prosperous[prάspərəs], distant[dístənt], indicate[índikèit]

4. 어미 없이 어두 + 어근으로 된 단어에서 악센트는 대개 어근에 찍힌다
(대부분 강모음 순서에 따른다.)
encroach[inkróuʧ] 침입하다, forbidden[fərbídn] 금지된, remove[rimúːv] 없애다, recommend[rèkəménd] 추천하다, compare[kəmpéər] 비교하다, disgrace[disgréis] 불명예, contempt[kəntémpt] 경멸, untruth [ʌntrúːθ] 허위, achieve[əʧíːv] 달성하다, expand[ikspǽnd] 확장하다, sustain[səstéin] 유지하다

5. 2음절 단어일 때 명사, 형용사, 부사는 첫 음절이 어두(접두어)라도 첫 음절에 대개 악센트가 찍힌다. 동사나 전치사는 강모음 순서에 따라 대개 둘째 음절에 악센트가 찍힌다
extract[ékstrækt] 명사; 발췌, [ikstrǽkt] 동사; 발췌하다
ferment[fə́ːrment] 명사; 효소, [fərmént] 동사; 발효시키다
recommend[rèkəménd] 권하다, comprise [kəmpráiz] ~로 구성되다
reward[riwɔ́ːrd] 보상, 보상하다, consult[kənsʌ́lt] 상담하다
fiscal[fískəl] 형용사; 재정의, simply[símpli] 부사; 단순히
among[əmʌ́ŋ] 전치사; 사이에, between[bitwíːn] 전치사; 사이에

6. 합성어에는 제1악센트, 제2악센트가 있는데, 악센트 음절은 각각 발음기호대로 발음되고 사이 음절들은 약모음 [ə]로 발음된다. 그러나 e나 i 음은 가끔 [i]나 [ə]로 발음되기도 한다

    모음 a, e, i, o, u는 강세를 받으면 본래의 소리가 나지만, 강세를 받지 않으면 약화되어 [ə]로 소리난다.
    undesirable[ʌ̀ndizáiərəbl], indicate[índikèit], insupportable[ìnsəpɔ́:rtəbl]

    제2강세가 없는 대부분의 단어에서는 악센트가 있는 음절과 강모음이 있는 음절만 발음기호대로 발음되고 나머지는 약모음 [ə]로 발음된다. 그러나 e나 i음은 가끔 [i]나 [ə]로 발음되기도 한다.
    imaginative[imædʒənətiv], composure[kəmpóuʒər] temperament[témpərəmənt], responsibility[rispɑ̀nsəbíləti]

7. 악센트가 찍히는 강모음 순서
    a〉æ〉e(ɛ)〉o(ɔ)〉ʌ〉i〉u〉ə

    * i:〉i, ə:〉i, u:〉i, i:〉o, i:〉e, ei〉a, ei〉æ, uə〉i

    ★ 단어의 어미와 강모음 순서로 악센트의 위치를 대략 유추해 낼 수 있다.
    contaminate[kəntǽmənèit]에서 어미 ate에 강모음 [eit]가 있으므로 단어의 강-약-강 리듬으로 mi는 [mə]로 약모음화 되고, ta는 강모음 [tæ]로 되고 con은 다시 약모음 [kən]으로 된다.
    다음절 단어에서 악센트 음절 이외에 강모음이 없을 때는 다른 음절은 모두 약모음화된다.
    temperament[témpərəmənt], intelligence[intélədʒəns]

8. 대부분 [æ]음에 악센트가 찍힌다

다음은 예외적으로 [æ]음에 악센트가 찍히지 않는 경우이다.

(1) 어미의 영향으로
application[ӕpləkéiʃən] (어미 ion 첫 음절에 악센트가 찍히므로)
anticipate[æntísəpèit] (어미 ate 둘째 음절에 악센트가 찍히므로)
anesthetic[ӕnəsθétik] (어미 ic 첫 음절에 악센트가 찍히므로)

(2) 2음절 단어에서
명사는 대개 첫 음절에, 동사는 둘째 음절에 악센트가 찍히므로
contract [kɑ́ntrækt] 명사; 계약, contract [kəntrǽkt] 동사; 계약을 맺다
extract[ékstrækt] 명사; 발췌, extract[ikstrǽkt] 동사; 발췌하다
aspect[ǽspekt] 명사; 모습, accept[æksépt] 동사; 받아들이다.

위의 두 가지 경우를 제외하고는 [æ]음이 강모음 [a]나 [e]와 함께 오는 경우는 매우 드물기 때문에 [æ]음에 대부분 악센트가 찍힌다. 단어에서 [æ]음을 찾기가 비교적 쉬우므로 [æ]음과 어미를 연관시켜 다른 음절의 음을 유추해 낼 수 있다.
compromise[kɑ́mprəmàiz]에서 어미 ise에 강모음 [a]가 있으므로 강-약-강 리듬으로 pro는 약모음화되어 [prə]로 되고, com은 강모음화되어 [kam]으로 된다.
benefit[bénəfit]에서 어미 fit에 모음 [i]가 붙고, 강-약-강의 리듬으로 ne는 약모음화되어 [nə]로 되고 be는 강모음화되어 [be]로 된다.

9. 다음 어미로 끝나는 단어는 바로 그 음절에 악센트가 있다
ee(eer, eed, eet), ette(ese), oo(oof, oon), bility(ality), ology(ogical), ometer

Ⅱ. 필수 기본 관용어(숙어)

〈시간이 있을 때 가끔 읽어(2시간 정도) 습득되도록 한다.〉

a bit of 약간의
above all 무엇보다도
absent from ~에 결석한
be absent from 결석(결근)하다
be absorbed in ~에 몰두(열중)하다
according to ~에 의하면, ~에 따라
account for ~을 설명하다
accuse of(criticize for) ~을 비난(비판)하다
be accustomed to ~에 익숙하다
across from(opposite) ~의 맞은편에
add to ~을 첨가하다(덧붙이다)
be addicted to ~에 빠지다(중독되다)
adjust to ~에 적응하다
advantage of ~에 유리한
advise to ~하도록 충고(조언)하다
be afraid of ~을 두려워하다
after all(in the end) 결국, 마침내
after class(school) 방과 후에
agree with(at) + 사람(사물) ~에 동의(찬성)하다
a head of(in front of) ~의 앞에

a kind of 일종의, 이와 같은
a lack of ~의 결핍(부족)
all along 처음부터, 죽
all at once(suddenly) 갑자기
all kinds of 모든 종류의, 여러 가지의
all right(O.K.) 좋아
all over 도처에
all over the world 전 세계에, 세계 도처에
all the time(always) 항상, 내내
all the way 내내, 시종
all the year round 일 년 내내
a loaf of 한 덩어리의
a long time ago 오래 전에
and so forth(and so on) 기타 등등
be(get, become, grow) angry about ~에 대해 성을 내다
be angry at(with) = be mad at ~에게 화내다(성내다)
be annoyed at(with, by) ~로 귀찮다(골치 아프다, 짜증나다)
answer for ~에 대해 책임지다
answer to ~에게 대답하다

a number of 많은, 다수의
be anxious for(about) ~을 갈망(열망)하다, ~을 걱정(염려)하다
anything but (never) 결코 ~아닌
apologize for ~에 대해 사과하다
apologize to ~에게 사과하다
apply for ~을 신청하다(지원하다)
apply to ~에 적용되다
approve of ~을 승인하다(인정하다)
argue with ~와 논쟁하다(언쟁하다)
argue about ~에 대해 논쟁하다
be armed with ~으로 무장하다
arrive in(at) ~에 도착하다(reach, get to)
as a means to ~의 수단으로
as~ as ~만큼, ~처럼, ~와 같이
a series of 일련의
as good as ~와 같은, ~이나 다름 없는
as it is 있는 그대로, 현 상황에서는
as it were 말하자면
as many as ~만큼 많은, ~와 같은 수, 무려 ~나 되는
as regards(as to) ~에 관하여
ask after 안부를 묻다
ask for ~을 부탁(요청, 청구)하다
ask(tell) + 목적어 + to부정사 ~에게 ~해 달라고 부탁히다(말하다)
assist with ~을 돕다

be associated with ~와 관련되다(연관되다)
as soon as possible 가능한 한 빨리
as well(also, too) 또한, 역시
at all (의문문) 도대체, (부정문) 전혀, 조금도
at a time 한 번에(한꺼번에)
at first 처음에는
at last(finally) 드디어(마침내)
at least 적어도(최소한)
at once 즉시
at present 현재는
attend to ~을 처리하다(돌보다)
at that point 그 당시에, 그 시점에서
at the risk of ~의 위험을 무릅쓰고
at the same time 동시에
at times 가끔은(때로는)
at Tom's 탐의 집에서
at the saying goes 속담에 있듯이
be attracted to ~에 마음을 빼앗기다, ~에 반하다
attribute to ~의 덕분(탓)으로 돌리다, ~때문이라고 생각하다
a variety of 다양한, 여러 가지의
be aware of ~을 깨닫다(인지하다, 알아차리다)
bad at ~을 못하는(서투른, 나쁜)
based on ~에 기초(근거)를 둔
be based on ~에 기초(근거)를 두

다
bear in mind ~을 명심하다
because of (due to, owing to, on account of) ~때문에
become(get) better 더 좋아지다
behind schedule 예정(예상)보다 늦게
believe in ~을 믿다
belong to ~에 속하다
bend over 허리(몸)를 구부리다
blame for ~에 대해 비난하다
blame on ~에게 책임을 전가하다, ~탓으로 돌리다
be blessed with 복(축복)을 받다
be bored with(by) ~에 싫증이 나다(지루하다)
be born 태어나다
be bound to 틀림없이 ~하다, ~해야 한다
break down 고장 나다
break into 침입하다
break out (전쟁이) 발발(발생)하다, 탈옥하다
break the ice 딱딱(서먹서먹)한 분위기를 깨다
bring about 초래하다, 야기하다
bring out 출판하다, ~을 꺼내다
bring to life ~을 소생시키다, 의식(기운)을 되찾게 하다
bring up 훈육하다(기르다), 화제를 꺼내다

bring up a subject 주제(화제)를 꺼내다
buckle up (안전벨트를) 매다
by accident 우연히
by far 훨씬
by means of ~을 수단으로, ~에 의해서
by mistake 실수로
by oneself(alone) 혼자서(홀로)
by the time 그때까지
by the way 그런데(대화에서 화제를 바꿀 때 씀)
by tomorrow 내일까지
call for 요구하다
call off 취소(철회)하다
calm down 진정하다, 조용해지다
cannot afford to ~할 수 없다, ~할 여유가 없다
be capable of ~할 수 있다
care about ~대해 염려하다(신경 쓰다)
care for(look after, take care of) ~을 돌보다(보살피다)
be careful about(of) ~에 주의(조심)하다
care to 좋아하다
carry on ~을 계속하다, 수행하다, 경영하다
carry out 수행(이행)하다
catch up with ~을 따라잡다(따라가다)

check in 탑승 수속을 밟다
check out 대출(확인, 조사)하다
cheer up! 힘내(기운 내)
be cluttered with ~로 혼란스럽다
collide with ~와 충돌하다
come across 우연히 마주치다(발견하다)
come back(return) 돌아오다
come from ~의 출신이다
come to(become) ~되다
be committed to ~에 헌신(전념)하다
come over 들르다, 건너오다
compare to(with) ~와 비교(비유)하다
complain about ~대해 불평하다(항의하다)
complain of ~을 호소하다
compliment on ~에 대해 칭찬(축하)하다
comply with ~에 따르다, 준수하다
be composed of ~로 구성되다(이루어져 있다)
come to mind = cross(enter) one's mind (갑자기) 생각이 떠오르다
come true 실현되다, 이루다
come upon ~와 우연히 만나다
come up with ~을 생각해 내다, 제안하다

concentrate on ~에 집중(전념)하다
be concerned about ~에 대해 관심을 가지다(걱정하다)
be concerned with ~에 관심이(관계가) 있다
confuse with ~와 혼동하다
congratulations ~ on ~을 축하하다(기뻐하다)
be connected to ~와 연결되다(연관되다)
connection with(between) ~와의 관계(관련)
consent to ~을 승낙(동의)하다
consider as ~로 간주하다
consist of (be composed of, be made up of) ~으로 이루어지다(구성되다)
consist in (특징) ~에 있다
contact with(between) ~와의 교제(접촉, 연락)
be content with ~에 만족하다
contrary to ~와는 반대로
contribute to ~에 기여하다(기부하다, 공헌하다)
be convinced of ~을 확신(납득)시키다
cool off 식다(식히다)
be coordinated with ~와 조화를 이루다
count on(upon) ~을 믿다(확신하

다, 의지하다)
be covered with ~으로 덮여 있다 (가득 차다)
crash into ~와 충돌하다
be crowded with ~로 꽉차다(들끓다)
cry over ~을 한탄(탄식)하다
be curious about ~에 대해 호기심을 갖다
cut down 베어내다
damage to ~에 손해를 입히다, 해를 끼치다
deal in ~(물품을) 취급(매매, 거래)하다
deal with ~(일을) 다루다(처리하다)
decide on(upon) ~으로 결정하다 (정하다)
decide to ~하기로 결정(결심)하다
be dedicated(devoted) to ~에 전념하다(헌신하다)
deliver(make, give) a speech 연설하다
deliver to ~에게 배달(전달)하다
demand for ~의 요구(청구, 주문, 수요)
depend on(rely on) ~에 의존하다 (달려 있다)
dependent on ~에 의존하는
describe as ~로 묘사(표현, 설명)하다

describe to ~에게 묘사(설명)하다
die of (병이나 노년으로, 직접적인 원인으로) 죽다
die from (사고나 과로로, 간접적인 원인으로) 죽다
different(differ) from ~와 다른
be different from ~와 다르다
be disappointed in(with) ~에 실망하다
disapprove of ~에(을) 반대하다
discourage from~ -ing ~하는 것을 못하게 하다, 단념시키다
be discriminated against ~에 차별 대우(냉대)를 받다
distinguish from ~와 구별(분간)하다
be divorced from ~와 이혼하다
do a good job 일을 잘하다(↔ do a poor job 일을 잘못하다)
do away with(get rid of) ~을 제거(폐지)하다
don't bother 걱정(염려)하지 마, 신경 쓰지 마
do one a favor 누구의 부탁을 들어주다
do one's best 최선을 다하다
dream of(about) ~을 꿈꾸다
be dressed in ~을 입다(입고 있다)
drive on (차를 몰고) 계속 가다
drop by(stop by) 잠깐 들르다
drop in ~의 하락, 잠깐 들르다

drop~ off(at) 차에서 내려주다
drop out 중퇴(탈퇴)하다
due to + 명사 ~때문에(덕분에)
due to + 동사 ~할 예정이다
each other(one another) 서로
be eager to 동사 ~을 하고 싶어하다, 열망하다
earn one's keep 생활비를 벌다
encourage to ~하도록 격려(장려)하다
end in(up) ~으로 끝나다, 결말이 나다
be engaged in(on)[occupied with] ~에 종사하고 있다, ~으로 바쁘다
be engaged to marry ~와 약혼한 사이다
enough to + 동사 ~하기에 충분한
enough for + 명사 ~에 충분한
be envious of ~을 시기하다(부러워하다)
be equipped with ~을 갖추고 있다(비치하고 있다)
escape from ~에서 도망치다(도피하다)
every time(whenever) ~할 때마다, 언제든지
excel in(at) ~에 뛰어나다(잘하다)
except (for) ~을 제외하고는
except that ~라는 것을 제외하면
excuse for ~을 용서하다

make an excuse (for) 변명하다
be exhausted from ~로 지쳐 있다(녹초가 되다)
be expected to ~이 기대(예상)되다
experiment with ~을 실험하다
explain~ to ~에게 ~을 설명하다
be exposed to ~에 노출되다(눈에 띄다)
face to face 얼굴을 맞대고
face trouble 어려움에 직면하다
fade away 앓다, 죽다, 시들어 죽다
fail to ~을 하지 못하다(않다)
fall asleep 잠들다
fall off ~에서 떨어지다, 줄다(감소하다)
be familiar with ~에 친근하다(친숙하다, 잘 알다)
famous for ~로 유명한
far away 멀리 떨어져
far from(never) 결코(전혀) ~이 아닌, ~에서 먼
fed up with ~에 진저리가 난
feel like ~을 하고 싶다, ~하고 싶은 기분이다
figure out ~을 이해하다(알아내다)
fill with ~로 가득 찬
be filled(packed) with = be full of ~로 가득 차다
fill out 기입(작성)하다
find out 알아내다(발견하다)
find time 시간(틈)을 내다

be finished with ~을 끝내다(마치다)
first of all 무엇보다도
be fit for ~에 적합하다
fit in ~에 어울리는(맞는)
fix up ~을 수선하다, 고치다, 개량하다
be fond of(like) ~을 좋아하다
for ages 오랫동안
for a moment(for a minute, for a while, for a second) 잠깐(잠시) 동안
for a short time 잠시 동안
be forced to 강요받다
for certain(sure) 틀림없이, 확실히
focus on ~에 초점을 맞추다
for ever 영원히, 언제나
for example(instance, as on illustration) 예를 들어
for fun 재미로
forget about ~에 대해 잊다
forget to ~할 것을 잊다
forgive for ~을 용서하다
for lack of ~이 부족하여
for the first time 처음으로
for the last time 마지막으로, 최후로
for nothing 공짜로
for short 줄여서
for the sake of ~을 위하여(때문에)

for the present 당분간, 현재로서는
for yourself 혼자 힘으로
four out of six 6명 중 4명
free from(of) ~이 없는, ~을 벗어난(자유로운)
be friendly to ~에게 친절히 하다(대하다)
be friendly with ~와 친한 사이다
be frightened of(by) ~을 무서워하다(두려워하다)
be from ~의 출신이다
from hand to mouth 하루 벌어 하루 먹는
from now on ~지금(이제)부터
from place to place 여기저기
from then on 그때부터
from now on 지금부터
from time to time(sometimes) 때때로
full of ~로 가득 찬
be furnished with ~로 갖추어져 있다(설비되어 있다, 꾸며져 있다)
get along with(on) ~와 잘(사이좋게) 지내다
get at ~에 도달하다
get away 도망치다
get back(return) 돌아오다
get hurt 다치다
get in(on) 타다(↔ get off 내리다)
get involved in(participate in,

take part in) ~에 참여(참가)하다

get lost 길을 잃다

get married 결혼하다

get off the phone 전화를 끊다

get out of ~에서 나오다

get out of hand 손이 미치지 않는다

get(make) ready to(for) ~을 준비하다

get rid of ~을 제거하다(없애다, 끝내다)

get spread around 소문나다

get(become) used to ~에 익숙해지다

get to(arrive at, reach) ~에 도착하다

get together 모이다, 만나다

get to know 알게 되다

get up(rise) 일어나다

get warmer 더 따듯해지다

give a hand 도와주다

give a lecture 강의하다

give a push 밀다

give back 돌려주다

give in ~에 굴복(항복)하다, 제출하다

give out 분배하다, 나누어 주다

give up ~을 포기(단념)하다

go ahead 계속하다

go a long way 많은(큰) 도움이 되다

go by(pass by) 지나가다

go -ing ~하러 가다

be going to ~에 가는 중이다, ~하려고 하다

be gone 사라지다

be gone from ~에서 떠나다(사라지다)

be good at ~을 잘하다, ~에 능숙하다(↔ be poor at ~에 서툴다)

be good for ~에 좋다

be good for nothing 아무 소용이 없다

go off 떠나다

go on(continue) 계속하다(되다)

go on America 미국 여행 가다

go on a picnic 소풍 가다

go on with ~을 계속하다

go out 외출하다(탈락하다, 불이 나가다)

go over 검토(점검)하다

go through 겪다, 경험하다

go to great length (목적 달성을 위해) 온갖 노력을 다하다

go to work 출근하다, 일하러 가다

go up to(approach) 다가가다(가까이 가다)

go with(fit in) ~와 어울리다(맞다)

go wrong (일이) 잘못되다

graduate from ~을 졸업하다

be grateful(thankful) to(for) ~을

고맙게(감사히) 여기다
grow up 자라다(성장하다), 성인이 되다
be guilty of ~을 범하다
hand down (후세에) 남겨주다, 유산(유언)하다
hand in 제출하다
hand in hand 손에 손을 잡고
hand(give) out 나눠주다(배포하다)
hand over 넘겨주다, 인계하다
happen to 우연히 ~하다, ~이 일어나다(생기다)
harmonize with ~와 어울리다(조화되다)
have a desire for ~을 열망하다
have a habit of ~하는 버릇이 있다
have an eye for ~을 보는 안목이 있다
have an idea of ~을 알고 있다
have an influence on ~에 영향을 미치다
have no idea 전혀 모르다
have nothing to do with ~와 관계가(관련이) 없다
have on 입고(쓰고, 신고) 있다
have one's own way 마음대로 하다
have stories read 이야기를 읽어 주는 것을 듣다
have the privilege of ~의 특권(특전)을 누리다
have to do with ~와 관계(관련)가 있다
have trouble ~ing ~하는 데 어려움을 겪다
have trouble with ~에 문제가 있다
hear from ~에게서 연락을 받다(소식을 듣다)
hear of ~대해 듣다
heat up 데우다, 덥히다
help oneself to ~을 마음대로(자유로이) 먹다
hide from ~부터 숨다(숨기다)
high time 꼭 알맞은 때
hold on = hang on = wait 기다리다, 전화를 끊지 않고 기다리다
hope for ~을 바라다(희망하다)
hope to ~하기를 희망하다
hurry up 서두르다
in accordance with ~에 따라서
in addition to ~일뿐 아니라, 게다가
in advance 미리, 사전에
be in a hurry(hurry up) 서두르다
in all 모두 합하여(합쳐), 총
in anticipation of ~을 기대하여
in a nutshell(in short) 간결하게, 한마디로
in a row 한 줄로, 연속해서
in a way 어떤 면에서

in bed(be sleeping) 자고 있는
in case of ~할 경우에
in charge of ~을 맡아서(담당해서)
in cold weather 추운 날씨에
in common 공동(공통)으로
in contrast 이와 반대로, 대조적으로
increase in ~이 증가하다
independent of ~와는 관계없이(별도로, 독립하여)
in despair 절망하여
in detail 상세하게, 자세히
in fact 사실은
in favor of ~을 찬성하여
in fear of ~을 두려워하여
inform of ~을 알리다(알려주다)
in front of ~의 앞에
in general(=generally) 대개, 대체로, 일반적으로
in haste 급한
in honor of ~을 기념(축하)하여
in light of ~에 비추어, ~로 미루어 보아
in many ways 여러 면에서
in memory of ~을 기념(추모)하여
in my opinion 내 생각으로는, 내 견해로는
be innocent of ~을 모르다(알아채지 못하다)
in one day 하루 안에
in one's shoes ~의 입장에서
in order to(so as to) ~하기 위하여
in other words 다시 말해서, 달리 말해서
in person(personally) 개인적으로
in place of ~을 대신해서
in itself 그 자체로서는(본질적으로)
in practice 실제로(실지로)
in private 개인적으로
in proportion to ~에 비례하여, ~에 비해
provide for(with) ~에게 ~을 제공하다
in public 공개적으로, 대중 앞에서
in pursuit of ~을 추구하여(쫓아서, 추적하여)
in reality 실제로, 사실은
in regard to ~에 관하여(관련하여)
in relation to ~에 관하여, ~와 비교하여
in reply to ~에 답하여, ~의 답장으로
in return for ~의 보답으로(답례로)
in search of ~을 찾아서
in shape 몸 상태가 좋은
in short 간단히 말해서
insist on(upon) ~을 고집하다(주장하다, 강요하다)
in spite of(despite) ~에도 불구하고
instead of(on behalf of) ~을 대신하여

intend to ~할 의도가(의향이) 있다, ~할 작정이다
be interested in ~에 관심(흥미, 의향)이 있다
interfere with ~을 방해하다(해치다)
in terms of ~면에서(관점에서)
in the course of ~하는 동안(사이에)
in the end 결국
in the event of 만약 ~하면
in the first place 우선(첫째로)
in the future 미래에, 장차
in the middle of ~의 한가운데
in the past 과거에
in these days 요즈음에는
in the way 방해가 되는
in those days 그 당시에는
in time 제시간에, 시간에 맞게
introduce to ~을 소개하다
be in trouble 곤경에 빠지다
in truth 사실, 실제로
in turn 차례로
in view of ~을 고려하여, ~때문에
invitation to ~에 초대
invite to ~에 초대하다
be involved in ~에 관련되다(관계되다, 휘말리다)
in want of ~이 부족한
It is necessary to ~하는 것이 필요하다
It is said (that) ~라고 한다
It is time to ~할 때(시기)이다
be jealous of ~을 시기하다(질투하다)
join in ~에 참여(참가)하다
judging from ~으로 판단컨대(미루어 보아)
keep a diary 일기를 쓰다
keep company with ~와 사귀다
keep down (억)누르다, 억제하다
keep~ from(prevent~ from) ~을 못하게 하다
keep(stop) from ~ing ~하는 것을 못하게 하다
keep house 집안일을 하다, 살림살이를 하다
keep ~ing 계속 ~하다
keep~ in mind 명심하다
keep in touch 계속 연락을 유지하다, 연락하다
keep on 계속하다
keep(break) one's word 약속을 지키다(어기다)
keep up ~을 계속(유지, 지속)하다
keep up with ~와 보조를 맞추다, ~을 따라 잡다
kind of 종류의, 약간
key to ~의 열쇠
know ~by heart(learn ~by heart) 암기하다, 외우다
know from ~에 관해서 알고 있다

be known for ~로 유명하다(알려져 있다)
lack in ~이 결핍한, 부족한
land on ~에 착륙(상륙)하다
be late for ~에 지각하다(늦다)
laugh at ~을 비웃다(놀리다)
lay off 해고하다
lead to ~로 이끌다, 초래하다
leave for ~을 향하여 떠나다(출발하다)
leave no room for ~의 여지를 남기지 않다
leave out 생략하다(빼다)
leave with ~에게 맡기다
lie down 드러눕다
lie in(consist in) ~에 있다
be likely to ~일 것 같다, ~하기 쉽다
be limited to ~으로 제한되다(제한하다, 국한하다)
line up 줄을 서다, 정렬하다
listen to ~을 듣다, 귀를 기울이다
live in ~에 살다
live on ~을 먹고 살다, ~을 주식으로 하다
live by ~로 살다
be located in ~에 위치하다
long for 열망(갈망)하다
look after(take care of) ~을 돌보다
look alike ~같아 보이다

look at ~을 보다(살피다)
look away from 시선을 돌리다
look back on ~을 회상하다, ~을 되돌아보다
look down on ~을 얕보다, 깔보다, 경멸하다
look for(search for, try to find) ~을 찾다
look forward to ~을 고대하다(기다리다)
look forward to ~ing ~하기를 고대하다
look into ~을 조사하다
look like ~처럼 보이다
look over 살펴보다
look up 쳐다보다, 올려다보다
look up to ~을 존경하다(우러러보다)
look on as ~라고 여기다(간주하다)
look over 훑어(살펴)보다
lose one's temper 화를 내다(흥분하다)
lose oneself in ~에 몰두하다(넋을 잃다)
be lost in ~에 열중하다, 푹 빠지다
love for ~에 대한 애정
make a career of -ing ~하는 것을 경력으로 쌓다
make a decision 결심하다
make a difference 차이가 생기다

make a fool of ~을 놀리다
make a living 생계를 꾸리다(유지하다)
make an apology 사과하다
make an appointment 약속(예약)하다
make an effort 노력하다
make a noise 떠들다, 시끄럽게 하다
make a reservation 예약하다
make fun of ~을 놀리다(비웃다)
make good 성공하다, 보충(수리)하다
make A into B A를 B로 만들다
make light of ~을 가볍게 여기다(다루다)
make much of ~을 중요시하다(중히 여기다)
make sense 이해하다, 이치(사리)에 맞다
make sure(ascertain) 확실히 하다(확인하다)
make the best(most) of ~을 최대한 활용(이용)하다
make time 시간을 내다
make up one's mind(determine) 결심하다
make use of ~을 이용(활용)하다
be made of (물리적 변화) ~으로 구성되다(만들어지다)
be made from (화학적 변화)~으로 만들어지다
manage to 가까스로 ~하다(해내다)
be married to ~와 결혼하다
may well 당연하다
meet a demand 요구를 만족시키다, 수요를 충족시키다
mention to ~을 언급하다
mind ~ing ~하는 것을 싫어(꺼려)하다
more and more 점점 더, 더욱더
more than ~이상
more than ever 더욱더, 여느 때보다 더
move into(to) ~로 이사하다
need for ~의 필요
most of 대부분의
most of all 무엇보다도, 가장, 제일
name after ~의 이름을 따라 이름 짓다
next door 옆집에
next time 다음 번에
next to(close, beside) 바로 옆에
nice(kind) of ~로 감사(친절)한, 고마운
no better than ~과 다름없는(나을 게 없는)
no longer 더 이상 ~아니다
be no match for ~의 경쟁 상대(적수)가 못되다
not~ anymore(no more = no lon-

ger) 더 이상 ~아닌
not at all 전혀 ~이 아니다
not~ but ~이 아니라 ~이다
be noted for ~로 유명하다
nothing but(only) 단지(오직), ~에 불과한
not to mention(not to speak of) ~은 말할 것도 없고
not(no) A until B B하고서야 비로소 A하다
now and then(occasionally) 이따금
now that ~이므로, ~이기 때문에
object to ~에 반대하다
of course 물론
of late 최근에(요즈음, 근래에)
be of good quality ~질이 좋다
of necessity 필연적으로, 부득이하게
of no use(useless) 쓸모 없는
be of service 도움이 되다
of use 유용한
on and on(on end) 계속하여, 쉬지 않고
on behalf of ~을 대표(대신)하여
on business 사업(업무, 출장)차
once more(once again) 한 번 더, 다시 한 번
once upon a time 옛날에
on course 예정(진로)대로
on duty 당번인(근무 중인)

one after another 차례로, 잇달아
one by one(one after another) 차례로, 하나씩
one day (과거의) 어느 날
order from ~에 주문하다
someday (미래의) 언젠가, 훗날
one morning 어느 날 아침
one right after another 차례 차례, 잇달아
on foot 도보로, 걸어서
on hand 수중에
on one's way to ~로 가는 도중에
on purpose 고의로, 일부러
on the beach 해변에서
on the contrary 그와는 반대로
on the ground of ~의 이유로(핑계로)
on the other hand (다른) 한편으로는
on the phone 전화로
on the point of ~하려는 찰나에, 막 ~하려고 하는 순간에
on the radio 라디오에서
on TV TV에서
on the right 오른쪽에
on the spot 현장에서, 즉석에서, 그 자리에서
on the verge of ~하기 직전에
on the whole 대체로, 전반(전체)적으로
on time 정각에, 시간에 맞추어

in time 제시간에, 늦지 않게
be opposed to ~에 반대하다
or so(about) 대략, 가량
be out 외출 중이다
out of ~의 밖으로
out of breath 숨이 가쁜(차서)
out of control 통제가 안 되는
out of one's mind(head) 제정신이 아닌, 미친
out of order 고장 난
be over(end) 끝나다
over and over again(repeatedly) 반복하여
over there 저기에, 저쪽에
owe to ~해야 한다, ~할 의무가 있다
owing to ~때문에
part company with ~와 헤어지다(교제를 끊다)
participate in ~에 참가(참여)하다
pass away(die) 죽다
pass up 놓치다, 포기하다
be patient with ~에 참을성(인내심)이 있다
pay attention to ~에 집중(주목)하다, 주의를 기울이다
pay back (돈을) 갚다
pay for ~을 지불하다(빚을 갚다)
persist in ~을 고집하다
pick out ~을 고르다, 선발(선택)하다

pick up ~을 집다(줍다, 집어올리다), 차에 태우러 가다
plan to ~할 계획이다
play a part(role) in ~의 역할을 하다(맡다)
play a trick on ~에게 장난치다, ~을 속이다
play on (경기를) 계속하다
be pleased with ~에 기뻐하다(만족하다)
be pleased to do ~하니 기쁘다
plenty(lots) of 많은, 충분한
point out 지적하다
be polite to ~에게 정중하다(정중히 대하다)
pour ~into ~을 ~에 붓다
pray for ~위해 기도하다(용서를 빌다)
prepare(ready) for ~을 준비하다
prefer to ~을 선호하다
prevail on(upon) ~을 설득하다
prevent from ~을 막다(하지 못하도록 하다, 예방하다)
pride oneself on ~을 자랑하다
prior to ~에 앞서, 먼저
proceed with ~을 진행(계속)하다
prohibit from ~을 금지하다(방해하다)
be protected from ~로부터 보호받다(지키다)
be proud of(take pride in) ~을 자

랑하다, 뽐내다
prove to ~로 판명(증명, 입증)되다
provide for ~을 준비(대비, 공급)하다
provide(supply) with ~을 공급하다(제공하다)
provided (that) = if 만약 ~라면
put down 내려놓다
put in(inset) ~에 집어넣다
put A into B A를 B에 넣다
put into practice 실행(실천)하다
put off(postpone) 연기하다, 미루다
put on(wear) 입다, 쓰다, 신다, 공연하다
put out (불 등을) 끄다
put up with(endure) ~을 참다(견디다)
be qualified for ~에 자격이 있다(적격이다)
quite a few 꽤 많은, 다수
rain cats and dogs 비가 억수같이(세차게) 쏟아지다
reach a conclusion 결론에 이르다
react to ~에 반응하다
read through 통독하다(꼼꼼히 읽다)
read to ~을 읽어 주다
be ready to + 동사
be ready for + 명사 ~할 준비가 되어 있다

reason for ~의 이유(원인)
recognize as ~로 인정(승인)하다
recommend to ~하도록 추천하다
recover from ~에서 회복하다(되찾다, 복구하다)
refer to ~을 언급(거론)하다, 참고(참조)하다
refrain from ~을 삼가다
reflect on ~을 심사숙고하다
be refused 거절당하다
regard as ~로 간주하다(여기다)
regarding(concerning, with regard to, in regard to) ~에 관하여
regardless of ~에 상관없이(관계없이)
register for ~에 등록하다
be related to ~와 관계가(관련이) 있다
relationship with(between) ~와의 관계
be relevant to ~와 관련이 있다
rely on(depend on) ~에 의존(의지)하다, 달려 있다
be remembered for ~으로 기억되다(유명하다)
remember to ~할 것을 기억하다
remind of ~을 생각나게 하다, 상기시키다
replace with(by) ~와 교환하다(바꾸다)

report to ~에게 보고하다
require to ~하도록 요구하다
rescue from ~에서 구조(구출)하다
respond to(reply to) ~에 응답하다
be responsible to(for) ~에 책임이 있다
result in ~을 초래(야기)하다, ~의 결과가 되다
result from ~이 원인이다, ~에서 기인한다
return to ~로 돌아가다, 복귀하다
reward with ~로 보상(보답)하다
rid of ~을 제거하다(없애다, 벗어나다, 해방하다)
right after 직후에
right away(immediately) 즉시, 당장
right here 바로 여기에
right now 바로 지금
rise in ~의 상승(인상)
rise to power 권력을 잡다
rob of ~을 빼앗다(강탈하다)
root out ~을 뿌리뽑다(근절시키다)
rule out ~을 제외시키다, 배제하다
run after ~을 뒤쫓다
run at ~에 달려들다
run away (from) ~에서 달아나다 (도망가다)
run into (우연히) 만나다, 부딪치다
run out 떨어지다, 만기가 되다
run out of 다 써버리다, 다 떨어지다 (바닥나다)
run over (차가) 치다, 넘치다
safe and sound 무사히(탈없이)
same here 동감이다
be satisfied with ~에 만족하다
be scared of(by) ~을 두려워하다 (무서워하다)
search for ~을 찾다
seek out ~을 찾아내다
see off 배웅(전송)하다
send for ~을 부르러 보내다
set a goal 목표를 세우다
set an example 모범을 보이다
set ~down 내려놓다, 밑에 놓다
set free ~을 석방하다
set off 시작하다
set sail for ~을 향해 출항하다
set the table 식탁을 차리다
set up 사업을 시작하다, 개업하다, 설립하다
share in ~을 나누다, ~에 참여하다
shake hands with ~와 악수하다
share with ~와 공유하다(나누어 갖다)
shoot at ~을 쏘다(사격하다)
shout at ~에게 소리지르다(야단치다)
show around 여기저기 안내하다(구경시켜 주다)
show off 과시하다

sick of ~에 싫증난
side by side 나란히
be similar to ~와 유사하다
sit back (의자에) 깊숙이 앉다, 편안히 쉬다
sit up 자지 않고 일어나 있다
so far(until now) 지금까지
solution to ~의 해답(해결)
sooner or later 조만간, 머지않아
sorry about ~에 대해 유감스러운 (미안스러운)
sorry for ~을 불쌍하게(유감스럽게) 생각하는
so~ that 너무 ~해서 ~하다
so to speak 말하자면
speak(talk) to ~와 이야기하다(~에게 말을 걸다)
speak(talk) about ~에 대해 이야기하다
specialize in ~을 전문으로 하다(전공하다)
spend on ~에 쓰다(소비하다)
stand a chance of ~의 가능성(가망)이 있다
stand by ~의 편을 들다
stand for ~을 대표(상징)하다
stand in the way 방해가 되다(훼방놓다)
stand opposed to ~의 반대편에 서다
stare at ~을 응시하다(쳐다보다)

start off(out) 출발하다, (여행을) 떠나다
start to ~하기 시작하다
stay at ~에 머무르다
stay up 안 자다, 깨어 있다
stay in line 줄에 서 있다
step by step 한 걸음 한 걸음, 점차로, 단계적으로
stick to ~에 집착(고수)하다
stop from ~을 중지시키다(그만두게 하다)
stretch out 뻗다, 쭉 펴다
strive for ~을 얻으려고 노력하다, ~위해 힘쓰다
be subject to ~의 지배를 받다, ~의 대상이다
subscribe to 정기 구독하다
substitute for ~을 대신(대용)하다
succeed in ~에 성공하다
succeed to 물려받다(계승하다)
such as ~와 같은, 이러한
suffer from ~로 고생하다, ~로 고통받다
sum up ~을 요약(묘사)하다
supplement with ~로(을) 보충하다
supply with ~을 공급하다
be supposed to ~하기로 되어 있다 (해야 한다)
be sure of(about) ~을(대해) 확신하다

surf the Internet 인터넷으로 정보를 검색하다
be surprised at + 명사, be surprised to + 동사 ~에 놀라다
suspect of ~의 혐의를 두다
switch on 켜다
switch off 끄다
sympathize with ~을 동정하다(공감하다)
take a break 잠깐 휴식하다(쉬다)
take a(the) bus 버스를 타다
take account of ~을 고려(감안)하다
take a class 수업을 받다
take advantage of ~을 이용하다 (~을 기회로 활용하다)
take a look at ~을 관찰하다(살펴보다)
take(have) a rest 쉬다
take a risk 위험을 무릅쓰다, 모험을 하다
talk about(of) ~대해 이야기하다
take(have) a bath 목욕하다
take after ~을 닮다
take a picture(photo) (of) 사진을 찍다
take a walk 산책하다
take as ~로 여기다(생각하다)
take away 빼앗다, 가져가다
take back 돌려주다, 반납하다, 취소하다

take care of ~을 돌보다(~에 주의하다)
take charge of ~을 떠맡다(책임지다)
take for ~이라고 생각하다
take ~for granted (take it for granted that) ~을 당연시하다
take in the situation 상황을 관찰하다
take into account ~을 고려(참작)하다
take it easy 일을 쉬엄쉬엄 하다, (명령문)진정해, 걱정 마, (헤어질 때) 잘 가, 또 만나
take leave of ~에게 작별 인사하다, ~에서 벗어나다
take notice of ~을 알아차리다(주의하다, 주목하다)
take off 이륙하다, 벗다
take offense 화(성)내다
take one's advice ~의 충고를 듣다 (받아들이다)
take out 꺼내다(인출하다)
take out a subscription to ~을 정기 구독하다
take over 양도받다, 인수하다, 떠맡다
take pity on ~을 불쌍히 여기다
take part in ~에 참가(참여)하다
take place(happen) 일어나다, 발생하다

take pride in ~을 자랑하다
take steps 조처를 취하다
take the initiative 솔선(주도)하다, 앞장서다
take the place of ~을 대신(교대)하다
take turns 교대하다
take up (시간, 장소 등을) 차지하다
teach oneself 독학(자습)하다
tell from ~을 구별하다, ~부터 알다
tend to ~하는 경향이 있다
ten to one 십중팔구(거의 틀림없이)
be terrified of(by) ~을 무서워하다(겁을 먹다)
thank for ~에 대해 감사하다
thanks to ~덕분에, 덕택에
that is (to say) 즉, 다시 말해서
that way 그런 방식(방법)으로
the day after tomorrow 모레
the day before yesterday 그제(그저께)
the other day 일전에, 최근에
think about(of) ~에 대해 생각(고려)하다
think out 생각해 내다(생각하다)
think over 곰곰이 생각하다, 숙고하다
be through with(finish) ~을 끝마치다(끝내다)
throw away ~을 버리다, 폐기하다

be tired of ~에 싫증나다
be tired from(with) ~부터 피곤하다
be to ~하도록 되어 있다, ~할 예정이다
to begin with 우선, 먼저, 처음에는
to date 오늘(현재)까지
to one's surprise 놀랍게도
to say nothing of ~은 말할 것도 없고
to the contrary 그와 반대로
transfer to ~로 옮기다, 바꿔 타다
translate into ~으로 번역하다
treat as(deal with) ~로 대하다, 다루다, 취급하다
be true of ~에 적용되다
try on 신어(입어)보다
try one's best 최선을 다하다
try to ~하려고 하다(시도하다), ~하려고 노력하다(애쓰다)
try out ~을 시험적으로 해보다, 테스트해 보다
turn around(round) 몸을 돌리다(돌아서다), 회전하다(회전시키다)
turn down ~을 거절(거부)하다, (소리를) 줄이다
turn(hand) in 제출하다
turn into ~로 바뀌다(변하다)
turn on (~을) 켜다
turn off (~을) 끄다

321

turn out 끄다, 드러내다(나타내다)
turn over 인계(위임)하다, 뒤집다
under control 통제(제어)되는, 통제 가능한
upside down 거꾸로, 뒤집힌
up to ~까지
used to ~하곤 했다, ~했다
be used to ~에 익숙하다
use up 다 써버리다
be(get) upset (with) ~에 화가 나다
vote for ~에 (찬성) 투표하다
wait for(await) ~을 기다리다
wait on ~을 시중들다(섬기다)
wake up 잠을 깨다, 정신을 차리다
wake up to ~을 깨닫다
walk around 돌아다니다
warm up (가벼운) 준비 운동을 하다
warn of ~을 경고하다
watch over ~을 보살피다, 보호하다, 지키다
what for 무엇 때문에, 왜

be willing to 기꺼이 ~하다
with a view to ~할 목적으로, ~을 위하여
with all(for all) ~에도 불구하고
with no war = without war 전쟁 없이
without fail 틀림없이, 반드시
with interest 흥미(관심)를 가지고
with surprise 놀라서
work at(in, for) ~에서 일하다
work on 착수(작업)하다
work out 운동하다, 계산(산출)하다
be worried about ~에 대해 걱정하다
would like to ~하고 싶다
would rather 차라리 ~하는 게 낫다 (~하고 싶다)
write down 적어 두다(기록하다)
write (to) ~에게 편지를 쓰다(편지를 보내다)

III. 불규칙 동사표

현재	과거	과거분사	의미
arise	arose	arisen	일어나다, 발생하다
awake	awoke	awoken	깨다, 깨우다
bear	bore	born	낳다, 참다
beat	beat	beat	때리다, 물리치다
become	became	become	되다
begin	began	begun	시작하다
bend	bent	bent	구부러지다, 휘다
bet	bet	bet	(내기를) 걸다
bid	bid	bid	값을 매기다(부르다)
bind	bound	bound	묶다, 감다
bite	bit	bitten	물다
bleed	bled	bled	피를 흘리다
blow	blew	blown	(바람이) 불다
break	broke	broken	부수다, 부서지다
breed	bred	bred	사육하다, 번식하다
bring	brought	brought	가져다 주다, 데려오다
broadcast	broadcast	broadcast	방송하다
build	built	built	짓다, 건축하다
burn	burnt(ed)	burnt(ed)	태우다, 타다
burst	burst	burst	터지다, 터뜨리다
buy	bought	bought	사다
cast	cast	cast	던지다, 투표하다
catch	caught	caught	(붙)잡다
choose	chose	chosen	선택하다, 고르다

cleave	cleft	cleft	쪼개다, 가르다
cling	clung	clung	매달리다, 집착하다
come	came	come	오다
cost	cost	cost	값(비용)이 들다
creep	crept	crept	기어가다, 다가오다
cut	cut	cut	자르다
deal	dealt	dealt	다루다, 거래하다
dig	dug	dug	(땅을) 파다
do	did	done	하다
draw	drew	drawn	그리다, 끌어당기다
dream	dreamt(ed)	dreamt(ed)	꿈꾸다
drink	drank	drunk	마시다
drive	drove	driven	운전하다
eat	ate	eaten	먹다
fall	fell	fallen	떨어(넘어)지다
feed	fed	fed	먹이다, 기르다
feel	felt	felt	느끼다
fight	fought	fought	싸우다
find	found	found	발견하다, 알(아내)다
fit	fit	fit	(옷 등이) 맞다
flee	fled	fled	도망치다
fling	flung	flung	(내)던지다
fly	flew	flown	날다
forbid	forbade	forbidden	금지하다
forecast	forecast	forecast	예측(예보, 예상)하다
forget	forgot	forgotten	잊다
forgive	forgave	forgiven	용서하다
freeze	froze	frozen	얼다, 얼리다
get	got	gotten	되다, 얻다, 받다
give	gave	given	주다
go	went	gone	가다

grind	ground	ground	갈다, 빻다
grow	grew	grown	자라다, 증가하다
hang	hung	hung	걸다, 걸려있다
have	had	had	가지다
hear	heard	heard	듣다
hide	hid	hidden	숨다, 숨기다
hit	hit	hit	때리다, 부딪치다
hold	held	held	잡다, 들고(쥐고) 있다
hurt	hurt	hurt	다치다, 다치게 하다
keep	kept	kept	계속하다, 막다
kneel	knelt	knelt	무릎 꿇다, 굴복하다
know	knew	known	알다
lay	laid	laid	놓다
lead	led	led	이끌다, 선도하다
leave	left	left	떠나다, 남(맡)기다
lend	lent	lent	빌려주다
let	let	let	시키다, 하게 하다
lie	lay	lain	눕다, 놓여 있다
lose	lost	lost	잃어버리다, 잃다
make	made	made	만들다
mean	meant	meant	의미하다
meet	met	met	만나다
pay	paid	paid	지불하다
put	put	put	놓다
quit	quit	quit	그만두다, 중지하다
read	read	read	읽다
rid	rid	rid	제거하다, 없애다
ride	rode	ridden	(탈것에) 타다
ring	rang	rung	(벨이) 울리다
rise	rose	risen	(해가) 뜨다, 증가하다, 오르다
run	ran	run	뛰다

say	said	said	말하다
see	saw	seen	보다
seek	sought	sought	찾다, 추구하다
sell	sold	sold	팔다
send	sent	sent	보내다
set	set	set	놓다, 배치하다
shake	shook	shaken	흔들다
shed	shed	shed	(눈물, 피)를 흘리다
shine	shone	shone	빛나다
shoot	shot	shot	쏘다, 발사하다
show	showed	shown	보여주다
shrink	shrank	shrunk	줄어들다, 수축되다
shut	shut	shut	닫다
sing	sang	sung	노래하다
sink	sank	sunk	가라앉다, 침몰하다
sit	sat	sat	앉다
sleep	slept	slept	자다
slide	slid	slid	미끄러지다
sow	sowed	sown	씨를 뿌리다
speak	spoke	spoken	말하다
spend	spent	spent	(돈을) 쓰다, (시간을) 보내다
spin	spun	spun	회전시키다, 회전하다
spit	spit	spit	침을 뱉다
split	split	split	쪼개다, 분열시키다
spoil	spoilt(ed)	spoilt(ed)	망쳐놓다, 망치다
spread	spread	spread	펴다, 펼치다
spring	sprang	sprung	튀다, 튀어 오르다
stand	stood	stood	서다
steal	stole	stolen	훔치다
stick	stuck	stuck	찌르다, 찔리다
sting	stung	stung	찌르다, 쏘다

strike	struck	struck	때리다, 치다, 부딪치다
strive	strove	striven	노력(분투)하다, 힘쓰다
swear	swore	sworn	맹세하다
sweep	swept	swept	휩쓸다, 청소하다
swim	swam	swum	수영하다
swing	swung	swung	흔들다, 흔들리다
take	took	taken	가지다, 받다, 데려가다
teach	taught	taught	가르치다
tear	tore	torn	찢다, 찢어지다, 뜯다
tell	told	told	말하다
think	thought	thought	생각하다
throw	threw	thrown	던지다
tread	trod	trodden	짓밟다, 유린하다
understand	understood	understood	이해하다
upset	upset	upset	뒤엎다, 당황하게 하다
wake	woke	waken	(잠에서) 깨다, 깨우다
wear	wore	worn	입다
weep	wept	wept	울다, 슬퍼하다
win	won	won	이기다
wind	wound	wound	(바람이, 나팔을) 불다
wring	wrung	wrung	비틀다, 쥐어짜다
write	wrote	written	쓰다

* -t(ed)에서 -t(UK), -ed(US)